The Nature
Instinct

Also by Tristan Gooley

How to Read Nature

How to Read Water

The Lost Art of Reading Nature's Signs

The Natural Navigator

The Natural Explorer

The Nature Instinct

Relearning Our Lost Intuition for the Inner Workings of the Natural World

TRISTAN GOOLEY

Illustrations by Neil Gower

THE EXPERIMENT

NEW YORK

THE NATURE INSTINCT: *Relearning Our Lost Intuition for the Inner Workings of the Natural World*
Copyright © 2018 by Tristan Gooley
Illustrations copyright © 2018 by Neil Gower

Originally published in the UK as *Wild Signs and Star Paths* by Sceptre in 2018.
First published in North America by The Experiment, LLC, in 2018.

The Experiment, LLC
220 East 23rd Street, Suite 600
New York, NY 10010-4658
theexperimentpublishing.com

Many of the designations used by manufacturers and sellers to distinguish their products are claimed as trademarks. Where those designations appear in this book and The Experiment was aware of a trademark claim, the designations have been capitalized.

The Experiment's books are available at special discounts when purchased in bulk for premiums and sales promotions as well as for fund-raising or educational use. For details, contact us at info@theexperimentpublishing.com.

Library of Congress Cataloging-in-Publication Data available upon request

ISBN 978-1-61519-479-7
Ebook ISBN 978-1-61519-516-9

Cover and text design by Beth Bugler
Author photograph by Ben Queenborough

Manufactured in the United States of America

First printing November 2018
10 9 8 7 6 5 4 3 2 1

To the kindest animals;
you know who you are

Contents

PART V—A WORLD OF SIGNS: DIGGING DEEPER

PART VI—EPILOGUE

To see additional images of this book's concepts as they appear in the wild, please visit: naturalnavigator.com/the-library/the-nature-instinct-images.

Introduction

I T IS POSSIBLE TO achieve a level of outdoors awareness—an instinctive ability to detect and interpret clues in nature—that, although once common, is now so rare that many would label it a "sixth sense." This is the practiced ability to make connections and then draw conclusions from all of the evidence presented to our senses almost without thinking. In this book, I will show you how to sense direction from stars and plants, forecast weather from woodland sounds, and predict the next action of an animal from its body language—instantly.

Anyone unfamiliar with this type of thinking may not spot a "missing" step until it is highlighted. We have become so distanced from this way of experiencing our environment that it may seem hard to believe that it is possible outdoors, although in more familiar settings it may seem less alien.

Have you ever felt you were being watched and later found out that you were right, but were unable to work out how you knew?

Imagine you are sitting in a café with your back to the window. You get a strange sense that someone behind you is looking at you. You may be right. If a friend is trying to catch your attention from the window of their car as they drive slowly past, this may register in the faces or body language of others in the café—perhaps the waiter looked up while pouring your coffee. Your friend's call later that day confirms you were being watched.

Psychologists have proved that we can gauge the mood of a person at the other end of a telephone conversation extraordinarily well as soon as we hear their first word. Our ears hear it, but our brain rapidly draws on a lifetime's experience, our knowledge of the character and situation of the caller, the time of day or night, and myriad other prompts to paint a much more inclusive picture than the word "hello." All day and all night, the outdoors whispers single words full of deeper meaning to us. We have grown a little rusty at painting more than the outline of the picture.

A sixth sense is not mysterious; it is expert intuition, a honed ability to join the dots offered by our senses to complete a fuller picture of our environment. And there are a lot more dots than we are aware of. In the past second your senses have picked up eleven million pieces of information. It could take years to analyze all of them consciously, so almost all of that information is filtered out by your brain without troubling you. But if your brain picks up anything weird, wonderful, or threatening, you will sense that something worthy of your attention is going on.

Recent research and popular books have convinced many people of our ability to gauge modern situations intuitively.

Look at the image opposite and imagine you are crossing the road. You will have seen that there are three cars and one is closer than the others, but that you need to be wary of the farthest one. And in reality you would do this instantly, without counting or measuring anything.

Nobody has considered what we are still capable of in nature. This is ironic, because the ability to judge situations intuitively springs from our need to survive in a wilder context. Humanity has used this type of thinking to experience the outdoors for most of our history, and evolution has ensured that we would not exist without it. The early human who had to rely on labored thought to work out what was going on around them was at a great disadvantage compared to one who sensed an enemy nearby, a dangerous predator behind, or a possible meal ahead.

I was once led deep underground by a BBC TV crew. We made our way, crouching, through dark, twisting tunnels into a cold slate mine in north Wales. There were no clues in our dank surroundings that were obvious to anyone in the crew, which was probably what prompted them to test me by asking if I could tell which way we were facing.

I peered at the damp rock, illuminated only by my headlamp, then answered, "East."

The safety consultant, who knew the mine intimately, confirmed that I was right, but admitted to being as mystified as the others by this "sixth sense." After a few enjoyable minutes, I revealed that I had noticed the alignment of the grain of the slate, known as "dip" to geologists. All sedimentary rocks begin as horizontal layers, but over millions of years, geological forces bend and tilt them; many end up with dramatic angles, and these have trends. I'd seen that the slate surrounding us in the Welsh valley sloped up toward the south and used this to find our direction deep underground.

In that case I used a "clue" consciously to answer a simple question. I have relied on this approach professionally for decades, and much of my writing has focused on this sort of logical, deductive thinking. However, something perhaps more interesting happens when the brain adopts the process and takes a shortcut. By the time we left the mine, everyone could sense direction instantly; it was reflected back at us in the slate. The idea that we might not have been able to do it was almost comical.

At the most basic level, we have not entirely lost these skills. Imagine you wake in a room that is perfectly dark, thanks to heavy curtains, and you hear a rooster crowing outside. It may not take any conscious thought to appreciate that it is growing light outside. The dog's bark at the usual time tells us that the mailman is arriving.

But these examples are infantile compared to what our minds are capable of outdoors. This book is about our great ability in this area, which has been allowed to atrophy, almost forgotten and steamrollered by our modern lifestyle.

But how do we know it is retrievable?

Because a few individuals have held on to these skills, mainly those who have immersed themselves in the study of particular creatures or certain landscapes out of necessity or desire. Indigenous tribespeople all over the world, expert hunters, and fishermen often retain extraordinary abilities and hold the torch to remind us of what is still possible.

I have sat with Dayak tribespeople in Borneo as they explained that a deer would appear over the brow of a hill, and was amazed moments later when my eyes met those of a muntjac in the predicted spot. Only after careful discussion did it become clear that the Dayak were subconsciously tuned to the relationship between the salt on a rock, the bees, the water, the time of day, and the clearing in the forest, all of which suggested that deer would come to lick salt at that time.

The Pygmy people of the Democratic Republic of the Congo are used to hearing honey. They know that when honey is available the sound of a particular animal related to the chameleon changes slightly. They can also sense when they are being watched by a leopard. The physical clues are in the tracks on the ground, but a pedestrian study of them barely relates to predators in the forest. Instead they have learned to associate certain prints with an intimate understanding of the likely resting places of a leopard. Fresh ones near a typical leopard resting place spell danger. When they sense they are being watched, they are usually right.

Inuit hunters have a word, *quinuituq*, that means the deep patience needed while waiting for something to happen. Through it, they develop a relationship with the land that transcends crude analysis. The Arctic expert Barry Lopez described Inuit hunters as going beyond listening for animals or looking for their hoofprints. They "wore" the landscape like clothing, and engaged in a "wordless dialogue" with it. It is important to emphasize that this is science, not mysticism. It is an ancient skill, not New Age, that we were all born to practice. Without any forecasts, many people can tell when rain starts whether it will be a shower or a longer downpour. They may struggle to explain it, but we grow accustomed to the changes in the sky that signify showers or otherwise. Our ancestors were tuned not only to broad changes in the landscape, but to finer ones, like the way the wood sorrel's bright leaves fold up at the approach of rain.

A fisherman may predict the exact spot a trout will rise to the surface, but initially struggle to explain how. On later reflection she realizes that her eyes and brain had worked together to notice that a cloud had blocked the sun. The black gnats had fallen out of the sky due to the lack of sunlight and the trout had come to the surface to feed. But the angler had sensed where the trout would surface.

It is not the location that is important, but the immersion. Recently I spent a few hours with David Baskett, a guide at a coastal reserve in the East of England. We were walking along the top of the longest shingle spit (a kind of jutting pebble beach) in Europe when a pair of dark shapes drew our eyes to the water. The grey seals played for a minute near the end of a groin (a shore-protecting seawall) that stretched down into the water. Then David said, "They'll come up onto the beach now."

The seals took their time, but they were soon wrestling inelegantly with the shingle and hauling their way upward.

"How did you know they would climb out?"

David look puzzled.

I tried again: "How did you know that they would choose this moment and this spot to come out of the water? Is it a daily habit?"

"Uh . . . no." David looked at his feet. "Umm, I don't know, really."

Ten minutes later we were talking about the birds' relationship with vehicles. Cars, vans, even buses will not scatter the birds at the preserve, but the second a car door opens, they're gone. I asked him about the seals again as we looked out over the Scrape (an area of mud and shallow water).

"I think it was the dog," David said.

"Was there one?" I tried to remember. "But don't dogs scare them off?"

"You'd think so, but the seals actually like to come up and investigate them. I think a dog was there when we were. That's probably what made me think that the seals would do what they did. I'm not sure."

Remnants of this ability can still be found in our relationship with domesticated animals. When you're walking a dog in a city park, it's fairly easy to tell from the way it turns whether the person approaching from behind has a dog with them or not. Time spent enjoying this way of experiencing the outdoors helps us to begin rebuilding our lost sixth sense. And if we make this a regular part of our outdoor experience, we soon find that our brain takes over, forging shortcuts and allowing us to draw conclusions without conscious thought. We stop having to think through each step, because our brains do it for us. We sense a dog behind us, and we sense that the weather will be fine tomorrow. It is only a small leap from that to sensing what we will find around a corner or what an animal will do next.

This book includes my experiences, but its main aim is to demonstrate how you can develop this sense in yourself. Central to this are the "keys," a collection of patterns and events in nature worth our attention. I have given each one its own name—for example, "the shear"—to make them easier to remember. Throughout the book, there is a progression from easy to more advanced. The keys will lead you from a raised awareness toward our lost sense.

In this book I bring a lifelong pursuit of outdoor awareness to its zenith, ever the goal of naturalists. It has been an exploration of meaning in nature, and I am indebted to that long tradition. Richard Jefferies, the nineteenth-century nature writer, believed there were messages in the brown, green, and red blotches on finches' eggs, an alphabet he found as alluring and puzzling as "the strange inscriptions of Assyria." All naturalists fail to reach the highest summit, yet we set off anyway, hoping with humility, but never enough, to glimpse nature from some uncharted plateau. Journeys under stars and across oceans, forests, and deserts have led me to the ultimate challenge: to gain a deep, intuitive understanding of my environment closer to home, a true sense of place.

Very little in our surroundings is random, and with a little practice we can learn to sense things that we may find astonishing. Understanding how and why this happens opens a new, and very old, way of experiencing our environment. It is a more radical experience of the outdoors than has been common for centuries.

Part I
Ancient and New

Wild Signs and Star Paths I

SIT ON A PATCH OF EARTH for ten minutes, and all manner of motion will appear. Leaves oscillate in the breeze, sun flecks roll over the undergrowth, birds fly by, insects introduce themselves through flight and wriggling, while ants or beetles may parade. If we choose to look, we will also see the world of the still, the shapes of trees, the colors of earth and flowers, the shades of leaves. When we stand up and walk briskly for ten minutes, our eyes may miss all but the bigger beasts and brightest butterflies. But our brain is busy noticing the things we think we miss.

I drove west along a road that was the blackest of wet tarmacs. There were hedges on either side that didn't register except as a speckled brown blur with the odd white burst of old man's beard, a type of lichen. The bare trees loomed as silhouettes, then raced by. My mind was on my destination, a mundane meeting an hour away, ready to gobble up my morning, then disappear from diary and memory. And then I felt it. I sensed south.

A few years ago, there was a collision between a tree and a star constellation in my head and the world has seemed different ever since. The south I saw on that drive was the result of a shape I have come to know very well. It is called the "tick effect." Phototropism, the way plant growth is influenced by light, leads to tree branches in the northern hemisphere growing closer to horizontal on the southern side and closer to vertical on the northern side. This creates a recognizable tick, or check mark, shape when the tree is viewed from one side.

I had sensed this shape in a tree by the roadside, one I wasn't even looking at, while traveling at about 30 mph. And its familiarity gave me the warm fuzzy feeling that comes with recognition of any pattern we know and like. It also gave me an instant sense of direction.

A couple of days later, I was running a course for a small group in southeast England and I led them to an ash tree. I had chosen it from hundreds of others because it was an exemplar of the tick effect. I gathered the group in the perfect spot to give the ideal perspective of the tree, then stood in front of it and pointed out the shape to them. I enjoy these moments, because others do: Something that may have passed unnoticed is highlighted and then it shines out from nature. It becomes surprisingly obvious.

There were nods and smiles. Most of the group saw it straight away, but two people didn't. I tried again, demonstrating the effect more slowly and deliberately, sketching in the air the silhouetted shape of the branches that made the checkmark. Not a flicker of recognition. During the third attempt, I felt a tinge of irritation—how could those two not see what was plainly in front of their eyes?

I quelled the irritation. There is no point in being a teacher of anything if you can't find the positive challenge in such situations. I tried another tack. I asked the pair to squint: This can filter out smaller details and help us to spot larger shapes. By the fourth variation, everyone in the group could see the effect. And by the end of the afternoon, one of the two who had struggled to spot it pointed out the effect in a distant tree before anyone else, including me, had noticed it.

Later that day, relaxing with a cup of tea, I tried to empathize with the two who had had difficulty seeing the shape. I thought about how I must once have been unable to detect it—I started noticing it in my late twenties, so before that it must have passed me by. Yet it was now announcing itself, leaping out of the blur to the side of a car I was driving. It was not just the shape that was now so easy for me to see, but its meaning. I was sensing direction from a tree, without even trying. How strange, I thought.

The constellation Orion straddles Earth's equator. As a consequence, it rises in the east and sets in the west. Also, it's visible all over the world, which makes it a favorite constellation for natural navigation. I have come to know it very well and have learned to sense direction from Orion without giving it much thought. But for many years I had to think about it. And to get from Orion meaning little to its announcing direction instantly, I must have followed the same paths of recognition that everyone traces with star constellations until something unusual happened.

First, we learn to recognize the pattern of a constellation. This must be why our ancestors concocted constellations; they were almost certainly invented in prehistory to give us something to recognize and help us to make sense of a complex picture. Our brains have evolved to find and recognize patterns, which allows us to impose and then find order in the thousands of stars that are visible at night. A night sky that would otherwise appear random and overwhelming is a collection of patterns we can identify.

The more familiar we become with the constellations, the more comfortable the night sky feels. But it is the recognition of the patterns that is vital. Recently, in an inflatable planetarium in Wales, I was listening to a talk by Martin Griffiths, a professor of astronomy, about the constellations and patterns that the Celts once saw in the night sky. It was a delightful talk but, however fascinating it was culturally, it became uncomfortable on a psychological level. I watched as the professor tore up the ancient patterns I knew and substituted different ones. It almost made me queasy. The telling thing was that none of the stars changed or moved, but he redrew the patterns. A bear mutated into a horse, a scorpion became a beaver. Small details perhaps, but it disrupted my comfort with the night sky. After the talk, I went back across the fields, guided by more familiar patterns.

Once we have learned to recognize a constellation, like Orion, the next step in natural navigation is becoming familiar with its meaning in terms of direction. In the case of Orion, it's not difficult to get started: Since it rises in the east and sets in the west, if you see it near the horizon you must be looking east or west. If, after half an hour, you notice it has gone up a bit, you're looking east, and if it has sunk, you're looking west.

The Orion method is a straightforward way of gauging approximate direction using a pattern in the night sky. I used to do it regularly. I never decided to stop, but it isn't what I do now. Now when I see Orion, I see direction. I'm not talking about numbers of degrees or words like "east" or "west" popping into my head: Those are labels of direction. I actually *see* direction. Which, I hope you'll agree, is a bit odd. But it *is* something you can see. And *you'll* soon be seeing direction in the night sky, but only as one tiny part of a new awareness. More importantly, you'll be regaining your sense of what's going on around you outdoors. I'll give you the nuts and bolts of the Orion method later, but first I'd like to share with you how it fits into the small revolution—perhaps renaissance is a better word, you decide!—in the way we can experience the outdoors.

The San people in the Kalahari desert report experiencing a powerful burning sensation when they are getting close to an animal they are hunting, and Aboriginal peoples of Australia have talked of orienting themselves using a "feeling." In 1973, when asked how he found his way, Wintinna Mick, an Aboriginal Australian, told the navigator and scholar David Lewis, "I have a feeling . . . Feel in my head. Been in the bush since small. That way is northwest." Lewis thought he was calculating this using the sun, but Mick was insistent that he was not: "I know this northwest direction not by the sun, but by the map inside my head."

We know that people who live in indigenous communities in wild places have an awareness of their surroundings that eludes those of us living in an industrialized society. A sense of direction is a small part of this, but by no means the most important.

During the Enlightenment, also known as the Age of Reason, rational thought was prized over the religious faith that had dominated for centuries. Cartesian rationalism and the weights, measures, and machines of the scientific revolution prevailed. Intellectual snobbery ensued, and any suspicion that the heart was being allowed to rule the head was viewed skeptically by the intellectual vanguard of the time. It was a decisive shift and, despite pockets of resistance and a determined fight by Romanticism, it has prevailed to this day. The savage was not noble, just ignorant. The gut was denied its feeling.

It's not only indigenous communities who have this awareness; animals have it too, of course. Which may explain why this form of thinking has unfortunately been seen as inferior historically, typical of the "lower" beasts and "natives." What sort of argument could be made in favor of the way tribespeople experience their environment when pitted against a civilization that gave us steam engines and a vaccination against smallpox? How hard is it still to value it from a culture of space travel and the Internet? We have gained so much through a more analytical view of the world, but at what cost?

This is not a new concern. We've had a nagging suspicion for centuries that we were becoming cleverer with each passing year, but perhaps not growing any more aware. William Cowper, the eighteenth-century English poet, expressed this in "The Doves":

Reas'ning at every step he treads,
Man yet mistakes his way,
While meaner things whom instinct leads
Are rarely known to stray.

He knew that as our maps became better, we were losing our deeper understanding of the territory.

Years after pondering tree shapes and my experiences with Orion, I began reading books and papers that I hoped would help me understand what was going on. Thanks to the work of many extraordinary researchers, such as the psychologists Gary Klein, Amos Tversky, and Daniel Kahneman, the mystery was solved. I could suddenly see a path to rediscovering our lost sense of awareness outdoors.

We have two ways of thinking and we need both, because each is excellent at certain things and rubbish at others. Consider this unlikely scenario: You are relaxing at home, watching TV, when a stranger kicks down your door and runs into the room wielding a knife. At this point your brain has performed a lot of assessments of the situation very quickly. You have made decisions about whether to run away, fight back, or stay put. Your pulse has risen, you are perspiring, and your breathing has changed. All of this has taken place automatically. At this point the intruder seizes you, holds the sharp, cold knife against your throat, and whispers in your ear, "A car drives at sixty miles per hour for two hours, then at forty miles per hour for another two hours. How far did it travel? Answer correctly and I'll let you go. Get it wrong and you're dead!"

"Uh . . . two hundred miles," you reply.

They let you go and disappear into the night.

In the space of one surreal minute you have used two different types of thinking. Some psychologists call the two ways of thinking System 1 and System 2. But I've found that's too dry to be memorable and quickly becomes confusing. Daniel Kahneman has better labels: fast and slow, as outlined in his book *Thinking, Fast and Slow*. If we need to compare or calculate things, follow rules, or make deliberate choices, this is "slow" thinking. If we are surprised by a sound, sense anger, feel beauty, or take fright, this is "fast" thinking.

How can we tell one type of thinking from the other? There is no perfect method, but the best clue is that if we can tell we're thinking about something, it's conscious thinking. It's slow. If we react to something "without thinking about it," then the truth is that we have thought about it, just using the system that we don't consciously acknowledge. This is fast thinking. When indigenous people show an instant awareness of their surroundings without appearing to think about it, they're using fast thinking. And I'm convinced that this was a far greater part of all humanity's outdoor perspective ten thousand years ago and at all times before the first agricultural revolution.

If we imagine there being a sliding scale from fast unconscious thought at one end to slow conscious thought at the other, we can picture our ancestors being closer to the fast end than contemporary indigenous people, and those of us who enjoy the odd Starbucks as being toward the slower end. It is important to stress that this has nothing to do with intelligence; there has been no significant biological change in our brains during the time period. The differences are cultural. Or, put another way, an average human of ten thousand years ago could solve *The Times* crossword as fast as his or her counterpart today, if they had led the same lifestyle and had the same influences. Ironically, according to eminent historians like Yuval Noah Harari, they probably had more free time than us, so they may have enjoyed the distraction.

Fortunately, there isn't yet a great wall between us and this experience of the outdoors. It is just that this faculty has shrunk to the point where it is a minor part of our experience. I remember giving a talk in a town in Essex, in southeast England, and staying in a hotel overnight afterward. During breakfast the following morning, I was thinking about the ideas in this book and a very cheery elderly waitress was pouring my tea for me when she said, "Looks like rain."

We were indoors and, to the best of my knowledge, she had not set foot outside for quite a while. Sure enough, by the end of my breakfast it had begun to rain. Because I was contemplating this book, I asked her how she had known it would rain. She looked pleasantly shocked to have been asked something so strange. But after a short pause, it transpired that there was no mystery: The skies had darkened a little, and this was evident even from the small amount of natural light reaching into a room full of neon. That may surprise or impress nobody, but that is the point: We all still have the ability. It is just that it has withered to a few short-term weather forecasts or similar. However, there is nothing stopping us from rekindling the deeper skills we once had. As we will see, few areas demonstrate the gulf between what we could once do and our ability today than our understanding of animal behavior in the wild.

Watch a bird flying toward a tree and you will be able to tell whether it is about to land on that tree or fly past it. This is not because you can read the bird's mind, but because you can read its body language. If you don't believe you can do this, try it. Watch a bird in flight and pick the moment you think it's about to land on something. It will be before its feet touch down. Now ask yourself, how did you know that the bird was about to land?

Birds fan their tails and change their angle of flying and their speed just before landing, which means that their bodies go from near horizontal to pointing slightly upward and this angle increases sharply just prior to landing. It is the way both birds and aircraft can go from flying quickly through the air to landing on something slowly and safely, without falling out of the sky.

Our brains are picking up these clues all the time and making sense of them as best they can. There are thousands of them around us, all of the time, and we interpret many without realizing it. Your brain can tell that the bird is about to land because it has enough information from your senses, but this is the interesting thing: If asked, you might struggle to describe exactly how you knew it. Your brain made sense of the bird's body language without bothering your conscious mind with the details, a classic difference between fast and slow thinking: The fast part knows things that the slow part can't articulate. Thanks to photography and careful studies, we now know that ducks have four distinct stages of landing, including a certain head angle and bringing their feet forward. But we knew this already; we know what a landing duck looks like, we just didn't have scientific labels for each of the stages.

Imagine you're walking in an area that you don't know well and you're being watched by a friend at the top of a steep hill. Your friend watches you walk quickly and confidently over the crest of a gentle hill, then slow down as you approach the crest of a dangerous precipice. Afterward they ask how you knew to slow down before the big drop.

"Well, I could see that there was a steep drop coming up," you answer.

"Yes, but how? Could you see what was on the other side of each crest?" she persists.

"Um, no. But one felt dangerous and the other didn't. I don't know why."

But, of course, you do know. Your brain has grown accustomed to noticing the subtle differences in the way the landscape changes as you approach a gentle hill compared to a sharper drop, even if you don't appreciate exactly what it's doing. The brain's not perfect at this. I'm sure you've had those experiences where you find yourself gingerly treading toward an edge, only to find that it is a small dip followed by a kind slope that rolls away. Your brain has picked up the steep edge and prompted you to take a safety-first approach in that situation. All it senses is that there is a sharp drop; it doesn't have the information to tell you that it's only a tiny one.

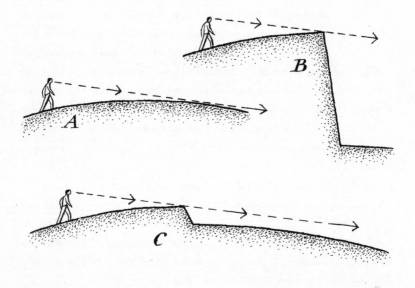

All of this so far is straightforward stuff, by which I mean that these are skills we have retained, even if we spend little time outdoors compared to our ancestors. But I shall demonstrate how it is possible to develop such skills to a much higher level.

People who still spend long periods outdoors, particularly if they are focusing on certain areas, talk of this greater ability. The language may vary, but the experience is similar and points to an ancient sense of extraordinary awareness. Rob Thurlow is the ranger in my local woods, and we often discuss our experiences there. He has spent thousands of hours monitoring deer behavior.

"Sometimes you just feel the eyes on you," Rob told me, referring to the fairly regular experience of knowing that a deer has clocked him, even though he's looking the other way. I know exactly what he means and have had the same experience, as have many others. Joel Hardin, who was a professional man-tracker with US law enforcement for many years, sometimes had a strong sense that he was very close to a fugitive: "I just had a feeling." And he was usually right.

When it is unclear how these sensations come about, they can be given labels, like "psychic" or "gut feeling" or "sixth sense," but whenever we use such words or phrases, we are alluding to the fact that the evidence has been sorted out using our fast thinking. There is no right or wrong with the labels we choose to use for this—it is hard to be precise in language about something that goes on inside our heads that we can't feel happening—but I shall describe it as "fast thinking" or "intuition," one being the active process, the other the general ability.

From suggesting that our distant ancestors would be able to do *The Times* crossword if they were given the cultural framework, it follows that we can regain our ability to sense the outdoors as they did. That may sound daunting, but it is the framework that is important. Besides, you are already using these skills every day in your work and at home. All we are talking about is moving us back along the scale outdoors. Let's look at a few examples that demonstrate that we can still do this.

If someone asks you whether it is night or day, it is not a taxing question to answer. If an insect lands on the back of your neck, you will swat it away without hesitation or contemplation. If you see the trees swaying outside a window, you instantly sense that it's windy. Through the same window on another day, you see the heat haze rise off bright pavement and your brain tells you it's hot without your asking it. Walking along a track down a hill, you see two small, bright elliptical objects on the ground in the distance that are colored like the sky. Before reading on, work out: What are these bright objects? That last question was a bit sneaky. Here, I have tried to lay a friendly ambush by asking your slow thinking to do something your fast thinking is better at. The answer is that you are looking at water, a pair of puddles on the track ahead of you. You may have worked that out by considering the evidence presented, the biggest clue being that these objects were the color of the sky—when viewed from a shallow angle, water acts like a mirror. But whether you got the answer to this before reading it or not is unimportant. The key point is that if you were actually doing the walk, you wouldn't have needed to consider the evidence or think slowly about it; your brain would have recognized the shape, color, and situation of the objects, automatically compared them to those with which it was familiar in that setting, and presented the answer to you. And this would have happened whether you wanted it to or not. In reality, you couldn't not have recognized the puddles.

Let's consider situations where we use both types of thinking. The other night I took my two sons out on a night walk. As we were returning home we saw the clouds suddenly brighten.

"Whoa . . . what was that? Was it lightning?" Vincent, my ten-year-old, said.

"Yup," I replied.

To me, it was obviously lightning, but my younger son hadn't yet built enough experience of it during night walks to recognize it instantly. He had to think about it. His cogs were probably sifting through a process like this: sudden very bright light in a cloudy sky . . . search memory for known images that fit . . . only one so far . . . lightning?

All three of us recognized the lightning, albeit in slightly different ways.

There was another strike.

"That was a big one! Is it close, Daddy?" Vinnie asked, a little anxiety in his voice.

"No, not close, but let's see how far. One elephant, two elephants, three elephants . . . fifteen elephants . . . twenty-five elephants . . . It's still a long way off, more than five miles away."

"How do you do that again, Dad?" Ben asked.

"We count the seconds, by counting elephants, until we hear thunder, then divide that number by five to get miles, or divide by three to get kilometers."

Because there was little wind, it wasn't raining, and the thunder had not arrived immediately after the lightning, I had known straight away that it was not a storm we needed to worry about yet; that was intuitive. By the time the elephants arrived in our conversation, we were all using slow thinking to build a more detailed picture of where it was.

When Vincent first asked me whether the flash was lightning, his fast thinking had sensed something that surprised and alarmed him. When that happens to any of us, our fast system bumps it over to our slow system to analyze. If you're walking down a street at night and sense that the person coming toward you is not behaving normally, you will begin to analyze the person and situation more deliberately. Fast (sense) to slow (analysis).

If you are at a party and hear your name mentioned in a conversation on the other side of the room, your attention switches to that conversation. You may then hear the rest, including references to your charm and good looks—let's give human nature the benefit of the doubt here. But if you then tried to remember what those people were talking about before they mentioned your name, you wouldn't be able to because you weren't listening carefully enough. The volume of the conversation hadn't changed, but by focusing your conscious slow thinking on it, you could make out what was being said from that moment onward.

Here's the weird thing: How did you hear your name being mentioned in the first place, since you weren't listening carefully at that point? That was your fast unconscious thinking constantly scanning your environment for threats, and nothing is more threatening to the modern tribesperson than gossip.

If all we could do was divide up the types of outdoor thinking into fast and slow, it would remain an academic exercise and do little to improve our experience or ability in nature. The next step is noticing how and where our brains engage fast thinking instead of slow. This is something to which I have given a lot of thought over the past few years. Incidentally, this thinking has been mostly "slow," sometimes painfully so. But there has been the occasional fast moment. We all experience sudden fast moments in our work and play. They are rare but delightful, and we call them "insights," or "aha!" moments.

"Yes! Brilliant! That's how we can solve the problem and meet the impossible deadline!" Or, "Of course! That's why Helen didn't react as I thought she would. She's in love!"

Gary Player, a very successful golfer, was practicing difficult shots out of a bunker. He managed to sink the ball in the hole twice in a row. A Texan who was watching and couldn't believe his eyes offered him a hundred dollars if he could do it a third time. In the ball went. The Texan handed over the cash, adding that he thought Player was the luckiest person he'd ever seen.

"Well, the harder I practice, the luckier I get," Player replied.

I'm sure he wasn't the first person to use that line and he won't be the last, because we all know that time spent doing things repeatedly hones our skills. That expression, "hones our skills," is another way of saying that our fast thinking becomes more adept through practice. Outdoor skills are no different from sports skills or any others; they take practice.

The Sun Anvil

THE AIM WAS TO, WITHOUT USING any maps or navigation instruments, touch the sea on the north coast of Crete, then head south until we could touch it on the south coast. It was about twenty-six miles as the crow flies, but we would be neither flying nor following many straight lines. I reckoned we needed to be ready to walk about double that distance. There was also the matter of the 8,000-foot mountain range in our way.

The real challenges were heat, water, and weight. It was September and the land would be parched. I wanted us to be able to walk for up to four days without relying on additional food or water from anywhere. But walking for four days in mountainous terrain with a pack in temperatures as high as 99 degrees Fahrenheit means you need a lot of water. And water is heavy. The more we started with, the heavier our packs, the harder the going, the slower we would walk, and the more water we would need. It was a teasing conundrum. The best compromise seemed to me to be four gallons each. To avoid a water emergency, the plan was that we were not allowed to touch our reserve gallon of water unless we had thrown in the towel, broken out the emergency map and GPS, and headed for civilization. And we were not allowed to touch the final gallon until the end was in sight. This may all sound a bit tough for a holiday walk, but I have known people who died from heat stroke and it can be sudden. In truth, it was the only risk I feared.

In Panormos, a small town on the north coast, my good friend Ed and I checked our own supplies and then each other's. We rammed water bottles into our packs, clipped them to the outside, filled our stomachs with fresh water, then touched the sea and waddled off into the hot hills.

One of the few great frustrations of natural navigation is that it is hard to assess rights of way in semi-wild environments. Nature does not map property rights in the way it does direction and terrain. It was not long before a shepherd emerged from a ramshackle outbuilding and began remonstrating with us in fast Greek. The words meant nothing, but the body language was fluent and easily intelligible—he was telling us to head back the way we had come. The simple plan did not allow for much retracing of steps; we had a time limit, enforced by our limited water, so we tried various ways of charming our way past him. He became angry. We tried a different tactic.

I had read a bit about the history of Crete, and I knew the hills are still stained with dark memories of the Second World War. During the Nazi occupation, there were brave pockets of resistance, then a wave of slaughter by the Germans. Guns are still widespread and there remains a proud, independent spirit to the Cretans, especially in the rural mountainous areas where we would be traveling.

"We're from London, England."

I don't know if this line helped or if its timing was coincidental, but the mood softened and we were soon waved on our way. All future meetings were very friendly. We were even offered a lift on an olive farmer's tractor—which we politely turned down. It was against the rules of the strange coast-to-coast game we had decided to play.

One heavy foot in front of the other, we made our way uphill.

"Clear."

"Clear."

One of the less savory routines we set up early on was to check in with each other about the color of our urine. We knew it would get darker as the paths got steeper and we risked dehydration, so we wanted to keep it the right side of amber.

The first day was always going to be hard. It was hot in the foothills, our packs weighed their maximum, and it was almost relentlessly uphill. Ed took my mind off the temperature by asking if the alignment of greenhouses might be used to help find direction. I wasn't sure, but made a note to check. It turned out that north-south is preferred, unless there is not enough light in summer, when east-west is better. So, maybe.

At the end of the first sweaty day we rolled out our foam mats and sat down by an outbuilding on the ridgeline of the mountains we were crossing. We had pushed ourselves hard and I wasn't sure that the heat would allow us to keep up the pace for the following days, but perhaps we wouldn't have to. And if we did, at least there should be some downhill and our packs would be about ten pounds lighter each day.

We ate some foil-packed curry and watched the stars emerge. I set up some transits—lining up the North Star over some rocks—to give us an accurate compass in the morning should the sun be hidden behind cloud. Then we lay down under a thousand stars.

Ed began the swearing, but I joined in soon enough. The mosquitoes arrived in waves. We plastered ourselves in repellent and lay down again. After a day like that, it would have taken mosquitoes the size of rats to keep us awake all night, but we did wake sporadically to sense them buzzing and biting our faces. It happened so regularly that we noticed a pattern. Every time we were woken by the mosquitoes, the sky was overcast. There were never any when it was clear. It was so dependable that we took to waiting for clouds to pass before closing our eyes, knowing we would wake again when the next bank arrived.

I carried with us the whole range of natural navigation techniques that my head has stored over the past couple of decades. But there was no doubting that, unless the weather did some very odd things, the sun would be our main compass.

In early September, the sun would rise and set a few degrees north of east and west and be due south in the middle of the day. The critical thing was how its bearing would change between those times. It is not a uniform process. The bearing of the sun changes more dramatically near the middle of the day than at either end. For any serious expedition, I try to keep a handle on this by calculating what time the sun will pass through southeast and southwest. This gives a good measure of its passage through the day—the closer to the middle of the day this happens (and it is always equidistant to either side), the more dramatic the change around lunchtime. I have found this to be the fastest way of accelerating a fresh familiarization with the sun as a compass.

It starts with a routine of cross-checking time with the direction of the sun. We had watches—our one concession to modernity. What time is it? That is, which side of the southeast time are we on? Half an hour early—OK, that means the sun must be a few degrees to the east side of southeast. We used that information to pick a point to aim for, ideally in the middle distance or beyond, and repeated the process perhaps a dozen times a day in open country, and much more regularly in woodland or difficult terrain.

Then something much more interesting started to happen. At some point, maybe toward the end of day two, the formal checks became less frequent and the informal ones much more common. That may not sound very profound, but I believe it is. The slightly slow deliberations were no longer necessary; we had a sense of where the sun was in the sky and the direction that indicated. Our brains had been gently hammered into a new pattern of thought. This is the sun anvil. The meaning we can find in the sun had become intuitive.

The following day, the change had become ingrained. It was hard to tell when we were even thinking about it; the sun was just there, guiding us silently and effectively in any direction we chose to go. This is how many indigenous people use the sun today, and how our ancestors once did.

At times the sun hid behind clouds, and we were even rained on briefly, which gave us the beautiful opportunity to navigate using a rainbow. The sky was a mixture of light and dark clouds, the sun well hidden behind a mountain ridgeline, and a rainbow appeared in front of us, adding welcome colors to the arid brown of the mountain range on the opposite side of a broad valley. It was extraordinary. I could feel the pattern unraveling again.

If we imagine a rainbow as part of a full circle, then the center of that circle will always be directly opposite the sun—this is why rainbows at the start and end of the day are big semicircles. To navigate using rainbows, we need only to think about where the sun is in the sky and the rainbow will be 180 degrees in the opposite direction. But this takes some conscious calculation. It is fairly straightforward, but it was striking how different it felt from the previous hours of wayfinding by

intuitive sense of the sun's direction. Practice had pulled the sun compass from slow thinking to fast, and the rainbow pulled it back the other way. If the rainbow had lasted long enough we would doubtless have learned to use it intuitively, as we had the sun, but the showers passed and the chance never came.

For our lunch break on the second day, we rested in the shade of a goat milking parlor. More for my own amusement than out of necessity, I placed a coin at the end of the shadow cast by a rusting piece of iron. After a lunch of cold chili con carne and dried banana chips, I placed a second coin at the end of the shadow's latest position; the line joining the two marked east-west on the ground.

A few hours later we passed a house with beach gear drying outside. It was satisfying to think that, unless we had gone horribly wrong, the signs of the sea that we were looking at had probably been driven up from the south coast, not the north.

The second afternoon was horrible. In an attempt to hold the high ground, usually a good tactic, we found ourselves caught in a maze of interlocking spurs. Steep climbs, steep descents, alternating in a brutal fashion for a few hours under a cloudy sky. They left us feeling tired and dispirited. We judged our progress in the distance we felt we had covered in a southerly direction. The spurs were forcing us east and then west, making us work hard for no south at all. We decided to pitch camp an hour before dark—whenever possible I like to have a bed and a meal, however basic, ready by the time the sun goes below.

We found a clearing among the trees, and it looked perfect. There were a few more animal bones than would have been ideal, but they were much easier to clear than the endless rocks in most spots we had considered. There were tunnels in the dense undergrowth nearby and it was obvious we were settling by a network of animal trails, but since we knew there were no animals in Crete that need concern us, we thought little more of it.

After supper Ed and I worked through the various compasses that were being formed by the stars: Scorpius and the summer, or Navigator's, triangle were pointing south, Cygnus, Cassiopeia, and the Big Dipper to the North Star. Again, we set up transits so that the following morning we could see the pointers marked on the ground.

The rest of the evening was far from relaxing. As we settled and said good night to each other, we heard a vehicle approaching over one of the many dirt tracks that laced the mountain. It sounded close enough for us to see headlights, but we saw none. Then we heard the first shot. The swearing at the mosquitoes the night before was nothing to the profanities that rang out around the mountainside then.

Hunting is the most popular pastime in these wilder parts of Crete. It was clear that someone was shooting if not directly at us then very close to us. In our exhaustion, we had accidentally made camp on a prime spot for targeting animals. Our headlamps went on and I broke out a spare one, setting it to flashing mode. Then I rummaged in the bag at the bottom of the rucksack that contained the things I hadn't thought we'd need and began breaking light sticks to hang from the trees. The adrenaline was intense. We were possibly trespassing, albeit in a semi-wild area, and it wasn't clear if we should be jumping up and down or keeping as low as possible. We opted for the latter, lay down, and listened. There were a few more shots and then we heard the vehicle start up and move off.

It was the sort of experience that would have kept me awake for an hour on a normal day, but at the end of two very physical days, I soon started to drift off.

Minutes later, I sat bolt upright and switched on my headlamp again. The beam lit the face of a startled cat. It was six feet from my face, staring at me. It was noticeably bigger than a domestic cat, but with some similar features. It paused for one second, as if assessing who was ascendant in this encounter. I remained still and stared back at it. Then it bolted into the undergrowth.

"What was that?" Ed asked.

"I don't know," I replied.

"What made you turn on your lamp?"

"I must have heard something." But I wasn't convinced. The animal was near silent in its retreat, and I doubted it would have made a noise that woke me. I may never know what caused me to sit upright and turn on the headlamp. I can picture the animal's face still, and there is only one species it can possibly have been: a wildcat sometimes nicknamed the Cretan lynx. It is extremely rare, thought for many years to be extinct. I treasure the memory now, but at the time I wanted some sleep untroubled by gunshots or rare felines.

Over breakfast the following morning, we looked for the tracks of the wildcat. They were there, but then so were hundreds of others. The whole clearing was a killing field, thousands of small bones. It was hard to tell what had done most of the killing, predators or humans.

We decided to give up on holding the high ground and dropped down into the valley. The sun came out again and we made good ground, heading south through wild, rocky landscapes, then olive groves.

By lunchtime on the third day, we could see civilization along a coastline, and it was welcome. Not least because water was already getting low. The temperature rose again as we dropped down, and we arrived at the coast that afternoon. Hobbling onto the beach, we dipped our hands into the sea and took photos of the moment. Then we studied signs on hotels and restaurants to work out exactly where we were. We discovered we were in a place called Agia Galini, meaning "Holy Peace." Neither of us had ever heard of it. Turned out it's directly south of our starting point in Panormos. But that was as much by luck as judgment. By which I mean that parts of our brains allowed themselves to be shaped by the sun anvil and we let them do the hard work. I am confident that we would have fared less well if we had relied on too much clever, slow thinking.

Wild Signs and Star Paths II

EARLIER I PROMISED YOU THE KEY to seeing direction in Orion. All you need to do is add a couple of secondary patterns to the shape of the constellation and then to practice noticing these. Your brain will happily do the rest for you—it is always keen to take fast, automatic shortcuts if it can, as this has been essential to our survival as a species. Sitting around a fire in the Amazon jungle, the sound of bird alarm calls in the trees sets a tribal group thinking slowly and consciously about its meaning. But the survivors of a jaguar attack didn't ponder the meaning a second time; they got out of there.

On his journey from east to west, Orion "rolls" up across the southern sky, then down. He is highest when due south. In practice this means that the orientation of the pattern we know as Orion and its height are clues to direction. And once we have had enough practice at recognizing these three patterns—the shape of the constellation, its orientation, and its height—the process becomes intuitive. We learn to see direction in the night sky "without thinking about it." The same approach can be applied to all the constellations. Some take more practice than others and many have seasons, but if we choose to, we can learn to see direction—that is, to sense meaning in constellations as we do with a compass needle. The first time anyone sees a compass, the needle holds no meaning.

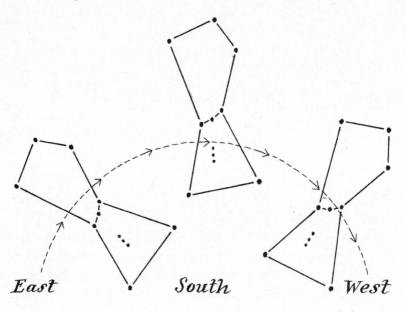

East   South   West

To start with, you'll want to keep the Orion method as straight-forward as possible. Height is a great help: The higher Orion is, the closer to south you are looking. Next, notice how Orion has a belt; it is easy to recognize as it is the only place in the night sky where you will see three bright stars form a short straight line. Below his belt hangs Orion's sword. As Orion rolls from east to west, through south, the angle of the sword changes relative to the horizon. If we think of it as a needle on a gauge, it moves from pointing east at the left side, via south in the middle, and finishes pointing west. Compare the illustrations above and below and this will become clearer.

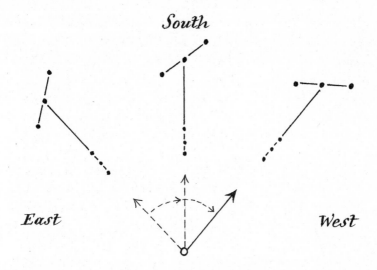

All you need to do now is to practice associating the sword "needle" with direction. It takes slow thought the first few times, but if you persevere you'll notice that the effort level drops. This can happen quite suddenly and is a sign that your brain has automated part of the process for you. Perhaps you struggle to identify Orion for a couple of nights, but within a week you'll find it hard not to spot him. However, at this stage it still takes a moment to work out which way he's aligned, and this may remain the case for a fortnight. Then, a few weeks later, you've parked your car, you're wondering what to have for supper, your mind is miles away from the night sky, and you suddenly see it: south in the sky.

Orion isn't visible from May to July; he reappears in August before dawn and leaves again after dusk in late spring. But all constellations follow regular patterns of movement, so we can develop this method with any stars we choose. Orion gets top billing because he was the first to point out to me how my understanding of the night sky had undergone the change that this book is about. In summer, I'd encourage you to look for the summer or Navigator's triangle, three bright stars—Altair, Deneb, and Vega—that form a triangle in the night sky. As it rises to its highest point, it forms an arrow that points south. Again, it may take a bit of scouring to find it the first few times, then longer still to see how it points south. But the moment soon comes when you will sense the sign and its meaning.

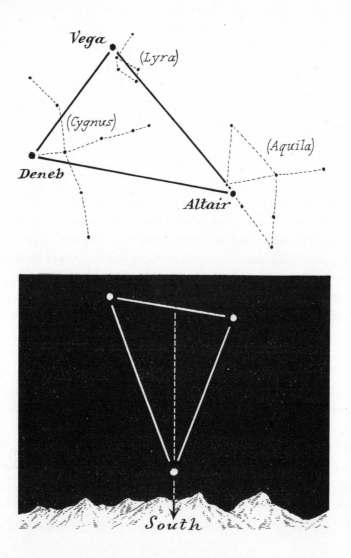

This is a moment to celebrate and savor. But soon after, I'd recommend explaining this method, step by step, to a willing victim among family or friends, because you will then get a great view of the road you've come along. You are sensing things they aren't. Not the stars; you're seeing patterns that they might have to search for, and you can instantly sense meaning in a sky that holds none for them—yet.

The night sky hasn't changed but, with a little practice, the way we perceive it has. As the Victorian polymath John Ruskin wrote, "The first great mistake that people make in the matter, is the supposition that they must *see* a thing if it be before their eyes." Knowing what to look for, and some practice, means we come to sense so much more than, at first, our eyes show us. And this applies to all our other senses.

A Royal Society for the Protection of Birds (RSPB) warden once explained to me that the most common word used to describe their reserve on feedback forms was "quiet." He found this "bizarre, given how noisy the place is." That is the difference between someone tuned to find meaning in sound and the more common modern experience, which is to filter it out as general noise. Richard Jefferies made the point that the seasons come earlier to those who are accustomed to sensing them: "It is very likely some ploughboy who thinks nothing of it—except to immediately imitate it—hears the cuckoo forty-eight hours before those who have been listening most carefully."

If we know that we have two systems, two very different ways of experiencing and making sense of the outdoors, it is natural to wonder about the biological explanation for them.

Different parts of the brain are tasked with different things. All vertebrates have "an ancient brain," a set of structures known as the limbic system. It allows fast reactions, emotions, and many things we might describe as animal-like thought or behavior; it is also involved in memory and learning, and it developed very early in animal evolution. It is the part of the brain that we share with most animals, even fairly primitive ones, which is why it is sometimes nicknamed the "lizard brain."

Within the limbic system, the amygdalae, two almond-shaped areas, are responsible for emotional learning and fear conditioning, including the "fight or flight" response. The group we met briefly in the Amazon ran from the bird sounds they heard for the second time in the jungle because the amygdalae had made a mental note that their best friends were eaten by a jaguar shortly after the last time that had happened. It was traumatic, and the amygdalae know that we don't like trauma. They do their best to help us avoid it by constantly registering patterns and their consequences.

Human brains also contain the neocortex. It is more ponderous than the limbic system, but very powerful. It can do things the limbic system can't, like work out the square root of 256, manage speech, compare the shapes and sizes of two objects, and decide to argue about politics and religion.

Imagine that a close friend who has always managed their finances appallingly asks you to loan them a large sum of money. Your limbic system will give you your gut reaction to that request. If you're OK with it, your neocortex will help you decide whether you can afford to make the loan.

The amygdalae constantly monitor our environment and trigger actions or other responses. It is this region that allows us to flick a wasp away before we are consciously aware of it. Whenever it picks up something it doesn't like or isn't sure about, it pings it over to the neocortex for a check. If you have ever felt uneasy about a situation, but not known immediately why, your neocortex is picking up a signal from your limbic system and trying to make sense of it. "Something's not right here" is part of the limbic system's vocabulary.

The Swiss psychologist Carl Jung believed it was this process that explained the rationale behind many omens, superstitions, and other behaviors that might be thought whimsical by rationalists. Pueblo Indians alter plans because of a change in mood; an ancient Roman who tripped on the way out of his house would abandon whatever he was leaving it to do. To Jung, these were not irrational actions, but decisions by people who were more in touch with the meaning of conflicting signals. According to this theory, we slip or trip because our brain is struggling with signals that we have yet to make sense of; in Jung's words, we are in a "distracted psychological state." We will see further evidence of the logic behind this theory when we look at how the wind influences our understanding of our environment.

We are homing in on the nuts and bolts of gaining a better sense of the natural environment. The limbic system is involved in our fastest reactions, our emotions, and our learning. This last part is crucial: Since our limbic system can learn, we can expect to get better at understanding situations fast. We all know the saying "Once bitten, twice shy," but the Bedouin go further than that: "He who's bitten by a viper jumps from a spotted rope." Past experience shapes our perceptions and future reactions.

This learning is not limited to simple emergency reactions. It can incorporate a lot more information from our senses and operates in much more complex situations. Experienced doctors zero in on diagnoses before they can explain to themselves, let alone their patients, how they got there. Detectives interviewing a suspect "know" something is not right before they can identify what it is. In 1856, in the early heyday of the English detective, a journalist eager to satisfy the public's curiosity about these new professionals interviewed one. The detective explained how he had recently apprehended a pickpocket: "I did not even know myself. There was something about him, as about all swell mobsmen [pickpockets working in groups], that immediately attracted my attention, and led me to bend my eye upon him. He did not appear to notice my watching him, but passed into the thick of the crowd, but then he turned and looked toward the spot in which I was—this was enough for me, although I had never seen him before, and he had not to my knowledge attempted any pocket. I immediately made my way toward him."

Charlotte Brontë described this skill as a "sensitiveness—that peculiar, apprehensive, detective faculty." The word "peculiar" here alludes to the skill being mysterious because its workings are not open to our own investigation. We don't find "peculiar" the ability of someone to work out the weight of butter or the surface area of a garden because the method can be described, written down, analyzed, and experienced by each of us, step by step. But intuitive thought doesn't subject itself to dissection so readily. That doesn't mean it can't be developed—and that is the game afoot here, as Sherlock Holmes might have said. By focusing our efforts and observation in certain areas, we can develop our awareness to a remarkable level.

Scientists have proven that we regularly reach conclusions about situations before we know it. It is possible to pick up on our earliest "lizard" responses by monitoring our palms, which will sweat before our conscious minds have assessed a situation. In a series of experiments with colored cards and gambling stakes, scientists in Iowa proved that gamblers can sense a pattern in the cards significantly earlier than they can explain it. In an experiment that involved turning over cards, participants spotted the pattern forty cards before they could explain it.

Psychologists have done a lot of work in laboratory conditions, but Gary Klein decided to focus his research on how people's experience shaped their perception and decision-making in real life, and often in risky situations. He made one of his most illustrative discoveries when he investigated how a firefighting team had narrowly averted disaster. The lead firefighter suddenly felt a sense of dread and ordered, "Let's get out now!" Shortly after, the floor they had been standing on collapsed into an inferno below. Klein was keen to understand what had prompted the decision to evacuate the building, but the firefighter was at a loss to explain it. He thought ESP—extrasensory perception—had saved him on that occasion and many others. But Klein was not convinced.

It turned out that there had been a series of small clues that the fire was not behaving as experience dictated it should. It was hotter than the firefighter would have expected, it didn't react to water in the way a fire like that should have, and it was quieter than normal. These were all indicative of a fire raging below, not just in front, but at the time they were "subliminal" clues, classic fast thinking; they are picked up by the senses and registered by the brain, but not in a way that an individual is conscious of. The firefighter's experience triggered the same deep sense of unease that Jung and others have referred to. It saved lives, which was great leadership, but we shouldn't be surprised by the psychology. This is precisely what that part of our brain has evolved to do: make fast decisions based on experience that allow us to live another day.

Most contemporary researchers acknowledge in passing that limbic fast thinking has its roots in evolution and stems from our original need to survive in a natural environment. However, there is a silent assumption that our original environment is no longer of any relevance. But many of us do still spend time outdoors, and these systems are still the key to taking that experience to another level.

The extraordinary ability to assess situations in firefights, doctors' surgeries, and detectives' interrogation rooms springs from our ancestors' ability to sense what was happening around them in nature. If professionals are still able to use it, it follows that outdoorsmen and -women can, too. In fact, since this ability evolved to help us thrive within the natural world, we are better placed than any of them to redevelop it.

"Once bitten, twice shy" means that we learn from situations we associate with bad experiences and hesitate or shy away from them. The expression is now used in a contemporary context: If we have been stung by a financial-scam email once, we hesitate rather than falling for the same trick again. But the habit stems from our brain's ability to learn from our natural environment; we hesitate before approaching wasps because we know what it feels like to be stung.

The first time I heard terrible nighttime screams, I turned to face them without thinking—my limbic system had told my neocortex that something alarming but unidentified was happening and it needed to work out what was going on. I raced toward the sounds, fearing that something outside in the dark was attacking our timid cat.

On reaching the source of the commotion, I heard rustling but then silence. I was bemused, worried, and at a loss to explain it. The following morning, I headed out to the scene and investigated. There were clear badger tracks in the earth and signs of trampling among the brambles. Aha! So that's what a badger fight sounds like. The next time it happened, it took a second to think, "Badger fight." The third time, I just grabbed my flashlight and raced on tiptoe to a place where I knew I could scan along the edge of the wood. There I enjoyed watching the two angry male badgers scuttle off in my full flashlight beam like a pair of quarrelsome louts thrown out of the pub.

The Building Blocks

Coming to understand the science achieved two things for me on a personal level. First, it explained my experiences with tree shapes and constellations. More excitingly, it illuminated the gaps in my experience: what I wasn't yet doing, and what must still be possible.

Animated, I headed outdoors, walked up into the hills, and stopped, suddenly deflated. There was still a big obstacle in my path: I didn't understand the building blocks of fast thinking. How could I hope to rebuild something if I didn't know what it was made of? I could now make sense of sporadic experiences with badgers, trees, and stars, but I couldn't see any means of developing this in a methodical way. It was as though I'd spent years admiring paintings of a great cathedral that had been lost to time, been given the architect's drawings, and decided to reconstruct it only to discover that I didn't know which bricks to use.

It was obvious that the senses were integral—we can't raise awareness of anything without them—but what do our senses feed into our brain that allows it to build this greater sense? I pored over the examples in the scientific research, as well as the areas of my own experience that had demonstrated this new yet ancient awareness, and looked for the common thread.

Not everything we sense is profound and imbued with meaning, but some things are: We call them signs. The detective picked up signs in the pickpocket's behavior, just as I had picked up a sign in the shape of a tree. Of course! I paced back into the hills, my mind racing with the possibilities of this new realization. The cathedral could be built, but only with certain bricks. Only certain signs work with our fast limbic system. Others must stay with the slow but powerful neocortex.

Just as I was starting to appreciate that the answers I sought were to be found in understanding nature's signs, another problem crept up on me, a wilder one. Like many before me, I had assumed that I would find those answers in remote places. And, if I'm honest, part of me was drawn to that idea because it was a good excuse for the sort of travel I've always cherished: weeks spent getting to places with names I struggled to pronounce.

On returning from Crete, I had begun the early research for an expedition to parts of Southeast Asia—a favorite region. I focused on the places where indigenous people and animals were reputed to have foreseen the devastating tsunami of 2004; there had been much talk of this ability, this "sixth sense."

A few days later, I was walking alone on the South Downs, a range of chalk hills in southeast England. I was a few miles from home. After stepping between bramble and bracken islands, I found my way to a clearer area at the top of a hill and sensed an oak tree behind me. It was a still day, barely a breath of air, yet I heard the tree. When I turned and saw the leafless dead oak, my plans for exotic travel were squashed beneath another insight.

I could hear a distant crow and a closer wren. But I was looking for a different bird. The scent of wildflowers was strong, marjoram swirling up from its home beside the long grasses. My eyes wandered to a familiar shape in a yew, then jumped back to the brimstone butterflies nearer my feet. Then I focused again and saw the great spotted woodpecker hopping around the oak's barkless trunk. Those woodpeckers favor the oaks near me—I rarely find them on the much more common beeches. Identification of the bird had been instant from its drumming sound, unconscious, and it had triggered another unconscious association—the oak. I had a clear sense of one particular species of invisible tree behind me. And it was at that moment, I realized I had come very close to barking up the wrong tree in my research.

I couldn't hope to develop this sense through interviews in a tropical wilderness. My only real chance lay much closer to home. Indigenous experience was the *inspiration*, not the solution, and I had collected enough examples of it over the years to know what was possible; any more would be self-indulgent.

The challenge was to prove my sixth sense could be rekindled. Fun though it would be, I didn't want to write a book talking about what others had achieved in faraway places. I didn't want to be a spectator. I wanted to relearn this lost skill and to share the keys to it. And for that to be possible, my best chance lay in the land I knew well.

I felt some early pangs of regret, but they were replaced by an appreciation that I was one of many millions to misunderstand what is wild. I have read authors' definitions of "wild" as any place you can walk for a week without meeting a road or fence. But I think that is a narrow view, a consumer view, a transactional perspective that expects a landscape to give us the sense of wilderness in return for our travel. It is one I subscribed to for many years, which is partly why I found myself in those places, but now I see it as lazy. A sense of wild is engendered by awareness, a sense of connection with and deep understanding of any landscape. A real sense of wild can come from relearning the keys to accessing that deeper sense in any landscape. The pavement of any city side street wriggles with enough life to terrify and delight us if we choose to immerse ourselves in it.

Soon, I was comfortable with my choice. It fit for another reason: If these skills are to have any relevance in our modern lives, they must be applicable closer to civilization. If I could find the keys to this deeper sense in a rural patch of southern England less than two hours from London, it remained relevant and was within reach.

The Wind Anchor

I MADE MY WAY ALONG A woodland path on a February afternoon of light snow. The wind rolled down from the highest ground, a northerly, pushing the flakes around the trees. They followed a curving path of their own as they sailed past. There was silver motion on the path ahead, and a single shimmer split to become three bouncing squirrels' tails. They made their escape along the path, then off into the undergrowth and up into a hazel tree.

The darkness of the path's wet mud was joined on one side by the dirty white of old man's beard and, behind it, the brown beech leaves had settled into a rhythm. A stronger gust made its way through a break in the trees and introduced a flicker to the red-flecked bramble below. A pheasant and I spooked each other; it launched away with its hiccupping call. The sound was a shock, but the direction it flew wasn't. As I watched it climb into the wind and toward the break in the trees, a snowflake landed on my eyelash.

Out of the woods, at the top of a gentle hill, I listened to the ever-angry crows cawing at the world behind me. The sun was setting behind thick clouds, but there was still enough light to notice the shifting colors and textures. A uniform blanket of high, light clouds covered the sky, but below them darker clouds with ragged edges passed by: the snow carriers. My eyes adjusted to the wrinkles of the landscape, and as it became familiar, it allowed the anomalies to shine through.

There was a blue that nature would never have permitted—a farmer's water hose half buried in the ground. A few minutes later my eyes rested on another color that was not quite right. It didn't scream like the hose's blue, but it was a tiny patch of color that seemed uncomfortable, a sliver of beige beneath an assortment of greens and browns. I walked over to investigate and found a small Tupperware container, nestled beneath a stack of rotting, moss-covered fence posts.

"Geocache. This box is part of a game. Please leave where found."

I did as bidden, tucking it back into its damp bed. Geocaching is a techno treasure hunt, a game of finding hidden boxes using GPS coordinates. I must have found a few dozen over the years, but never in the way I was supposed to.

I was too conspicuous for my liking, too obvious to the surrounding wildlife: Anyone standing where I was would seem a distinctive predator to all around. I moved to a soft, grassy bank and settled there. Despite the thickening clouds, I sensed the sun setting in the lowering light levels and no less in the chinking of the blackbirds, then the roosting calls of the pheasants as they headed to bed.

The lights of distant farmhouses were sprinkled across the dark hills and a broader orange glow rose from the southern coast. It was time to venture off the path and across the fields. I walked into the wind and the snow nibbled at my face as it formed a thin layer on my coat.

There was not much settled snow, not enough for me to look for patterns in the low light, and I made a mental note to be up early the following morning to hunt for these seasonal gems. Continuing north, I kept my fingers moving in my gloves as my eyes began to water. And then the warmth embraced me. It was such a dramatic shift, taking place over only a few steps. The wind seemed to have dropped altogether, and its chilling effect was gone. The snow was no longer biting and I was enveloped in an invisible duvet. I sensed the copse ahead and lifted my head to see the dark wall of trees.

The clouds parted, allowing a sight of Sirius being hauled up by Orion, which now burned brightly between the higher branches of the trees. Nearing the edge of the woods, the changes in light and breeze married; as the light began to force its way through the trees, so did the wind. I turned back toward the heart of the wood and the wind dropped away, although it still rattled the ash trees. There was a cool sensation on my right cheek, and, turning, I could just make out an animal track. The animals had followed a natural parting in the trees and ironed some of the undergrowth. The trees and animals together had formed a delicate wind valley.

From the cool on one cheek to the sway of the trees, the dust on the march to the waves out at sea, the birds facing one way to the smoke and the chimney, the signs of what the wind is doing will always be there. But the habit to notice them may not, until we demand it of ourselves. We need to know what the wind is doing. From this our sense of weather, landscape, navigation, animals, and so much else flows. The memorable encounter with an animal depends on our accepting the gift of a feather that floats past.

The wind shapes the route taken by many animals, but also the direction they face when stationary, and their ability to sense us and other animals. If we hear a bird call from the tree behind us, our awareness of wind direction allows us to sense the direction the bird is facing and the direction it will take off if we clap our hands without turning.

This relationship among wind, human, and animal behavior is deeply rooted within many indigenous cultures. The mood of hunters may change with a shift in the wind and a hunt may be canceled. From the viewpoint of a post-industrialized society, this can seem whimsical, but there are good practical reasons behind it. If the wind changes to come from a direction that makes hunting less likely to be successful, perhaps to blow from an area of good cover instead of toward it, we can see why hunters, whose livelihood may be tied to their prospects, will become less cheery and less inclined to venture out.

The potential for misunderstanding and misinterpretation across cultures in this area is great, and I'm as guilty of it as the next person. In Borneo, a Dayak hunter once pointed to a river beach where deer regularly came to drink. He added that they would only hunt mouse deer on this beach and would leave other species alone. I leaped to the wrong conclusion, to the lazy assumption that this might be explained by superstitions or religious reverence for certain animals. It turned out that the beach's topography meant it nearly always had to be approached downwind, which meant it was only practical to hunt animals that were not sensitive to scent. The mouse deer is one such animal; the other deer would be alarmed by the whiff of a human.

The wind we feel is part of a map. We can sense its dramatic shifts easily whenever we step from exposure or shelter into the opposite. But these paragons are the introduction to a richer, subtler world of wind

maps. If the wind is fairly constant, every shift we feel suggests something in the landscape, usually on the windward side, but not always: The wind is shaped by large obstacles on the downwind side, too. Spend a moment on the windward side of a building or dense wood and you will notice that you are sheltered from it, as the wind is forced over that obstacle and begins its climb farther out than many might guess.

The higher winds travel unmolested, but we need to be sensitive to the way that our low wind is having to make its way around hills, trees, or buildings. Any substantial obstacle will have some effect on it, and bumps in the landscape impact the wind over much greater distances than might be expected: We will still feel their effect ten times the distance downwind of their height. In practice, this means that we sense this wind by sampling, by repeatedly tuning in to it and forming a picture from lots of little snapshots. This may sound laborious, but it quickly becomes effortless and enjoyable. The satisfaction comes in two different ways: predictions that are fulfilled and surprises that trigger insight.

Imagine you have been sensing the wind on and off over the course of half an hour and developed a really good feel for where it's coming from—you have "anchored" the wind because you have a memorable sense of where it comes from. Many like to describe the anchor by one of the cardinal directions—"The wind is coming from the *west*." Here, "west" is the anchor. But it is more helpful for our intuition to create an anchor out of the landscape—we feel the wind coming from the *church on the hill*—because we can sense it without labels. Providing your anchor isn't something you will lose sight of for long periods, there is no right or wrong. You will probably find that you do both in many situations. Names and labels are never the important part; they are slow additions, happy baggage at best. The wind and its meaning will not be slowed or moved one inch by them.

There will be slight shifts in the wind direction over time, there always are, but once you have an anchor for where your wind comes from, you have given yourself a weather station, map, compass, and insight into animal behavior.

Predictions flow from building familiarity with each wind. Once we feel we have our anchor, then every time we pass any obstacle that lies between our path and that anchor, we should expect to sense changes in the strength and direction of the wind. We notice the lone spruce tree and anticipate a drop in wind speed and fluctuation in direction; think of it as a "wobble" in the wind. We feel the wobble a full two hundred yards away as we walk past the tree. It is surprisingly satisfying to sense this simple and logical pattern.

One of the best ways to accelerate an appreciation of the effect is to stand at the edge of some still water, a lake or a large pond, with your back to the wind. Look out across the ripples that the wind has formed in the water, then map the changes in them back to the obstacles along your side of the shore. You will notice a mix of rougher and calmer patches and begin to see from how far the obstacles are able to shape them. Now you can have some fun spotting your own wind shadow in the ripples and confirming that you've gotten it right by taking a few steps to the left, waiting until the patterns change, then a few steps to the right and repeating.

When the surprise comes, our new awareness is beginning to pay dividends. The wind bends when you weren't expecting it, giving a sense of change in the landscape. Turning reveals the small withered oak among the field of oats. We sense the change instantly, and a slower analysis adds detail to the picture. By nurturing an awareness of bold changes, we become attuned to the ever-subtler ones. Walking in a city, we feel a gust and sense the side street; the following week, a strengthening breeze indicates a firebreak in the distant woods.

This sensitivity brings an automatic improvement in our awareness of where we are and where we have been. Every time we tune in to the wind, we gain a sense of our heading relative to it—perhaps we know we have walked for about an hour with the wind on our backs. We're not talking about a perfect recollection of exactly where we have been, just a good sense. We know we have walked with the wind for an hour and begin to sense we're looking back toward our starting point when we feel the wind on our faces.

We can develop this awareness without moving anywhere. If there is a spot near home or work where we can spend a minute tuning in to the wind a few times each day, we'll reap the benefits. The Inuit check the wind first thing in the morning, when they step outside for their first pee of the day, then report its direction and any changes to the group. They can sense from it what the moving ice will be doing, where cracks will be appearing, and whether the conditions are suitable for traveling or hunting.

The modern outdoors person wears layers to shield themselves against the vagaries of the weather. The ancients sensed the vagaries as their shield. Major weather changes are the result of a "front" going through, the name given to the leading edge of a different air mass. Whenever this happens, there is a significant shift in wind direction and speed. If we have grown sensitive to the little fluctuations caused by something as small as a bush or boulder, any front will announce itself brashly. It refuses to be ignored.

All over the world, fronts are also preceded by cloud changes. Blue skies are replaced by the wispy cotton candy of cirrus, followed by the milky blanket of cirrostratus. The sun or moon wears a halo—"Guard your herd, O Amr, from the rings around the moon!" the Bedouin say. When accompanied by a change in wind direction, this is a strong indicator of a front about to go through.

It becomes a fast two-step process: We notice the wind direction change, then check the sky for cloud signs. It's a habit that is conscious at first, then automatic. It works the other way, too: once we're aware of the cloud signs, they will prompt another check of the wind.

Below the clouds, the moisture in the air will fluctuate with any change in weather or wind direction. The sea and many coastal land-marks are visible from the ridge of the South Downs, and it is rewarding to watch them disappear and reappear with shifts in the wind. Prior to vanishing, distant features lose brightness, color, and clarity—they become ghosts. And from these fluctuations other insights follow.

In August, as humidity rises and the distant coast fades to white, I know to look for roe deer. They become more active in late-summer mugginess and will venture out onto the stubble of harvested fields. The sense of a wind change, to one that now rises very slowly up the hills, triggers my look to the coast, where the whiteness tells me to expect deer. It happens in less than a second.

Each landscape has these pairings, and the wind is the key to unlock-ing many of your own. It starts with a general sense of change, but progresses toward a keener, more precise, and faster idea of what that change means. Perhaps you notice that the wind has shifted to come from the dark rocks on a hillside and that shortly after you find pheas-ants sheltering on the lee side of the woodland around the corner. Four hours later it rains. The pattern is repeated a couple of times. You come to think of the pairing of the wind with the dark rocks as a sign of where you will spot the pheasants and of the weather to come. You might even choose to nickname the rocks the "wet pheasants." But, with or without the name, your brain will be joining these dots for you. You have gained an intuitive sense of what is about to happen.

Wild Signs and Star Paths III

FIREFLIES RECOGNIZE EACH OTHER through their flashing messages, trees warn each other of attack through fungi networks, and bacteria send and receive signals. We live in a world of signs. But most of them pass us by. Are we lost within a beautiful Enigma machine?

We are alive because our brain has evolved to make sense of the complexity by finding signals in the noise. Each species has done the same. The trees need not concern themselves with the sounds a large mammal makes, but we must. We will instantly react to a surprising bark or roar, or even the loud crack of a branch underfoot, turning to face it. Even if we don't want to, our limbic system will focus our attention; it is out of our control.

Certain things are hardwired, like a healthy wariness of snakes. We recognize snakes more quickly than we do other animals, and researchers proved that when the level of camouflage is steadily raised to the point where we lose sight of most animal shapes, we can still make out the snake's. This is part of our innate pattern-recognition system, one that may vary from species to species, but we share with the rest of the animal kingdom. Leopards prey on macaques, but these monkeys are finely tuned to leopards' patterns and can tell when their spots are "wrong." Researchers using models of leopards to test macaque behavior discovered that the macaques gave fewer calls, their sign of recognizing a leopard, if the spots were not in a true-to-life pattern.

But only part of our awareness is built in. Much of our reading of signs is based on experience. We learn to pay more attention to certain things in our environment, which leads to a faster reading of situations. The sound a sheep makes triggers a different response in the rambler walking through the field from the one evoked in the shepherd, as would the walker's dog's bark. This is because they have had different experiences and have attached different meanings to each sign.

If we concede that we can't expect to pick up and decipher everything in our environment quickly, our task can be simplified by understanding the types of signs that are profitable and steering our attention toward them. To do this, we will pass through the realm of semiotics, the formal study of signs and symbols. Within this we find the exotic underworlds of zoosemiotics, phytosemiotics, and ecosemiotics: the studies of signs among and across animals, plants, and landscapes, respectively.

The first time I encountered the work of semioticians, it was a revelation. I had long felt in my gut that the world was extravagantly rich with signs, but for years this had been based on personal experience. Many thousands of hours outdoors had led to my spotting patterns, asymmetries, and trends; they were beautiful, but often hard to explain. I would scrabble about in haphazard research, trying to make sense of the forms and feelings pressed into my mind. When I was lucky, I could pair the fruits of dirty hands and sore knees with any science I could scavenge.

I was lucky in other ways, too: Word of my work has spread a little, and I'm grateful to correspondents who have pointed me toward signs across the world. At the end of our time together, I often say to a group I'm leading, "You will have seen and will go on to see more of the world than I possibly can, so please share it!"

I have received emails about foxes that pounce into the snow in a northeasterly direction, and one from France about *Pyrrhocoris apterus*, the "firebug" or "gendarme," which my correspondent, Alban Cambe, had spotted congregating on the warmer south side of trees. Alban revealed another French nickname, "cherche midi," "midday searchers," an acknowledgement of their love of the sun's light and warmth.

But however warming and delightful these signs were, my approach and good fortune had given me a narrow, bug's-eye view of their richness. I realized, later than I might have, that the work of semioticians, who followed a very different path, offered a valuable overview.

Zoosemiotics, a word coined in 1963, helped me toward a broader understanding. This niche discipline is dedicated to understanding the signs flowing among animals, within and between species. Sex, predation, territory: All of the key domains of animal life are marshaled with the help of signs, and many are available to our senses.

Soon I found my gut feeling echoing back at me in the words of early semioticians like Charles Sanders Peirce, who declared that the "universe is perfused with signs." I am not qualified to comment on the veracity of the statement by the American philosopher John Deely that semiotics is "perhaps the most international and important intellectual movement since the taking root of science in the modern sense in the seventeenth century." But I can say that it feels that important to me. I know I am not alone; the search for meaning must have started further back than we can trace, and any new promise of it stirs passions and intrigue. Signs are a promise of meaning, and humans are "meaning-seeking creatures," so we find signs treasured, lauded, and woven through the foundation of any new religion.

Religions may divide, but the search for meaning in nature unites humanity; cultures as diverse as early Christians in Ireland and Native American tribes have seen the tree not just as a plant, but also as a "pan-semiotic web of cosmic meaning." The search is for pattern in the mess, for signification in the chaos and overload. Nothing is more uplifting than to feel we live in a universe that is a "musical harmony of varied shapes and colors with a certain order and rhythm," as St. Gregory of Nyssa believed. Because the alternative is less appealing, to put it mildly. Who would want to view their life as a meaningless interlude between two infinite stretches of oblivion? Even those who believe it to be true cannot wish it so. It is a search that recurs throughout the ages in art and writing, and always will. As long as a thirst for meaning in life survives, signs will be valued.

The personal challenge that remained was to sift through all of the signs I was sensing, understand where they fit into the larger family of semiotics, then decide which ones *worked*. I needed to know which were available to the learning of our fast-thinking system. If the task was enormous, it was at least now definable.

We have already seen that snakes, trees, and constellations have one characteristic that the brain can make fast use of: shape. You have been making use of this outdoors every day already, many times, usually without realizing it. We can tell ominous clouds from friendly ones partly by their color, but also by their shape. A "fluffy sheep" cumulus cloud will register with everyone as harmless—it has earned its nickname from its shape and because it is benign. But a giant tower of a cloud, one that is many times taller than it is wide, will ignite consternation. As we investigate shape, the animals can be our inspiration.

Many animals need to be able to identify an aerial threat from birds as fast as possible. This is a good example of where slow neocortex-type thinking would not work. It would get animals killed. Imagine that you're vulnerable to birds of prey, like hawks; you could compile a list of all the attributes of each of these birds, including their various sizes and the colors of their wings, legs, and bodies. And then you could monitor the sky for birds that meet these criteria. Or evolution could teach you that they have a common attribute in their shape.

Shape is especially suitable for the fast recognition of birds because we, like their prey, so often see them as a colorless silhouette against a brighter sky. But even within shape, there is a danger that animals might complicate the issue by focusing on how certain birds of prey have "fingers"—spread feathers at the wingtips—and others don't, or some have fanned or forked tails and others don't. This detail is great for developing the later stages of recognition, when we are trying to identify individual species, but for the animals and us, simplicity is the aim at first, and the one shape characteristic that birds of prey share is a short neck.

Experiments have shown that creatures vulnerable to birds of prey, like ducks and geese, will react to any roughly bird-shaped silhouette with a short neck, but not to those with a long one. And they will react to models of birds that have a short neck, and even to models of bird shapes that don't actually exist but still have a short neck. For the ducks and geese, the "key" to fast recognition is that one simple shape.

It's not a perfect system. The birds may mistakenly identify swifts as predators, even though they are harmless to them, because swifts happen to have a short neck. But in evolutionary terms, that is a false alarm worth enduring—embarrassing though it doubtless is for the drake who has to laugh it off afterward among its macho friends.

I believe the importance of neck shape may still be more deeply rooted in our psyche than we realize. Ask someone to sketch any flying bird of prey and a flying goose for you and, even if they protest that they can't do a good job, a difference in necks will probably feature strongly.

The simplifying approach of animals is instructive, because it's the opposite of what most naturalists encourage today. All communication aiming to improve our understanding of nature over the past few centuries has, by definition, aimed at our slow thinking. The neocortex is king because it handles speech and reading. This has accelerated our move away from an intuitive understanding of nature. In the past, we were more likely to have learned about animal behavior by twinning the crack in the forest with the freezing of the person in front of us and their subsequent body language—areas that our fast thinking makes sense of, then learns from. We can see this difference clearly in the contemporary approach to bird identification.

The assumption is that we are keen to identify individual species, which may be the case later on, but this approach is aimed at our neocortex, not our fast thinking. The RSPB has produced an excellent handbook on British birds, complete with an identification section for each bird. In it we learn that the merlin, a bird of prey, can be identified by knowing that it is "25–30 cm . . . with short, broad-based, pointed wings and shorter tail than Kestrel. When perched, wing-tips reach about three-quarters along the tail length . . ." This is fantastic detail, but quite difficult to use intuitively. For that we do better to think of very broad groups and the shapes that unite them. An animal that might get eaten by a bird of prey can't tell one from another; our "lizard brain" loves to keep things simple. There are few birds with a popular image that jars more with their personality than the robin. Far from being a touch of color on a winter scene, with sweet song and a willingness to appear on Christmas cards, robins are psychopaths. They are fiercely territorial and devote huge energies, including their war cry of a song, to establishing and maintaining their turf. If a robin arrives within the territory of another and is not deterred by song or aggressive flight and body language, conflict will follow.

It is very tempting to think that the robin is incensed by the interloper and inspects it carefully before deciding to attack. But in the middle of the last century, the British evolutionary biologist David Lack led studies of the robin that remain the benchmark to this day. They revealed what in particular about an intruder robin will trigger an attack. Was it the motion, the sounds, the behavior, the recognizable shape, the colors of the bird, or something else?

Lack placed a stuffed robin in the territory of a real robin. This motionless model was viciously attacked until its head came clean off. The attacks continued. Curious to see at what point the resident robin would consider the job done, Lack and his team deliberately removed the tail of the stuffed robin. The headless, tailless torso was attacked again. Its wings were then removed; it was attacked. This bizarre Russian doll of an experiment continued; they removed the body and back of the model robin. All that was left were some red feathers of the breast and some white feathers below, supported by wire. The aggression continued. After many more experiments, the team had their answer: The trigger was the red feathers. If the red color was changed to brown, the attacks stopped.

The old saying "a red rag to a bull" is a myth; it is the motion of the cloth that can trigger aggression in a bull. But red is a trigger to a robin, which is not so much *incensed by this interloper* as programmed to rid its territory of other birds of the same species by a simple sign: the red on their breast.

The world is pulsating with color signs, from messages sent between octopuses to the vivid hue of a fungus. My task was not to expect to find meaning in all color, in the lurid tints of inner organs, as the ancients might once have done, but to accept the signs that were on offer and of fast value. The white flash reveals the rabbit's rump, just as I sense its story in the darker prints on the white frost. The eruption of wildflowers in a wood is a sign of sunlight and therefore direction.

I gained a valuable insight into the importance of motion as a sign on the side of a small Spanish mountain. It was a strange and enjoyable sortie. I was accompanying an artist I knew only as Long as he set off up the arid slopes to erect a temporary art installation at the summit of a mountain in Almería. From the surrounding area, he had collected beer bottles that locals had abandoned over many years. He had smashed the bottles into smaller pieces of brown glass and had then cut out from paper the template of a soaring eagle. He was going up the mountain to make an eagle out of broken glass before taking a photo of it, then collecting the glass and returning down the hill. As we carried the glass up through the pines, we exchanged stories about nature, and I pointed out how the almond blossoms were making a compass for us, the flowers coming into bloom first on the south side of the trees.

Long told me that the black squirrels near where he lived in Canada would approach you if you imitated the motion of their tails with your hand. His hand undulated in front of his chest as he explained that it drew the animals closer to investigate. I'd never heard of this before and, on returning home, I researched it. Sure enough, there were documented instances and even a film of it on YouTube. The motion of a hand was clearly acting as a sign. I have since tried it with the grey squirrels that live near me, and it seems to have an effect; they watch the motion very carefully, but they neither approach nor run away from it. Sometimes it appears to have a mildly hypnotic effect on them. The science explaining animals' perception of motion as a sign is plentiful, and the squirrel's tail is indeed part of a sign system; it passes a message to other squirrels and tells some predators that they have been seen, for reasons that will become clearer later on.

Evolution has taught animals the simplest signs and therefore fastest keys for each task. In the interests of simplicity they also use different signs for different stages of the same task. Butterflies that are searching for particular flowers might use the scent as the sign that they are near them, but then use the color of an individual flower to fly toward and land on it. They use the scent as a rough map and the color as a homing device.

The tasks and therefore signs change with time and season. Hawk moths use colors to guide them to their destination, and these change with the seasons. They fly toward yellow and blue objects when they're looking for food, yellow-green objects when laying eggs, and dark or grey places when preparing to hibernate.

There is a powerful sign that does not like to fit in. It is the anomaly. Even when we don't think we see a pattern, our brain is brilliant at finding one. And having spotted one, it is then great at noticing when something doesn't fit into it. Rake up a pile of leaves or twigs, then ask someone to scatter them again in a way that appears natural. They will find it surprisingly difficult; they are likely to create something that doesn't look "right." There is a pattern to leaves on the ground or sticks on the forest floor, one that is hard to describe.

One of the universal sign rules is that of dependence: If an animal or plant depends on certain other animals or plants, then our noticing the first is a sign of the presence of the other. There may be gaps in either distance or time between the two, but these must close at times, and experience can give us a sense of those times. The hatching of the fly is the sign of the fish.

My understanding of the types of signs that would work grew, but I still needed to gain greater insight into the mechanics of how we can learn to sense them intuitively. I knew there might be no perfect shortcuts—we value experience for a reason, and practice and observation must be the largest part of the challenge. We may need to learn *quinuituq*, the deep patience of the Inuit as they wait for animals, but that doesn't mean we shouldn't seek to accelerate the learning. Educators, trainers, coaches, and mentors have roles in all areas of life because we learn faster when we are shown the way to go.

It turns out that the process is simple and there are only three parts to it. We need to know what to look for, then look for those things, and we need to care. The three parts can be thought of as knowledge, experience, and emotion. The first two are obvious and combine to form wisdom; the third less so, but all three are logical.

The first part is the simplest: Our brain cannot make any sense of things it is not aware of, so the more we sense, the more raw material there is. But we have limited ability to notice things—we can't see what is behind us, for example—so we can think of the things we focus on, with each of our senses, as being like money spent. It is a finite resource, we need to spend it wisely, and if we know where to focus, that will accelerate the learning and awareness.

The second part is practiced observation. Our brain stores images, events, and their consequences—that is, their meaning—and makes sense of the world by sifting and comparing those we receive through our senses with those we have experienced in the past. We stop at the red traffic light "without thinking" because our experience of that sign quickly reached the point where the image and meaning were paired with our fast unconscious thinking.

Time spent practicing noticing things builds an area of our fast thinking called "associative activation." Everything we notice triggers our unconscious mind to evoke things that have been associated with it in the past. If you read the word "cloud," your brain automatically launches into a process of retrieving associated concepts, experiences, and emotions. It will be more attuned to anything associated with the sky than it is with caves. Equally, the word "cave" will trigger a very different collection of associations. You are more likely to think of the colors blue or white in the first instance and of bats in the second, but your exact associations will depend on your experience.

If you have had a bad accident in a cave, the word itself will set off a lot of powerful associations, emotions, and physiological responses. Before you have had time to think about it consciously, your fast thinking has initiated a pulse rise, with a lot of other very different physiological and emotional responses—your facial expression will change involuntarily.

The good news is that this process is automated. If the first few times we hear the jingle of an ice-cream van we get an ice cream a few minutes later, our brain will pair them without prompting. The jingle makes us salivate. Once we experience a connection, the brain will do the rest. The more frequent the experience, the more automated it becomes. Our challenge is only to notice these connections, which takes us back to knowing what to look for.

The philosopher David Hume identified three ways in which we build associations:

1. Things that resemble each other.

2. Things that occur in the same time or place.

3. Things that cause or are caused by certain other things.

The second two are especially relevant to us.

Nature is not randomly scattered; everything has an association with time and place and other parts of nature. Where we see rabbits, we find grass; where we find deer, there are ticks; where we see stinging nettles, we find dock; where we see granite, we find bogs; where we see and smell wildflowers, we find moths; when we see the stars, it is cooler; when we see Orion high in the sky, it is near winter; and when we see Scorpius return, we smell the fragrant wild mint by the path.

Animal behaviors have certain causes, and we come to associate the behavior with the cause. Once we know to associate the two, our brain can forge the fast appreciation. We accelerate the process because we are forewarned to look for the association and therefore notice it, instead of picking it up very slowly, having spent decades outdoors. We may already pair the dog's bark with the stranger approaching, but we may not have thought to pair the stranger's approach with the earlier change in the distant bird's flight. Next time we do, and the time after that the dog's bark seems tardy.

Knowing what to look for and practice come together in a process called "feedback." If the consequences of any situation become apparent soon afterward, we form an intuitive feel for that situation more quickly. We have all been burned by a hot pan in the kitchen, often after someone else has been using it, but very quickly we come to associate the smells and sounds of a hot stove with the need for care around everything on or in it. The consequences of carelessness around hot stoves are instant and unambiguous. The opposite is also true: If the feedback is slow, like when we try to work out what grows well in a garden, we can gain intuition, but it will be slow to build.

In nature, most things we observe fall somewhere along this spectrum. The faster and more accurate the feedback, the more worthy of our attention. The alarm calls of songbirds can easily be paired with threats in the environment—perhaps you hear the racket in the garden three mornings in a row and see the cat walk past a minute later three mornings in a row. You quickly come to sense the cat before seeing it. However, even though the sounds of crows doubtless have richer meaning, the feedback is poor and slow because of the complexity of their lives and language. It is so much harder to pair the sounds of corvids with exact meaning; something's going on, we think, but what?

If an event is too infrequent, it is hard to build a fast sense of its meaning. We may know that certain behaviors in animals indicate that a tsunami is approaching, but unless we live in an area threatened by tsunamis and develop a practiced eye for those behaviors, including false alarms, this will remain slow thought. It follows that the more common the plant or animal, and the more common the association, the better our chances.

The third part, caring, may seem vague until we think about how and why our limbic system has evolved as it has. It handles emotion and learning, and the two are connected when it comes to our understanding of environment. Historically, many more experiences in nature would have been associated with opportunities or life-threatening situations. Think of the times you have smelled gas or burning unexpectedly at home; this is a fair guess at the sort of reaction our ancestors would have paired with certain sounds in the forest, although they would doubtless have reacted faster due to having much more practice.

We wouldn't want to endanger ourselves in order to attach more meaning to situations, but caring is more complex than life or death. The firefighter still relies on intuition for their safety, but the surgeon much less so—it is mainly others who are at risk. But surgeons still care, if they are good at their jobs. The same is true of most professions: Good teachers care, and because they care, they feel the outcomes of different approaches. Over time they develop an intuitive sense of what will work best for each pupil or group. We don't remember our best teachers because of their academic knowledge, but because they sensed what worked for us.

There is also a psychological trait we all share that helps turn practice into caring. We attach greater importance to the things we recall most easily, and these are the things we are most exposed to. Therefore, the more time we spend outdoors, the more importance we will attach to natural phenomena and the more we will care about them. If you recognize certain animal tracks or leaf shapes, you will be familiar with the positive feeling that comes from spotting them.

We cannot invent a care for something, but since you are reading this, the desire and care are already there and will grow. Knowing what to look for and experience bring successes, which can nurture an interest toward a passion. The care flourishes. A hunch or sense of unease goes from being something we dismiss to something we cherish and pursue. The more we care, the more our brain registers the consequences and the faster our intuition builds. If we care enough to notice that a constellation appears higher three hours after we first see it, we are on the path to sensing meaning in that pattern.

There is a tipping point. The desire to see the connections grows: We feel more, we learn more, and this improves our chances. The satisfaction that comes with growing successes kindles the care. This is the best sort of feedback cycle. We go from hoping that we will find signs and meaning in the things we see in nature to sensing that everything in nature is a sign with meaning. We feel it.

Part II

Above and Below: Sky and Land

The Shear

ONE COLD MARCH DAY I SAW an invisible wind. The seventh-century English monk Aldhelm claimed that the wind was invisible. He was right and wrong. The wind gives us an opportunity to watch our thinking move from slow to fast. Try gauging wind direction by watching the motion of distant clouds. It's doable, but it takes a few seconds, and the first few times we try, it reveals nothing intuitively. If, however, we practice recognizing one particular shape in the clouds, we can develop an intuitive method.

Wind speed nearly always increases with altitude, causing a shear at the tops of tall clouds. If we think of tall clouds as a deck of cards, the top cards slide farther with the stronger winds, revealing the direction of the wind there. We don't need to worry for now about gradual differences between wind direction at altitude and on the ground; at this point we are interested in the psychology of experimenting with a new method.

Whenever you see clouds with a shear at the top, just make a mental note that they are revealing the wind direction. Do this as regularly as you can and fairly soon something interesting will happen: There will come a moment when you see the wind direction in the sky. You will have sensed something instantly without having to think about it.

The Ramp

I T WAS A DAMP SUMMER'S MORNING. Rain had passed through, and I took the coast path away from the beach. It led up through mixed woodland until only a few trees were left, isolated between the scrub of brambles, gorse, and grass.

I continued uphill and now felt the wind's full strength. Out at sea, the water was raked with cats'-paws. Around a mound of brambles, there was a hollow Second World War gun emplacement. Drink cans and snack wrappers occupied one corner, as they always do.

I sat on the concrete roof and looked out to sea. The wind was being funneled between two headlands, forging waves in a corridor. They were fanning out as they passed through the mouth of the bay. I watched them parade past, with their shallow backs and steeper fronts. Familiar patterns formed around the proudest rocks below me. The sea surged and scattered with each shift in the wind.

Farther along the path I met a jaded sycamore. It had paid the price for the exposed spot and wore the marks of a tyrant. Its scars howled direction at me.

Every landscape endures the elements for the weeks, months, and years that we choose not to. Our lives and work show in our faces and hands, and each environment has its wrinkles, too.

Once we are attuned to what the wind is doing in the present, and the temporary shape it creates in clouds, we need to become sensitive to longer-term trends. There is a law of nature, beautiful in its simplicity, dictating that the wind gives everything it sculpts a familiar shape. We can think of it as "the ramp."

From snow and ice, to sand, dust, water, trees, shrubs, grasses, and even rocks, the wind is happy to carve its ramp shape in all it meets. Everything in nature that has been subjected to strong enough winds for long enough periods will develop a shallower angle on the side the wind has come from and a steeper one on the side it is blowing toward. The ramp is everywhere in nature; it is even found in sediment ripples on Mars. The only things that change are how dramatic the shape is, how long it lasts, and the names we give it. It may last seconds in water or thousands of years in rock.

To begin with, we will find it easiest to spot this effect in trees in exposed locations. They are swept over from the windward side. But look at the grasses around them, and we soon start to see the effect there, too. The same is true at sea, and in sandy or icy deserts. The effect is given different names when it appears in each medium—water waves, sand dunes, rock yardangs, and ice sastrugi—but this need not worry us. The sense we are rebuilding does not concern itself with vocabulary.

There are almost infinite subtleties within the ramp. In a small wood on a hillside, I call it the "wedge effect"; trees on the windward side of a copse will not grow as tall as those on the sheltered downwind side. But for our fast sense of awareness, all we need is to tune in to the ramp: the way in which the shallow side of these shapes points consistently in the direction the wind has come from, and the steeper side points away from it.

The Ramp

Wind direction

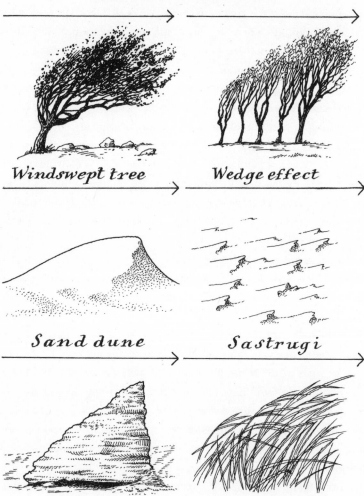

Windswept tree

Wedge effect

Sand dune

Sastrugi

Yardang

Windswept grass

Now we have a shape that pops up all over the place and gives us two things: a sense of direction and the prevailing wind in our landscape.

As soon as we have learned to notice it, we will find its direction is consistent across the landscape.

We may choose to add one other piece to the jigsaw: a name for where this wind comes from—that is, the cardinal direction of the prevailing wind. Where I live in northwestern Europe, this tends to be from the southwest but, again, the label is not important. The ramp is not so much a clue to direction, it *is* direction.

If we notice the ramp in trees or grass, we have a sign that gives us an instant sense of direction. We can travel using this sign as our sole concept of direction; perhaps we have walked with the grass ramp for an hour, then against it to find our way home. The moment we translate the ramp into cardinal directions, we step away from an intuitive sense of the landscape toward an analytical one. This is not a right or wrong decision, just a choice. There are times when we will want to do this; it is a modern way of looking at the world, so it is hard to resist. So long as we remain aware of what we are doing, we can switch between the two modes. But we won't develop an intuitive sense quickly if we feel the need to analyze and label everything we see.

Sometimes a strong prevailing wind will be reinforced in its power by salt and sand or ice and snow, which will have an exaggerating or secondary effect on the landscape. The sycamore on the coastal path showed two clear signs. First, it had the ramp; it had been forcibly sculpted by the prevailing southwesterly winds. But it also bore the marks of salt, with an effect known as "burning." The leaves on the windward side were smaller, shriveled, and dying at their edges. Those on the downwind side were bigger, greener, and healthier.

It takes practice to sense it intuitively, but once familiar with the shape of the ramp, we will notice it appearing within every landscape on Earth, from downtown Tokyo to Transylvania.

The Pink Compass

THE RAIN CLEARED THROUGH, LEAVING A ragged assortment of tall, lopsided clouds. At the end of the day, the sun set behind the wooded hills. I saw direction in pinks scattered along the horizon.

Most people have some familiarity with the idea that the sun rises in the east and sets in the west. But there are many levels to this awareness, and it's one of the things that divides the modern viewpoint from the ancient.

After learning where the sun rises in a general sense, we might get to know that it is due south in the middle of the day. Next, we might learn that it rises closer to northeast in June and southeast in December. After growing comfortable with these cornerstones, the rest of the sun compass is familiarity and interpolation. If we know the sun is due south in the middle of the day and sets near southwest in late December, we can accept that it will be close to south-southwest halfway between midday and sunset.

As we have seen, it is possible to find our way using the sun without thinking of cardinal directions or a modern compass and, with practice, this becomes intuitive. The ancients used various labels or none, and often viewed the relationship from the other perspective: The direction of sunrise from a fixed location revealed the time of year, not the other way around. The principle that the sun was an indicator of direction and time was ubiquitous, and we find it in all ancient cultures.

Once sensing the direction of the sun becomes second nature—that is, intuitive—everything lit directly by it and the shadows it casts can, with practice, take on that familiarity, too. If you sense that it is near the middle of the day, so your shadow is cast north, and you follow that shadow as your guide for half an hour, by the end of that short period the shadow will have assumed the same confident intuitive association with the direction north that the midday sun had with south.

The next step is to notice how the sun reflects off many things that we may never have considered compasses. Deep in a wooded valley, look up at the highest and tallest trees near the end of a sunny day and you will find bright compasses sprinkled across their tops, long after you lose sight of the sun itself. Now look higher, to the clouds; spend time observing how they have brighter and darker sides and how this is accentuated near the start or end of the day.

Distant tall clouds can hold on to sunlight on one side for hours after we lose sight of the sun. And if we have practiced associating sun with direction, the bright side of the top of a distant cloud doesn't just point to the sun but forms a compass, too. The bright pink side of a cloud soon offers as fast a sense of direction as the midday sun.

The Sky Map

I HAD BEEN ON THE WATER for a few hours that Saturday morning, experimenting with a new family toy, an inflatable sailing dinghy. The harbor is strewn with moored yachts that made tacking up and down the channels during our maiden voyage an enjoyable challenge. I tried harder than normal to read the harbor breezes, studying patterns in the water and the sky as our single-sailed plaything wove this way and that. I noted each small eddy and every bubbling cloud over the land so that I could meet the unambitious twin goals of not getting wet or laughed at by those on proper boats.

I survived and succeeded, avoiding capsize and ridicule. By the time I set off for home, my eyes were sharpened, my forensic muscles were flexed, and it was this readiness that made the sight of a hill floating in the sky so exquisite. There is a euphoric sensation that accompanies the moment when heightened awareness is greeted by a bold sign.

Clouds form if there is more moisture in the air than can be sustained as gas. When this point is reached, the transparent water vapor condenses to form tiny liquid droplets, which scatter the light, creating clouds. It is the scattering of the light that gives us the white color. The larger the water droplets grow, the more light they absorb—making the cloud grey—and the more likely they will start to fall as rain. So, we associate dark clouds with imminent rain.

Two main factors influence whether clouds will form: the amount of water vapor in the air and the temperature. The warmer the air, the more water vapor it can hold as gas. This means that if the amount of water vapor in the air keeps increasing, at some point a cloud must form. Or if the temperature of any air with water vapor in it reduces, at some point—the dew point—a cloud must form.

In nature both things happen regularly, which is why we see so many clouds. It is also why we don't associate fog with hot days—fog is just very low cloud, and when the air temperature is warm, it can hold lots of water vapor. It is also why we get more fogs in the early morning and late evening than we do during the warmer middle of the day.

The air over the sea is very moist, as water is constantly evaporating from it. This makes fogs over the sea likely if the air cools sufficiently. But it also means that if anything lifts the moist air to a level where the air is cooler, clouds will form. This is why all countries with a coastline and large sea in the direction that their prevailing winds come from are likely to experience lots of rain, especially on the side of that sea.

When sunlight hits land and sea, it doesn't have exactly the same impact on both because land heats much more quickly than water. This means that the air above the land also heats more quickly than the air over the sea, and warm air rises. If warm, wet coastal air rises to a level where it cools sufficiently, clouds will form.

Clouds over land are obviously much higher than the land itself and, for thousands of years, this simple physics has allowed ocean navigators to spot islands long before the land itself becomes visible. An island that rises to 100 feet above sea level will be visible from twelve miles away, but a cloud that is 2,000 feet above that same island will be visible from at least fifty miles away.

One of the key things about island-formed clouds is that they look and behave differently from any others. They will have a different shape but, more critically, they don't move in the same way: If you see a horizon scattered with clouds moving with the wind, and a cloud that changes shape slowly but refuses to budge, then the chances are that there is land underneath it. The island cloud is constantly being formed and dissolved by the air, but the net effect is a cloud that doesn't appear to go anywhere. My joy at seeing these clouds over the Caribbean islands after twenty-six days alone at sea is a fond memory, only surpassed by smelling the sweet verdancy of Saint Lucia a few hours later.

The wind travels at slightly different speeds and angles over land and sea, which means that very moist air can be corralled along the coast, creating long bands of cloud marking a coastline and visible from a long distance. When walking on the South Downs, it is very common to see the coastline painted in the sky to the south, even when the sea itself remains invisible. It was an altogether more rapturous experience when we saw a long line of cloud and realized we were seeing a map of the south coast of Crete in the sky, after days of hard walking.

On a smaller scale, forests, cities, and even airports will heat markedly quicker under intense sunlight than the lighter-hued surrounding countryside. This can create much smaller local clouds. Coniferous trees release chemicals called terpenes, and scientists have discovered that they help in "cloud seeding" by forming aerosol particles that enable condensation and make cloud formation more likely over coniferous forests.

I used to fly small airplanes out of a grass airstrip that was alarmingly close to Heathrow and noticed how often the dark tarmac temple of the airport had more clouds over it than our green runway. The sun heated the tarmac faster than the surrounding greenery, causing local thermals and clouds. This is also why you will often see birds of prey soaring on the thermals above coniferous woodland. On a smaller scale still, Alaskan hunters have reported being able to locate caribou herds from miles away, before seeing them and before dogs pick up the scent, by the small bank of cloud that their breath creates.

In places where there is a clear difference between the color of land and sea, it is also possible to detect color variations on the undersides of clouds. In the Arctic, this form of sky map is used regularly, particularly an effect called "water sky," where an area of open water will give clouds over it a darker color. Seasoned Arctic people can read other colors in the clouds: Pack ice gives a true white, sea ice a grey hue, while snow on land adds a yellow tint to the clouds. Out in the Pacific, navigators searching for islands rely on the same principles, but a different palette. A cloud over white sand will be brilliantly white, over forested land it appears darker, over dry reef we might detect a pink tinge, and over a lagoon, perhaps a hint of green.

The day I saw the hills in the sky after sailing was especially memorable because I was looking at a favorite sky map sign. Whenever a wind encounters high ground, it is forced upward and turbulence is created. It's exactly the same physics as the whorls that are formed in the water when a river passes tree roots; eddies are always created when any fluid passes an obstruction. Winds passing the corners of buildings create dust vortices, and water flowing over rocks generates standing waves, water that appears to want to go against the flow.

When wind flows over hills, it is lifted and eddies are created. If the winds are strong and encounter steep land, they can be very powerful and have been known to overcome light aircraft, leading to disaster. But much more commonly there will be enough lift and turbulence to carry some of the air into higher, cooler regions; if it is moist enough, this flow will be marked by clouds, such as the lenticular or "lens" cloud, altocumulus lenticularis—its shape reminds many of a lens or even a UFO. The first few times we spot this effect, it is normal to marvel at the strange shapes we see, but as we get used to spotting them, we start to see hills in the sky.

The Invisible Handrail

I'LL SLEEP IN ANY POSITION THAT works in the woods, but I like it when I wake on my back because I'm reminded of the belief that jaguars in the Ecuadorian rain forest do not attack a person who sleeps face up. On seeing eyes and a face, the jaguars recognize a being, like themselves, but they will sink their teeth into someone facing down, as meat. There are no jaguars in the south of England, but it's a stirring thought to wake to.

It was still early evening as I followed a wide track east over the hill, toward Leo, with Orion marking south off to my right. Then I took an animal trail to the south, before curving back to the east and Leo. When I was walking with the moon ahead, the visibility outside the densest woodland and away from monolithic yews was good. It made the wrinkles in the land easier to read. It is tempting to think we will see more wildlife under bright moonlight, but many nocturnal animals are less adventurous then, preferring to keep to cover. The woodland edges are alive on such nights.

I took a detour, scrambling up a bank to avoid the awkward dense undergrowth along one part of the dry streambed.

Longer, kinder routes are the easier choice at night. *Imshi sana wala tihutt rijlak fi gana*, as the Bedouin say. It's better to go the long way for a year than risk stepping into a ditch.

Then that feeling arrived. A sense not of disorientation—the stars and moon gave me a dozen easy compasses—but of not having any landmarks within sight. I was low, between the hills, and their form was not clear, except the dark undulating lines that touched the sky. The shape of the woods was lost, too, and no streams or rivers were within sight or earshot. Twenty years earlier, in some remote place, I would have felt a quickening of the pulse. I might have ridden the first waves of dread and looked over their crests at an approaching panic. But no longer: I knew "the handrail" was out there. (The word "panic" comes from the ancient Greek mythological figure of the wild, Pan; it is the feeling we experience when we have strayed and don't belong in his realm.)

In navigation, a "handrail" is a linear landscape feature that can easily be identified and followed, such as in rivers, paths, roads, railway lines, or mountain ridges. It is one of the universal navigation techniques, used by everyone from indigenous people to casual walkers, all over the world, because it is so effective.

It will come as no surprise that we can avoid getting lost by following one of these clear lines in a landscape, but here we are considering how we can learn to derive a strong sense of where we are relative to those lines *even when they are invisible*. One of the greatest advances in natural navigation is confidence, when we appreciate that knowing exactly where we are is a rare treat. Most of the time, even in a familiar landscape, we will learn to revel in the sense of being uncertain of our precise position but at the same time fenced in by friendly lines and shapes. This is true even when it has been a long time since we set eyes on them.

If we know we are to one side of a road, railway line, river, track, forest edge, ridgeline, or other linear feature, and we have developed a sense of where this runs, we are set free to play. By adding one other sign, from sky or land, we can roam to one side of this "handrail" and never feel lost. We can cover trackless land, or even sea, and feel secure, knowing that the stars, wind, or gradient may give us a sense of where our invisible handrail lies.

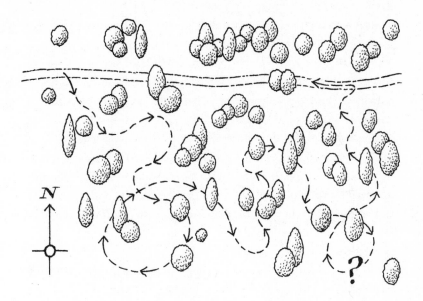

If you know there is a track to your north that runs west-east, as I did in the example above, you can always find this feature by heading north; it doesn't need to be perfect north. If the feature is long enough, you can head northeast or northwest, or one then the other, and you will find your handrail.

It can be done without any reference to star or constellation names and without even using cardinal names, like east or north. On any short excursion, if you leave a handrail of any kind while keeping a constellation to your left, you must be able to find it again by keeping that constellation on your right. The stars help us forge a path and the handrail forms part of a mental map.

Exactly the same method applies if we know where a handrail is, relative to the sun, wind, land, or animal sounds. Over short distances we can find our way back to the edge of the wood by holding on to the sense of where it is relative to gradients, the breeze, even the sounds of sheep.

To gain this sense, all you need to do is experiment with a clear handrail and a strong supporting sign. For example, having chosen your guiding sign carefully, you can venture off a clear track in the woods, then gradually increase distances. As soon as your handrail has disappeared, use your sign to point to it. Now walk back a few steps until it reappears. Walk a bit further away and repeat. You will notice that you start by doing some basic conscious calculations: "I walked downhill, so the track is uphill." Or "I had the sun on my face, so I must turn toward my shadow." But your brain won't let you work that hard for long; soon you'll gain a sense of where the track is. This is an exercise that works well in city centers, too; lose the main street—your handrail—and wander down winding backstreets with your sign in mind, then pick your moment to regain the main street.

There are risks in this sort of navigation, but the bigger and bolder your handrail and sign, the easier and safer this method is. You will want to start by avoiding ambiguity. Practice makes a mile as easy as fifty yards. More practice can stretch this out to the days of walking that indigenous navigators manage.

The only thing that changes if we venture farther from the path is that, as the hours tick by, constellations move across the night sky, winds change, gradients fluctuate, and animals move, so a constant familiarity with these motions allows greater ranges. But the principle of a sense of handrail never does. It works with almost all natural navigation clues, including the way grass is bent.

It can be as simple as knowing we left a river in the direction of a distant coastline. When we sink down between hills and lose sight of both, it needn't rob us of the sense that the river is still there; it is still a handrail that can be found if we climb to gain a view of the sea and put it on our back. We can feel the handrail even when we haven't seen it for hours or even days.

Soon the sun rose over the eastern hills and I squinted. I descended into the shadows again—dawn starts earlier higher up and marches down into the valleys. There was more uphill before I found the track, my handrail, and held on to it as I walked back toward my long shadow and home.

The Light and Dark Woods

MY FACE WAS SCRATCHED AND CUT by the time I emerged, and my jacket was dripping with resin. At one point, I'd become properly disoriented. My instinct was to go in one direction, but the sky disagreed. The clouds, visible though a narrow break in the canopy, kept me on course.

There was a moment, about two hours after I'd stepped into Kielder Forest in North East England, when I began to feel a little disheartened by the lack of clues to direction that I was able to find. It shouldn't have been a great surprise; an old plantation forest is a natural navigator's desert—far harder to navigate in than a real desert. But, still, it's not a feeling I like, to look around and find only one or two weak clues. Then I heard the direction I needed to go.

We can think of deer as having two broad types of habitat: open or closed, moorland or forest. Most deer use scent to monitor their surroundings and any threat that might be near, but a deer's habitat will determine the sense it pairs this with. Deer in moorlands rely on scent and sight mainly, whereas forest deer rely more heavily on scent and hearing. Our sense of smell is not strong enough for it to be such a powerful tool, but we can still take a lesson from the deer: in dense woodlands, we need to use every clue our ears offer.

During my crossing of Kielder Forest, I was helped near the end when I noticed a gentle eruption of birdsong and that it was only coming from one direction. A sharp increase in bird numbers, varieties, and songs could mean only one thing: I was nearing the edge of the forest. I emerged into moorland after scrambling toward the birdsong for five minutes. There is also a rise in the sound of the wind on the trees when you near the edge of woodlands. It is a sound I think of as "the fizz."

Beyond a general aim of trying to listen actively in woods, a more practical suggestion would be to practice identifying trees by their sounds. Identifying the tree itself is not the aim, but this is an effective way to practice active listening. If there is enough wind, each tree has its own sound, and some are easier to recognize than others. Start with the ash, whose signature gentle clacking is hard to mistake, then progress through the radio static of a beech and the whispering of an aspen toward the more taxing conifers. Once this collection of sounds is feeling healthy, you can add another: the sound of each tree in the rain. Logophiles might like to know that there is a word for the rustling sound of the leaves in wind: psithurism.

Long- and middle-distance vision is of limited use in dense woodland—in fact those who live exclusively in such forests lose a normal relationship with this type of sight and can struggle with scale and perspective upon emerging. In the Congo, decades ago, a Pygmy stepped out of the forest onto open plains, where he confused distant buffalo with nearby insects. Those who work in forestry sometimes talk of "wood blindness," a temporary condition where everything appears identical.

In less dense woodlands, or deciduous woodlands in winter, our sense of sight becomes paramount. Look across the wood in all directions and you will notice how the light levels fluctuate. It can be surprising how great the variation is. It is caused not just by changes in the density and depth of the forest, but also by the shape of the land: Where it rolls downhill, light increases, and vice versa. If we practice looking for changes in brightness, we can develop a type of x-ray vision. We start to sense sudden changes we may not have noticed before and, through this, pick up forest edges, clearings, hills, and gradient changes that previously went unseen.

Paths, tracks, and firebreaks in woodlands create a surge in light along their length from the opening in the canopy and also because the ground around the track tends to be of a more reflective color. Forest floors absorb light, making them dark, while paths and tracks reflect light more effectively. Grass is a much better reflector than the undergrowth and plant litter of the forest floor.

After you have been looking out for these shifts in light, you will start to notice the firebreaks and wider tracks at greater distances than you may have thought possible. Standing in the wood and picking up bands of brightness, you may feel fenced in by light. After lots of practice, smaller paths appear, too, and even animal tracks emerge.

Remaining aware of shifts in woodland light levels also makes us more sensitive to weather changes; we are less likely to miss the dimming that heralds any deterioration. And tuning to the sounds and light of the wood adds a richness to the changing of the seasons.

If we have been crossing woodland for a while and notice we are about to step onto a track, firebreak, or other natural parting of the trees, it is a good idea to slow right down and move silently. These breaks allow us to see long distances and offer rare opportunities to slice through the woods with our eyes. If we have been struggling to spot wildlife, despite having the breeze on our face, it may be because the sounds we make as we travel alert the animals before they come within sight.

At breaks, though, we can turn the tables—if we move slowly and quietly. Stepping carefully out of the edge of the wood, we may suddenly see ten times the distance we were able to a moment before, which lifts the likelihood of spotting animals by a similar factor.

The husks crunched underfoot and a pigeon took flight ahead. I stopped and looked up at the canopy, then turned slowly. I was surrounded on all sides by beeches, their thin upper branches threading the gaps between the thicker lower ones. I dropped my gaze and let my eyes adjust before turning slowly again. I saw the color north.

Lichens are sensitive to nutrients, water, acidity, air quality, and light. There are some general trends we can look out for. We will notice the numbers and varieties of lichens shoot up as we near any woodland edge, where the light levels increase. We sense their numbers falling sharply as we draw nearer to cities, and their characters change toward the sea. One bright-orange maritime lichen found in the US, *Caloplaca scopularis*, is tolerant of salt spray and can be found along New England's marine shores, and so is nicknamed "seaside firedot."

In 1970 the Hawksworth & Rose scale was introduced to deduce air-pollution levels from the lichens that were present on trees. It could help you gauge how close you were to industrial areas because lichen reflects sulfur dioxide levels, each species having a different tolerance for its effects (the gas and accompanying acid rain were considered more of a threat in 1970 than they are today).

There are thousands of lichens in the world, and many require analysis to identify or understand them. Most favor slow thinking and are not easy to sense intuitively. So, we can either become lichenologists and launch ourselves at their fruiting bodies with a magnifying glass, or choose to notice their colors, shades, and textures, and get to know them steadily until we build an intuitive sense of the species we find and their meaning. One approach pays great dividends.

Light is one of the decisive factors in determining which lichens will thrive and where. In mixed deciduous woodland where the sun is allowed to break through occasionally, its influence is painted all over the bark of the trees. Lichens give color and character to each side of the trees' bark. Many shades of green are punctuated by whites, greys, yellows, oranges, rusty reds, and blacks. The aspect of the bark determines its color, which means that we see different colors and shades as we face in each direction in the wood.

Near the middle of the day, the southern sky is brightest, even when it's overcast, so the trees to our south appear darker, more contrasted, more silhouetted. Since the brighter lichens are often on the south-facing side of trees, which we see when we face north, the color effect is compounded.

If we practice pairing the direction in which we are looking with the colors we see on bark during any walk through the woods, the moment will arrive when the colors offer direction without effort. You will know that this stage is near when you find it extraordinary that you once saw tree bark as one shade and color.

The Edge and Musit

I'D WALKED TWELVE MILES AND THE April sun was low. I didn't feel ready for the indoors and took a detour away from home, threading my way under a pair of dark yews, then pausing to sit on a rotting trunk.

The sun lost one edge to a distant bank of cloud and was soon below the horizon. A rabbit hopped along the fence line and wood pigeons popped their way in and out along the skyline woodland border. I scanned the undergrowth along the far edge of the trees. On the third passing, my eyes picked it up. There was a dark slit among the brambles, which reached up about two feet from the ground and was noticeably wider in the middle, tapering at the top and bottom.

I was rewarded soon after, but the direction of travel surprised me. The badger lollopped along the edge of the brambles, then turned into the dark gap and disappeared.

In a landscape, the ecotone is the line of tension and friction between two types of environment. We pass over an ecotone when crossing from water to land, high ground to low, woods to open country, coniferous forest to deciduous, or fresh water to salt.

The whole length of a river is an ecotone, a broad line where land meets water, and it is distinct enough that it has earned its own name: the "riparian zone." In drier parts of the country, you will be able to see this band of greater verdancy from quite a distance away. Ecotones are, in short, edges, hence our key name "the edge."

Edges help us find a pattern in randomness and give us insight. If you were able to list the last twenty times you went outdoors and saw something of interest, and then list the last twenty times you saw little of interest, the first would include more time spent near edges.

The edge key helps to explain the sixth sense of the seasoned naturalist. The first time you read works by any expert naturalist of the past few centuries, you will think them extraordinarily lucky: Why is it that they watch barn owls swoop past and the foxes trot by, when all I see are nettles swaying in the breeze? The answer is that they know this pattern, this key.

At all times of year we should expect to notice more happening at the edges than at the heart of woods, water, or wide-open spaces. Since there is more intense animal and plant activity at the edges, it makes sense for us to give them more of our attention.

The edge can work over varying scales: some stretch for miles, others just a few yards. We will see more wildflowers at the edges of paths and tracks than in the middle or ten yards away. Small islands are in permanent contact and tension with the surrounding water, making each island one big edge. This is one reason why islands are areas of relatively intense activity. There may be ducks on an island in the middle of a pond, but thousands of birds on a rock out at sea.

Why are edge areas such magnets for life? Part of it is simple math: The border areas are suitable for all of the creatures on either side and some that need both. Imagine the edge of a wood that meets pasture. For simplicity, let's say the wood is a suitable habitat for five hundred species and the pasture is suitable for a different five hundred, while another five hundred need both. It's conceivable that we will see any of fifteen hundred species at the contact zone, but only a third of them fifty yards in either direction.

Also, most prey animals prefer some cover and will not take to open ground unless they have to. Animals tend to follow and cling to edges: boundaries, walls, and hedges. So, all edges are natural highways. And it follows that where there is greater activity there is opportunity; studies have revealed that predators are more active at the edge than in the interior.

The edge is a sign that things will happen.

When agriculture arrived in the UK between 5000 and 4000 BCE, there came with it the challenge of keeping animals and plants separate. The hedge was born. Hedges are also edges—double-sided ones, at that. They won't offer shelter to larger mammals, but the thorn-rich consistency makes an ideal refuge for many smaller mammals and birds.

To this day, hedges are not planted to segregate the smaller animals. They are there as a barrier to the bigger domesticated ones, such as sheep and cattle. Smaller animals can't pass at will through a hedge; they have to find their own workable route between the maze of stems, branches, and thorns. Trial and error has led rabbits, foxes, badgers, and others to prefer certain crossing points. Over time, small natural passageways become established; each edge and hedge has its share. They will go unnoticed unless we look for them, but they are surprisingly easy to spot. Run your eyes along the bottom of any hedge, a few inches off the ground, and they will start to show. If you are struggling to find them, bend down to change your perspective and allow more light through the hedge. With practice, these gaps begin to shine out.

If we combine the high levels of activity at edges with the fact that many animals will be forced through certain natural gateways, it gives us a means of predicting action. We have a sense of where an animal will appear.

This focal point has been known to those who care, mainly hunters and poachers, for centuries—it has always been the logical siting of a snare. It is such an important feature that it has earned its own name. You may hear it referred to as a "run" or "pinch point," but historically it was called the "muse" or "musit." As one sexist Middle Ages, and possibly middle-aged, wag put it: "'Tis as hard to find a hare without a muse, as a woman without a scuse."

I prefer "musit" to "muse" because it doesn't conjure images of inspirational goddesses, so I call this key "the musit."

The Fire

I THREADED MY WAY ALONG THE sandy path, between the heather and toward the line of pines in the distance. Out of the corner of my eye I sensed fire. The impression was unmistakable, which is only remarkable because the fire had gone out. Probably about three years ago.

We have evolved to pick up any clues of active fires. The distinctive smell seizes our attention to this day, probably because fire has always been significant. When it is raging out of control, it is, of course, lethal, and countless numbers of our ancestors must have perished in forest infernos. But smaller fires are just as significant, since they point toward human activity. The hint of smoke on a breeze is impossible to ignore, like a flare sent up to windward.

Nature notes fire, too. It kills most plants and scatters wildlife, but that is only the tip of the change. Landscapes have long memories of fire. When a fire is built there is a concentration of minerals in one place that remain in the ash long after the flames have died down, changing the ecology of the area, deterring many plants and favoring others. Rings of phosphate-loving stinging nettles may be joined by fireweed and thistles.

Fireweed's fondness for colonizing areas cleared by fire has earned it its name. Lower down, mosses and pixie cup lichens thrive on former bonfire sites. *Funaria hygrometrica*, the bonfire moss, paints the ashy soil with its tiny egg-shaped leaves. A bonfire site left to nature will stand out from the land around it for at least a decade, and often much longer.

The Browse, Bite, and Haven

ONCE WE HAVE GROWN FAMILIAR WITH the plants that colonize these sites, they continue to gleam, as if the fire never died. Sitting by a fence at the edge of the wood, I scanned the farthest edge of a field for movement. Nothing. My focus lowered and came closer, settling on the rough undergrowth. I sensed rabbits. I became restless after a few minutes and sought out their burrow.

In all green landscapes, there will be a tussle between animals and plants. We find traces of it and signs of invisible animals in the foliage all around, like tracks that hover between our eye level and the ground, because every animal betrays their presence in the marks they leave on plants. The ungulates, hoofed animals like deer and cattle, and the rodents, rabbits, and hares, are the ones we are most likely to sense.

Grasslands are a sign of grazers being dominant, as the land will revert to forest if saplings are not "nipped in the bud," but this is at the macro end of the scale. The more interesting signs are to be found in places where neither animals nor plants have seized the upper hand. Common signs include browsing, stripping, and fraying.

"Fraying" is damage to tree trunks and foliage caused by the habit all male deer have of rubbing their antlers and scent glands on them to mark territory. It's quite an aggressive treatment of a tree and marks not only the bark, but also the lowest branches. Another sign of fraying is a ring, whole or partial, of disturbed ground at the base of the tree. Look more closely and you will see where a deer's front hoofs have dug into the soil for purchase, as he presses hard against the tree. Also, the rough, abrasive nature of his actions will leave small hairs in the areas affected. The height of the fraying is an obvious reflection of the size of the beast, as noted by Edward of Norwich in the fifteenth century: "Furthermore ye should know a great hart by the fraying (for if ye find where the hart hath frayed), and see that . . . the tree is frayed well high, and he hath frayed the bark away, and broken the branches and wreathed them a good height, and if the branches are of a good size, it is a sign that he is a great hart . . ." The damage to lower branches caused by fraying will scream, "Deer!"

Deer, squirrels, rabbits, and hares will strip bark off trees for food. The height that the stripping starts and finishes, the width of the teeth marks, and the species affected all point to likely culprits. It is possible, especially if you are a ranger or forester, to identify the animal responsible for fraying or stripping at a distance. Evidence of bark being stripped well above ground level, and where a branch meets the main trunk, especially in trees like oak and sycamore, is a strong indication of squirrels—they like to use a side branch for grip when gnawing at the bark.

Browsing is the eating of young shoots or leaves. It is the standout sign in this category for two reasons. First, it is very widespread, and second, we can gain fast insight without long immersion. It is going on somewhere quite close to you right now.

Browsing is part of a natural culling of young plants. Within a stone's throw of where I sit to write, there are possibly a thousand tiny ash saplings. In twenty years, perhaps a dozen will be trees. Browsing and humans will have accounted for the rest. (Saplings may survive browsing and grow to be mighty specimens, but the signs of browsing can still sometimes be seen many years after the event. If the apical bud, the topmost growing part of the tree, is bitten off, the tree may continue to grow but with more than one main stem. A century or more later, the result may be a tree with a forked trunk.)

The two keys to fast recognition of browsing are height and bite profile. Animals can stretch their necks up, stand on their hind legs, or even rest their forehooves against trees, but they cannot defy physics: The height at which the browsing takes place will be a strong clue to the animal responsible. The next time you are in a field and notice that the trees have a canopy with a suspiciously tidy bottom, which perfectly mirrors the ground, look to the animals that are keeping those trees company and you will see how a stretched neck reaches to the level of the lowest surviving foliage. Repeat this exercise enough times and you will start to see the animals in the flat-bottom shape of the trees.

My favorite example of a browse line, one that is obvious when you know to look for it but remains invisible to most, is the ivy on trees. When you walk anywhere near the edges of woodland, you're likely to pass lots of ivy. Look at the trees and notice where the ivy leaves start: If it is below waist level, few deer are roaming in the area. If you see a line of ivy across several trees starting at about chest height, this will tell you that deer are probably close by. If you practice looking for this over a few walks, you will find that the line starts to stand out. You might also notice how the deer like browsing the leaves on stems that grow up trees, but are less keen to eat the ground-carpet ivy, which spreads unchecked.

Whenever an animal browses, it bites, but no two bites are identical. I sensed the rabbits in the rough undergrowth because there was a clean diagonal (oblique) bite in the brambles, close to the ground. Rabbits and hares leave a clean cut after browsing because they have upper and lower incisors. Deer and many other ungulates, including sheep, press the plant stem between their lower teeth and a hard part of their upper mouth, then tear off the end. This leaves a ragged, messier end to the shoot. (To work out if hares or rabbits have been about, look at the broader browse pattern rather than just the bite. Rabbit browsing is radial, it fans out from cover or burrow, but hares often follow a natural line, like a field or forest edge.)

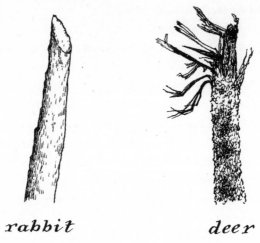

rabbit   *deer*

Browsing signatures

Roe and fallow are the two deer I see most regularly, more days than not. Roe are shorter than fallow, but the trees and undergrowth both species browse fall within a range. Brambles are a staple for these deer, accounting for perhaps 80 percent of their diet in my area, and form a dependable instant map of deer activity on my walks.

"The haven" is my name for any area that is protected from browsing. Every animal has its preferred food and every animal has physical limitations. If we put these together, we find that the way in which certain plants thrive or struggle in each area will give us strong indications as to the presence of particular animals.

When gardeners, foresters, or conservationists want to allow trees to regenerate, one of their main strategies is to fence off browsing animals. Near where I work, large areas have been fenced off as part of a plan to allow 185 acres of farmland to return to the wooded landscape of a century ago. The area is only accessible via high, self-closing metal gates. This is a giant haven; the deer have been sealed out, and it shows. After only a couple of years, those spaces already look markedly different from the neighboring farmland, woodland, or verges. There are no big trees yet, of course, only a sprinkling of young saplings, but the main difference is in the density and height of the undergrowth. Grasses, spurges, myriad wildflowers, brambles, and many other species have formed a carpet that undulates between knee and waist height across the fenced-off area.

Only ten yards outside the fence we find undergrowth shorn down to ankle and shin height: the contrast between the browse and the haven writ large. But it doesn't take a formal regeneration project to see this contrast; there are small pocket havens throughout every landscape. Anything that either physically excludes the browsers or deters them can help us build an instinctive feel for the animals around us, even when the animals remain well hidden. The deterrent you are most likely to see frequently is human activity—notice how brambles and other undergrowth rise in height near paths, buildings, and other hives of human activity. (This will be influenced by light levels and nutrients, like dog feces by paths, too, but stinging nettles will be the giveaway if nutrients are the cause.)

If a browser, like a rabbit, is dominant, you will find another sign of this in the species they avoid. Rabbits rarely eat ragwort, so close-cropped ground with eruptions of certain plants is another animal-species indicator.

You will have noticed that some of the signs in this section are fast and some take a bit more thought. As a rule, browsing and the likely culprit can be picked up instantly, as can a haven. You will spot a bite quickly if you happen to be down low. Everything else will follow at its own pace. Precise species identification can take a lot longer than the instant awareness that deer or rabbits are nearby.

The Celebration and Shadow

MY FACE AND HANDS FIZZED WITH pins and needles as the tiny raindrops were blown onto them. Dark stratus clouds stretched in all directions. The wind gave a thin whistle, working its way around the corner of a barn. A path by the corrugated metal wall led into a wood.

It was late July and the full beech canopy hogged the light, leaving little for the forest floor. Small twigs yielded instantly underfoot, old beechnut husks resisted for longer before cracking. I walked for ten minutes over a woodland floor that held the full range of greens and browns.

My footsteps were now silenced by moss. I smiled as a line was drawn from the ground to the sky, stretching from the corner of each eye, forming a perfect compass in the air before me.

The greenery we see is governed by two sets of influences: genetic and environmental. One dictates the species we will see and the other shapes their character. In cold, wet, exposed, shady places, we will see few of the same plants that we see in hot, dry, sheltered, bright places. But between the extremes we find smaller or taller, bushier or skinnier, even uglier or more beautiful examples of each species.

With the exception of a small number of carnivores or parasites, all green plants, from short grasses to mighty sequoias, derive the energy they need from light. This leads us to expect more plant life where there is more light, and this is what we experience. Find a clump of conifers standing in an otherwise open area and walk into their midst; you will witness the lower plants giving up around your feet.

There is an important secondary boost to the abundance of life from sunlight: It raises the temperature, which increases the rate of most processes within plants. Life is made possible, then accelerated by light and warmth. We all know there are limits to this at the extremes, in hot deserts, but we overlook many subtleties, too.

Leaf size and color, stem growth, sturdiness, roots, shoots, and the appearance and timing of flowers are all strongly influenced by light. Broadleaf trees have broader, thinner, darker leaves on the shadier northern side and conifers have thinner, darker needles on their northern side. The most appealing difference is that more light leads to more flowers in many plants. A few flower well in shade, like lesser celandine and wood avens, but they are the exceptions. In plants that rely on insects for pollination, the flowers are more likely to face the light, too. They rely on insects seeing the flowers, and the more light they reflect, the better their prospects.

Aspect is significant, not least for natural navigation. In northern parts of the world, we get most of our light from the south, so we see more life in south-facing places—the southern side of a hill can receive twenty times more light than the northern. East-facing slopes receive more light in the morning, and west more in the afternoon, which we would expect, but they also experience spikes in irradiance at these times, too, which some plants can't tolerate. Light also bounces off any reflecting surfaces—permanent ones, like rocks, or transient, like clouds. A north-facing slope opposite a bright cliff face might harbor some plants that would struggle without the cliff's sharing of the light.

The level of sunlight also influences the amount of moisture available to plants, with southern aspects often markedly drier than northern ones. Together, these factors lead to noticeable differences in plant life on each side of any hill. The exact species will depend on the geography of the area—including the soils, latitude, and climate—but we can quickly come to recognize our local regulars and the favorites of any new terrain, too. Beneath woodland canopies there is a full range of light levels and colors, from the deep darkness of yew shadows, to the brighter, greener light of beeches and ash trees, while the birches even might allow a little sunbathing on a hot day.

Every landscape has a thousand varying light levels and intensities. We cannot be expected to sense all of these subtle shifts, and the accompanying segueing of the plant life, but if we take an interest in the relationships between light and plant species, the boldest shifts begin to announce themselves.

On my walk through the drizzle, I had spent some time in a low-light environment on an overcast day, passing among shade-tolerant species, like dog's mercury. By focusing on the subtle shifts, I had noticed places where the sunlight was sometimes too intense for these light-shy specimens, which had begun to wither and brown. Just a few feet away, though, the trunk of a tree must have cast a midday shadow because the plant had thrived in a narrow strip.

The compass line in the sky was formed when I saw the small eruption of brambles, wild marjoram, and other wildflowers. This little community indicated plenty of direct sunlight, which was only possible because the hole in the woodland roof pointed south.

If you turn the outdoors into a "laboratory," you can accelerate the revelation stage. Find a place where there is a stark difference in light levels—a break in a woodland canopy is ideal—and go there in the middle of a sunny day. Look at where the sunlight hits the ground, study the plants there, and see how they differ from their neighbors in the nearby shade. Keep doing this and you will quickly start to "see the light" on overcast days and sometimes even at night. If you practice drawing a line from the light-loving plants to the source of their light, you will soon begin to develop a sense of direction. With this key, "the celebration," we can sense direction and meaning from the way plants reveal a sudden rise in light levels.

Its counterpart is "the shadow," where shade-tolerant plants, like arum, announce a drop in light levels among otherwise sun-loving ones. The shadow indicates a shade-casting obstacle between those plants and the south. Both belong to the broader family of environmental clues.

Just as plants reveal truths about light, they also show the levels of nutrients and water in their environment. Stinging nettles, dock, and elder signal artificially high levels of nutrients—in an otherwise wild landscape, they are a sign of human or animal activity. Alders, willows, and many plants, like sedges, indicate wet ground.

I called this key "the celebration" because the discovery of wildflowers, when accompanied by an instant sense of light and direction, is joyful.

The Friend, Guest, and Rebel

I
T HAD BEEN A FRUSTRATING HOUR. A crossing of a
spruce plantation had left me with a hunger for signs. There had
been compasses in the storm-felled trees, pushed over from southwest to northeast, and older clues, too, in the tumultuous earth. The
storms of centuries past had left mounds where old root balls had once
been, and dips where they had been pulled from the land, a southwest to
northeast line from dip to mound. But I had been spoiled over previous
days, plucking at clues and signs on more open land, as if it owed me
such. Now I was irritable and greedy for them.

The edge of the forest was foretold with light, lichens, and ivy. Stepping past the last of the spruces, I saw an oak with its lower branches
spread wide. Now I knew there would be signs aplenty.

Every tree we meet is a friend, guest, or rebel. Each species is either
a long-established part of the landscape, a recent addition, or simply
doesn't belong there. And once we recognize which category each tree
falls into, we gain an instant sense of what else it might reveal. Native
species have grown in partnership with the landscape; every native tree
we see plays host to a large number of much smaller organisms. These
mosses, lichens, fungi, and insects can give us as rich a sense of our surroundings as the tree itself.

Every time I see an oak I feel a lift, first from its familiarity, but also because I know it will provide many small signs. Oaks have history; they've existed for millions of years and have lived in Britain for millennia, which always leads to a more complex web of life on the tree. I know that an oak will give me dozens of compasses in the lichens that have made their homes on its branches, with insights from galls—the odd growths and lumps—and other members of its community.

Invasive trees are guests. They have arrived, often uninvited, and the partnerships are immature in an ecological sense: the smaller organisms haven't gotten to know them as well. They are poorer hosts and form weaker ecosystems. We must expect to see less life on invasives such as a Scots pine or tree of heaven than we will on the natives like maple, walnut, beech, or oak.

If we encounter an ecosystem that is rich with a mix of native species, the possibilities grow exponentially. And if we stay true to our philosophy that every living thing is a sign, then the wealth of meaning that one short stretch of hedge can offer is tantalizing.

The rebel is a tree that does not belong in any natural context, one that is neither native nor a late accidental arrival.

It says more about human activity than wilderness. If we are traveling across a landscape and find a tree that stands out as ill-fitting, it should trigger a sense of human activity. I have enjoyed the fruit of such a tree in the heart of Borneo, where it was a sign of a long-vanished village. But closer to home, anomalous trees are more common.

Rows of Lombardy poplars are a sure sign of human landscaping. They are unmistakable, with their distinctive narrow columns, even from a distance, one of the few trees that stand out even from the air and are used as landmarks by pilots. The Norway spruce and many other species are planted to hide ugliness in a landscape, perhaps a sewage-treatment facility, but there are more pleasing examples, too. Scots pines were once planted in clumps in the UK to send a signal to drovers that they could stay for the night and graze their animals—a more alluring version of today's great neon signs that throw colored light across our roads and point to service stations. In this instance, it is the landscaping, the isolated clumps, that stands out, not the species, which is native to the UK.

My favorite example of a rebel is described by Richard Jefferies:

> *By old farmhouses, mostly in exposed places (for which there is a reason), one or more huge walnut trees may be found. The provident folk of those days planted them with the purpose of having their own gunstocks cut out of the wood when the tree was thrown. . . .*

> *The reason why the walnuts are put in exposed places, on the slope of a rise, with open aspect to the east and north, is because the walnut is a foolish tree that will not learn by experience. If it feels the warmth of a few genial days in early spring, it immediately protrudes its buds; and the next morning a bitter frost cuts down every hope of fruit for that year, leaving the leaf as black as may be. Wherefore the east wind is desirable to keep it as backward as possible.*

If we get the feeling that a tree doesn't belong, we can also sense the human hand behind it.

The Reaper

I REACHED THE TOP OF THE hill on a warm, overcast day and sat down between two lines of foxgloves. As I drank some water and ate a few almonds, my body began to cool and the landscape came into clearer focus. A red admiral butterfly jinked away from me as it followed the track in the direction I had come. I saw a scar on the side of an ash tree; it was the shape of south.

Nature is an abundance of life despite the odds. The chances of any plant or animal succeeding from its first moments to adulthood are minute, and if it reaches this milestone, thousands of organisms are keen to deprive it of life. Whenever we see a plant or animal, including when we look in the mirror, we are witnessing disease and death being held at bay temporarily. This is not a cheery thought, but life is not a bedtime story; it's a temporary, unlikely, and exquisite flourishing.

Part of the sensitivity that allows all the other signs to stand out is an awareness of the well-being of the nature that we pass through. Nature does not have hospitals, hospices, retirement villages, or bowling greens. When the balance starts to go against an organism, it quickly reaches a tipping point and death follows.

Our ancestors were tuned to this sense of well-being for immediate practical reasons: Diseased animals or plants were avoided as food and a camp was not built under trees that were near collapse. But this awareness is also part of a wider sensitivity. Just as a parent will notice before other adults that their child is catching a cold, so those fully immersed in nature will remain attuned to fluctuations in the well-being of this broader family.

The awareness is also a window into the interconnectedness of our environment, since plants and animals succumb to other organisms or the elements. A patch of dying woodland is a sign of the fungi that killed the roots, and these fungi are a consequence of the flood that deprived the roots of aeration. A thin, weak, and ill animal may have poisoned itself, forced into eating something toxic that it doesn't normally touch.

An animal with recent injuries may have sustained them as a result of conflict with another animal, a clue to a territorial dispute, usually linked to food or sex. An animal that is nearby and protecting its territory is worth knowing about and can often be identified from the injuries. A dead bird will reveal whether it was taken by a mammal like a fox—look for gnaw marks on the quill of the feathers—or a bird of prey, with a more surgical removal of the soft tissues and feathers that have been plucked.

There are hundreds of signs that an organism is in trouble and, as with all signs, there are levels of complexity and richness. If we start by noticing the clearest, time allows more layers to be added. The sign that we are seeing something succumb is "the reaper."

As with so many plant-related signs, trees are the best place to start, because things happen on a grand and helpful scale; trees put on such a show.

You will already be aware that one of the most glaring signs of a tree's distress is its shape. All deciduous trees should have straight main trunks; any deviation from that will have a cause and is a sign of stress. The shape of the canopy is also a measure of health. Before trees die they become vulnerable to parasites and pathogens. Deciduous trees that are under attack die at the top first; conifers lose needles and thin out dramatically before withering high up.

Mature trees that have a gentle twist may be exposed to more wind on one side, but younger trees that show a more pronounced corkscrew effect have become victims of climbers like honeysuckle. If the climber is no longer on the tree, it may have left its fingerprints at the scene. Honeysuckle grows clockwise, while others, like bindweed, grow counterclockwise.

The saprotrophs, organisms that feed on dead or dying organic matter, are the sign you will spot most regularly. There is no shortage of them. One fifth of all living things rely on dead wood, and among these some of the easiest to remember and recognize are the fungi. King Alfred's cakes earned their nickname from their dark, burned, rounded appearance. They grow most commonly on ash trees and are a sign of death; occasionally they will be found on other deciduous species, but never on healthy branches. They are also known as "coal fungus" and "cramp balls" and are familiar to bushcrafters and survivalists as an abundant natural tinder for fire lighting.

Jelly ear is easy to identify from its name alone and is a sign of an elder tree that is dead or in trouble. Once known as "Jew's-ear," elder is said to be the tree from which Judas Iscariot hanged himself. The fungus responds to changes in the weather, shriveling in dry times and growing more gelatinous after rain. Yellow brain fungus will be found on dead deciduous wood, especially birch, hazel, and gorse. Beech woodwart, hemispheres that turn from pink to brown and then almost to black, is to be found on dead beech branches.

These fungi appear regularly as part of the cycle of an environment in balance, but everywhere in the world also suffers from epidemics, when invasive species take advantage of populations that have evolved little resistance. Dutch elm disease and sudden oak death are two recent examples in the US.

Wet wood, also known as slime flux, is the tree equivalent of an animal wound that has gone septic. Any rupture in tree bark leaves sap exposed to infection by bacteria. It becomes toxic, gives off a sour smell, and reacts to moisture, foaming after rain and drying to a white crust. If you see a wound with evidence of "bleeding" below it, the tree is fighting for survival. The wound may heal in time or branches may die.

Suckers, lots of young shoots, emanating from the base of an oak mean it is struggling. They represent a bid for a better life and can result when an oak has been overshadowed by another tree. On some other species, like linden trees, suckers are common and should not be seen as a sign of weakness. You will often see suckers growing from a recently felled stump. The stress that this tree has experienced is obvious, and here the suckers represent a desperate bid for survival.

Bark may be shrouded in mosses and lichens, in their many colors. They can look ominous, but are harmless residents. Ivy is not a parasite or saprotroph—it does no direct harm to trees—but it can make them more vulnerable to gales, when it acts as a sail, and occasionally competes for light, too. Mistletoe is more of a threat, being a partial parasite: It commonly kills branches and at best gently hinders the tree.

Animals, such as squirrels, hares, and deer, will cause patches of damage to trees low down, but a long, vertical scar is more likely the result of lightning. It is sometimes accompanied by the darkness of burning. The scar I saw on the ash at the top of the hill, which pointed south, was caused by something different: sun scald. In northern temperate zones, the south side of trees is exposed to dramatic temperature fluctuations in winter, going from below freezing to hot in the midday sun. Research has shown that the temperature difference between the south and north side of trees in winter can reach 45 degrees Fahrenheit. Sun scald can lead to permanent scarring, normally forming a vertical line on the bark of the tree that faces between south and southwest. It is sometimes referred to as "southwest winter injury" and is more common in young trees because of their thin bark. They usually survive, and as they grow, contusions may develop around the vertical scar.

Trees are attacked on many fronts, so it is nice to know that they are not without defenses. Pioneer species, like birch, grow fast in places where they are vulnerable to animals, intense sunlight, and pathogens. Silver birches grow thick, rough bark quickly, which protects against animals; the silver part of the bark contains betulin—a compound which is antibacterial, antiviral, and acts as a sunscreen. Spruce and pine trees contain chemicals that act as antibiotics; they are so effective that the air in these forests is near germ-free and the needles can be added to water to kill protozoa.

Signs of ill health in animals are either physical, and therefore obvious, or relate to a deviation from normal behavior. Our chances of spotting this will depend on our familiarity with those patterns. I know when any of our dogs or cats is sick, usually from their feeding habits. I'm much less likely to spot it in our chickens; my wife spends more time looking after them than I do. The animal we all have the most familiarity with is the human. It's quite common to ask someone we know well if they are feeling okay when they lie down or go quiet for a while.

I don't doubt, dear reader, that you are immune to the temptations of excess, but your friends and colleagues may not be so abstemious. You will have noticed how people become more or less loquacious and restless after a big night out. One person sits motionless and silent, the other paces up and down and gibbers; the following day they revert to their norm. Something similar has been noted in animals in captivity: birds and fish get to know their boundaries in cages and tanks, and any out-of-character brushing up against them is a sign of discomfort. Similar changes in behavior are happening in the wild, but our lack of familiarity may make it a little harder to spot. A wild animal that fails to respond when you would expect it to do so is probably in poor health (or, as we will see later, it may be feeling threatened). The difference will be seen in energy levels; an ill animal will be uncharacteristically agitated or lethargic, like us.

Many animals, including apes, elephants, bears, and birds, are capable of self-medication, or zoopharmacognosy. Our dogs regularly nibble grass on our walks, which doesn't warrant a trip to the vet, but other animals sometimes eat larger amounts of grass to clear a gut problem by inducing vomiting or diarrhea. Carnivores, including dogs, nibble at green plants to supplement their diet, and herbivores, like deer, will occasionally lick carrion. Female woolly spider monkeys in Brazil can raise or lower their fertility by adding certain plants to their diet.

PART III

Creatures of Meaning: The Animals

The Perch and Sentinel

I N THE CENTER OF A FIELD of stubble there was a long-dead oak tree. Its skeletal frame loomed over the rabbit that was following the fence to my left. I stepped carefully along the grass at the perimeter. Grass that is too long or too short can be noisy, but in different ways. Long blades crunch, but the short ones won't cushion the sound of twigs, nut husks, or stones when trodden on.

The silhouette of a crow stood out near the highest point of the tree. My eyes flitted between the still, dark shape and the rabbit as it hopped slowly away from me. I watched the crow turn, pause, and then take off. Before I looked back to the rabbit, I knew it would be gone.

As a rule, we want to sense the ephemeral before the more permanent. It would be strange to spend a minute studying a tree's shape and colors and only then to glance up to see if a hawk is patrolling above.

In any open country, there will be at least a few local high places—a tall rock, a hedge, or a tree branch—that offer vantage points. They will form part of an animal's reading of a landscape, and need to be part of ours. Predators and prey view these perches differently, aggressively or defensively. Birds, like hawks and barn owls, will use them as lookouts to survey their domain, scanning for hunting opportunities. Prey that has become alert to the presence of predators on those perches will be sensitive to the danger of travel within sight of them.

Height is such an advantage that these perches are not hogged exclusively by predators. Many other species of mammal and bird will take advantage of the better view to survey the landscape for danger. When this is a specialized role within a group, the animal or bird becomes known as a "sentinel." Species of crow, blackbird, pigeon, and wren are known to use sentinels. To be in that position is like drawing a short straw; foraging time is lost, but it also exposes the bird or animal to greater risk of attack. Most species with sentinels have evolved a rotation of the duty.

In some species, we may even pick up the changing of the guard as the sentinel returns to foraging and the substitute takes up the post. Meerkats are famous for sentinels; they rise on their haunches and emit constant soft noises when on duty. When it is time for the sentinel meerkat to stand down, the sounds alter, announcing the shift change. When the male red-winged blackbird is guarding a nest, he gives constant calls that reveal he is keeping watch and that there is no immediate danger. If he detects any threat, his call changes.

The height of any sentinel determines how much it can see, which will influence the behavior of others in the group. The higher any sentinel is, the more those in the group know they can rely on it and the more time they spend focused on foraging. If you see a group of birds pecking away at the ground, apparently without a care in the world, there is a good chance that if you look up and around you will find that one has found a high perch.

As you enter open country, remember to scan for the perch and sentinel. They are key to understanding why the birds or animals seem to have eyes in the backs of their heads, and one of the fastest ways of telling whether or not your presence has been detected. They also reveal our chances of getting closer to the animals on the ground and the route to take if you want to advance with stealth.

The Return

ALL WAS QUIET AROUND ME, BUT I knew that all was not quiet.

Emerging from the wood into a clearing, I sat down beneath the oak, my back against its trunk, and waited. Deer-browsed ivy formed cover over my head, shielding me from aerial eyes. After five or more minutes, a bullfinch landed on the holly tree twenty feet in front of me. It was soon joined by other birds. There was a rustle and a bounce in a hazel on the other side of the clearing: a squirrel leaping from one thin branch to another. Seconds later, the lightest of thuds: A young acorn dropped through the canopy above my head to land near my feet. More acorns followed, one landing on my thigh, as the invisible squirrel flitted among the tree's seeds. A pigeon sang out from high in a beech. A quarter of an hour had passed before I heard the first crack of a twig.

However stealthily we walk into the breeze, even if we tiptoe across soft earth in softer shoes, we send a bow wave of alert through the land-scape around us. The animals are often too sensitive for us to hoodwink them into failing to notice us altogether. We may get close enough to see them as we walk, sometimes even within touching distance, but we have to concede the likelihood that, when we are moving, the wildlife in the immediate environment is aware of our presence. This awareness suppresses natural behavior, triggering alarm calls, flight, or often just silence. Their sounds and motions melt away and they disappear from our senses.

But if we tuck ourselves away, motionless and silent, life slowly returns to normal. This is "the return." Just as the animals pick up on each other's signs of alarm—their calls, flight, or body language—so there is also a communal language to communicate safety. The presence of the first bird encourages the others, then the squirrel, the deer, the fox, and the badger.

After I'd spent an hour beneath the ivy, the oak's root began to bruise my backside, so I stood up and shook myself down. The life melted away again.

The Face and Tail

THE SQUIRREL SAT IN THE MIDDLE of the path, about a hundred yards ahead. I wasn't sure at first if it had detected me, and I took another few steps toward it. As soon as its tail started to flick, I knew I'd been detected. Sure enough, one more step and it was gone.

A friend of ours with kids about the same age as ours shared a sneaky parenting trick with us a few years ago. It is a form of lie detector and it works like this: If you suspect a young child of telling a fib in answer to a question, say to them, "I can always tell when you're lying because your nose begins to twitch." Then ask them the original question again. If they're telling whoppers, their face takes on an unnatural look of concentration as they simultaneously try to work out if their nose is twitching and suppress the sensation that it might be about to. It's hilarious to watch and I believe leads only to passing psychological damage.

Nowhere is our intuitive ability to read meaning in visual clues more apparent than in faces. Before we venture into the wild, we can learn a lot by considering human faces and the Facial Action Coding System (FACS), developed by anatomists about forty years ago.

Anatomists have studied human faces and deconstructed the individual actions that lie behind our expressions. We know that a smile includes the corners of our mouth rising, but anatomists have gone many steps further and learned the dozens of actions that make up expressions of anger, happiness, sadness, surprise, fear, disgust, and more. Happiness is one of the simplest: It involves raising the corners of the mouth with a raising of the cheeks. Fear is much more complex, involving a selection from seven facial actions: inner and outer brow raising, brow lowering, eyelid raising or tightening, lip stretching, and jaw dropping.

But you already knew this, even if you'd never heard of FACS. You can tell instantly whether a stranger is angry, happy, or sad without knowing or being able to describe the actions their face is undertaking. It is part of our intuitive tool kit: Life would be a struggle if we were unable to tell when someone is unhappy long before they articulate it. But there are hundreds of subtler nuances within relationships where we go, with practice, from the basic tool kit to a much more refined one.

Imagine someone whose upper teeth rest on their lower lip just before they're about to sing along to music, but rarely at other times. If you successfully predicted to a neutral observer that they were about to break into song, it might be regarded as psychic or a sixth sense (or just weird). But it is just the practiced pairing of a facial expression with an emotion or action. The neutral observer would be able to perform the same trick with a stranger, even if they had never met the singing lip-biter, provided they were aware of this sign in that individual. What begins as a conscious analysis of a simple clue in one person quickly becomes an intuitive sense of what is happening and about to happen. And it is this that brings us back to the wild, where these signs are plentiful.

We can learn to make these pairings purely through observation, as many of our ancestors did, but the process can be accelerated. You need to know how not to waste your time. You could spend a lifetime looking for telltale clues in the facial expressions of birds or reptiles and glean little or nothing; they give little away in their faces. Fish, on the other hand, would make terrible poker players as the same nerve—nervus facialis—that controls our facial expressions also controls the gill covers of fish, leading some experts to argue that the speed and rhythm of fish gills is the best window to their thoughts. The splaying of gills is a sign of imminent attack in some species, while amphibians' state of arousal is best gauged by looking at the skin of their throat. Snakes coil the front third of their body and may increase tongue flicking prior to a strike.

The best head start, forgive the pun, comes from knowing where it is worth focusing your attention. Horses, cats, deer, and elephants reveal a lot through their ears. Cats, dogs, and sea lions can reveal emotions through their whiskers. Predators open their mouths more widely than grazers, so any unusual opening of the mouth of ungulates, like sheep, is a possible sign of distress or excitement. The jaw and lip position of bears and rhinoceroses can reveal the level of aggression.

Much of this will already be intuitive: Snarling in any animal is not a welcoming sign, and the human grimace finds its roots in these animal expressions. But there are counterintuitive signs worth knowing about in case you encounter them. Monkeys and hippopotami that yawn are not getting ready for a nap, but more likely preparing to attack; this sign is called a "temper yawn." And the most famous false sign is the crocodile's smile: It's fixed, not a token of friendship. Crocodiles give clues to their level of excitement in their eyes, which are narrow slits in a calm beast but widen to circular when it is aroused.

We glean a huge amount from animals by following their gaze. Animals can't defy the laws of physics, so they have to point their eyes at anything they want to see, which often means aligning their heads, too. Obviously, the more visually led any species is, the more we will gain from considering their eyes. There is little value in gauging where a badger is looking, but a lot to be gained from following a dog's gaze. Birds may lack expression in their faces, but their eyes are powerful, and even if we are too far away to make out where their eyes are fixed, their body language can reveal it. A hovering kestrel will point with its head and beak at activity on the ground (and into wind).

A common sign that we all use with people and can grow more aware of with birds is a turned back. It is common for birds to land nearby, spot us, then spend time assessing us with regular head tilts, giving one eye or each in turn a good look at us. Once they turn their backs it is a sign that they are no longer worried by us. Any movement we make that they detect will bring them quickly around again. We can see them doing this daily on bird tables or lawns.

There is great potential for us to develop our ability in this area, as research with the Australian magpie has revealed. Scientists in Australia discovered that it is not so much whether the magpie is looking at something that reveals its next action, but the eye it uses. If a magpie is preparing to fly away, it looks at a threat using its left eye; if it uses its right eye, it is more likely to approach for a closer look. Lesley Rogers, a professor of neuroscience and animal behavior, and her team at the University of New England in Australia, who conducted this extraordinary research, believe there may be an explanation for this close to home. Information from our left eye is processed by the right side of our brain, which is used for novel situations or potential threats. The left side of the human brain, receiving information from our right eye, is better at analysis. Perhaps this offers an insight into fast or slow thinking in birds through their head tilt and choice of eye.

There is debate within the scientific community about how much of this is a two-way street. It is generally accepted that many primates and dogs can follow our stare and work out what we are looking at, but it is not known how widespread this skill is in the animal kingdom. If dogs do, but wolves apparently don't, could this be one of the lines between domestication and the wild?

Some old hands recommend looking at animals out of the corner of your eye, and I often feel an instinctive urge to do this, particularly if that is where I have detected a flighty creature, like a fox. But we have detailed vision only when looking at something directly, so I use the sidelong glance to monitor general movements. I'm still not sure which animals are able to deduce things from the target of my gaze, but my personal experience is that head position and motion have a strong bearing on the behavior of many animals. Many birds seem to grow quiet when I look up at them in a tree, and squirrels often freeze, but it is hard to know whether my head movement and body language or my gaze triggers this. Corvids and pigeons are known to recognize individual faces, so they're likely to be sensitive to where we are looking.

Many deer face something directly if curious, but turn to look from side-on if alarmed. This is often a two-step process: The deer hears me and pops its head up, facing and staring in my direction, then, on discovering that a human is close by, bounds a few paces away, then turns to look from side-on. I always try to focus on the tongue and ears of deer to predict the second step: A deer licks its nose when alert, as the moisture improves its sense of smell. Its next move is nearly always preceded by increased twitching of its ears.

At the other end, a tail is less complex than a face, but it can reveal an animal's state. A squirrel's tail is well worth watching: when we are still and spot a squirrel before it sees us, the slightest movement of our head, arms, or body can send nerve impulses though the animal and set its tail flagging.

The wagging of a dog's tail is not a sign of happiness, as is commonly supposed, but can be seen as a greeting or a sign that the dog knows it has company. A tail held high is a sign of a dog that feels assertive or dominant, while one that is low is more submissive. When the tail is tucked between the legs, this is a sign of surrender or appeasement: You win—please don't hurt me.

Deer and antelope, as well as some lizards and many water birds, flick their tails to indicate that they are aware of a predator's presence. Some monkeys will hold their tail out horizontally behind them when afraid, but baboons signal fear by holding theirs vertically upward.

The Point

VENUS REBELLED. NORMALLY A COMFORT ON an early-evening walk, it surprised me by sitting further south on the horizon than I had expected. Venus can set as far south as a winter sun, so I shouldn't have been shocked. It was a reminder that there had been few clear evening walks of late.

I followed the riverside path out of Arundel on the last day of October, stepping off regularly to investigate the many diversions that water creates. The sound of a coot led to the discovery of a tiny tributary, both hidden and announced by its cloak of reeds.

I turned with the path and passed through a meadow. There were a few cows standing to graze and two lying down. A pair of crows passed high overhead, and I watched their disciplined track until I lost them over the crest of a hill. There were no stars out yet, but it wouldn't be long.

When I lowered my eyes to the meadow, it was obvious that something interesting was about to happen.

There is much debate about the direction in which animals choose to align themselves. We know from research that there is a north-south bias in cows and that many prey animals prefer the wind coming from behind when foraging, as it allows their sense of smell to fill in the narrow void of their peripheral vision. But there will always be a dose of variability too. All it takes is a noise or even one small patch of lush-looking grass to turn an animal.

Trends are common, but it is unusual for cattle or horses all to face the same way in a regimented fashion—unless there is good cause. If we see two or more animals perfectly aligned, standing still with their heads up, this is "the point" key, and it tells us something of interest lies in that direction. It was one of the many techniques poachers and gamekeepers of old used to sense each other, even when well hidden.

From an evolutionary perspective, the point has a dual function. It allows an animal to monitor anything of concern, but the body language also signals to a potential predator that it has been spotted. Predators rely on an element of surprise for most hunts, so any animal that makes clear they have spotted the hunter reduces the chance of an attack. A meal that is aware and ready to run for its life is not as attractive as waiting for one that is less cognizant, which is why this strategy is so widely used by mammals and birds. On detecting danger, hares face the threat, stand upright, and prick their ears, which improves vision and hearing. It also signals that this hare has no intention of being caught by surprise.

The two cows that had been lying in the Arundel meadow were now standing. Their bodies were parallel and both they and their comrades were facing the same way. The grazing had stopped. I followed the direction of their bodies and found the source of their consternation.

At the far edge of the meadow a fox was walking along the line of a scraggy hedge. It disappeared behind a clump of grass, then reappeared, a pattern it repeated until it had covered about twenty yards. The cows shifted to track it. Their attention did not wander from the auburn motion in the grass.

As the fox approached the corner of the field, one of the two cows that had been lying down began to walk, then trot toward it. The fox appeared oblivious. It was focusing elsewhere and now seemed to be stalking some small prey among the tufts. It jumped once and then again, but was unsuccessful. Then it turned to see two cows approaching and, as it did so, the leading cow broke into a run. The aloof fox trotted off and disappeared through a musit in the hedge as the faster cow closed the distance to a few yards.

The Peek

A FTER A DRY MONTH AND A few flirtatious showers, the rain arrived in May. The woods seemed greener within hours, but unless the wet sheen on the leaves was enhancing the color, I must have imagined it. I didn't imagine the sounds.

There are three levels of rain sound in any area with trees. The faintest whisper of rain hitting open ground will be drowned by the static of it landing on the leaves. The hissing sound is like that of an untuned analog radio, a white noise that is both fluctuating and constant at the same time. Then there is the lower, louder plopping of the rain running off the leaves and hitting lower ones or the ground below. You can see the prints of the fat run-off drops in any wet mud as it becomes pocked. Get down low and look toward open sky across the patches of pocked mud and you will see a mottled tapestry in the ground, one that shifts with each new plop.

Any long period spent in the open under rain is a balancing act between motion and stillness. Too long sitting still in rain becomes a trial, but too long walking in it makes us oblivious to what is going on. Move and pause: that's the way to play the rain. If it is cold, motion will rule.

I can't pretend to prefer rain, but as one more dollop of cold water hit my neck, I warmed at the thought of our pond reversing its decline and creeping back up. I was also warmed by the sight of a horse chestnut tree. A few days earlier, I had noticed for the first time how its flowers' pink-tinged white pyramids did not grow vertically, but were tilted toward the southern sky. How many times had I seen the flowers on this tree and not noticed that? A blackcap sang nearby, echoing my thoughts. The last flourish of its song always sounds to me like "I told you so."

I rested, leaning against a tree. My focus drifted into a forest gaze until some small motion harnessed it. A blackbird was hopping through the ivy undergrowth. Peck, peck, up, peck, peck, peck, up, peck peck, up, hop, hop, peck, peck, up, hop, peck, peck, up. I watched until I had a sense of the bird's rhythm, which told me when to take my next steps.

For many years I would have seen the collection of bird actions as a part of a single entity called a blackbird, in the same way that a handful of sand is just sand, until we look closely and realize it is a compilation of different-colored particles, quartz, shell, dark volcanic specks. The individual motions of animals are wrapped up within the package of the names we give them. A blackbird is not just its signature yellow beak, or its sweet song, or the way it flies: it is all of these things and more. This is the purpose of identification—to recognize the whole, nothing more. But to get a deeper sense of what an animal is doing and about to do, that is not enough. We have to see through the package to the behavior.

All animals are capable of different levels of alertness, but we can think of them in one of two states: the animal is either vigilant or not. An animal that is focused on any of its daily habits, like feeding or the various stages of sexual reproduction—from advertising or defending territory to copulation—is not being vigilant. In human terms, we might say that the animal "has its head down and is getting on with things." This idiom is more pertinent than it might seem: One of the basic indications of how vigilant an animal is being is its head position. Watch any two people in conversation as they walk along a pavement, then notice how their head positions change when they prepare to cross the road—cars are the closest things to predators for many. If we hear any loud, unexpected noise, we are startled into a state of vigilance and our heads rise. Think of the rabbit or squirrel up on its haunches. As we have seen, there are good, practical reasons for the head rise: We can see and hear farther and better, and the smaller the creature, the more dramatic the impact. Try lying on your chest in undergrowth, looking at and listening to your environment. With one press up, the world opens around you.

There are two types of vigilance, routine and induced, and each is determined by whether or not an animal is aware of a threat. It is either taking precautions or has reason to heighten its awareness. If an animal is foraging and unaware of any threat, it will still alternate between feeding and vigilance. This is sensible, evolved behavior; just because it hasn't sensed a predator ten yards away, that doesn't mean there isn't one. Routine vigilance is easy to spot because there is a rhythm to it: Feeding and alertness alternate. It's never a perfect beat, but it has a shape. Notice how all ground-foraging birds peck at their food, but alternate this with a raised or cocked head movement.

The moment an animal becomes aware of a threat, it will stop what it's doing and enter into a deliberate state of vigilance. Again, this is easy to spot, if we've been watching it, because of the break in its routine. Watch squirrels for any length of time and you will witness both types of vigilance many times. A squirrel that lifts its head while on all fours is probably still in routine mode, but one that is up on its haunches is more likely to have picked up on something of concern. Squirrels will also climb onto logs, tree stumps or rocks to gain a few extra feet for improved vigilance.

Many deer, including the roe I see so often, have their own pattern of deliberate vigilance. As we saw earlier, if roe deer sense something of concern they will lift their heads and trot a few yards away before turning broadside on to the threat. This may seem odd, as it exposes their flank to attack by a human or animal hunter, but there's logic in this strategy. A deer doesn't want to trot away and keep its rear toward a threat as this makes vision awkward, but neither does it want to face the threat as that makes running in the opposite direction difficult. We don't have to understand the evolutionary pressures or thought processes of the animals we see, we just need to practice noticing the state and thinking: short trot, then broadside on—ah! That's induced vigilance. Quickly the words disappear and we sense what is going on.

Predators are finely tuned to vigilance and will target animals that are foraging over those that are vigilant. For prey, it is always a balancing act—which is the greater threat? A predator or starvation?

Studies of mammals and birds have shown that the animals are tuned to risk levels and tailor their alertness accordingly. Many birds, including favorites such as sparrows, starlings, robins, and blackbirds, become more vigilant as their distance from cover increases. And animals enter into a vigilant state more frequently if they have detected a predator or other threat, which is what we would expect.

Vigilance also increases when animals realize they are entering terrain that makes them more vulnerable. Grey squirrels will pause more frequently when moving out of woodland and into open ground than when moving back into cover. And it appears that vigilance comes with maturity: Adults are more alert than youngsters.

The behavior of different seal populations shows an extreme example of sensitivity to the likelihood of danger. In the Arctic, ringed seals have to be wary of predators, like polar bears, wolves, and foxes, and will startle at the least trigger. Weddell seals live relatively carefree lives in the Antarctic, untroubled by such predators. They sleep so soundly that humans can approach within touching distance.

The burden of vigilance is shared within a group, but also across species. Willow tits scan their surroundings less when they are in a flock with coal tits. And both birds and mammals are sensitive to the size and shape of the group. House sparrows scan less as the flock increases in size, but they scan for longer the farther away other birds are. Rabbits are similarly sensitive; a solitary rabbit will appear more jittery than one in a group, as a result of its frequent bouts of vigilance.

The house sparrows' reliance on their "neighborhood watch scheme" may explain why they, along with many other animals, advertise discoveries of food. You'd think a hungry animal would just tuck in, but house sparrows make a specific call, a chirrup, that announces the find to other house sparrows, which will then flock together, feed together, and take turns being vigilant. Mallard ducks extend group vigilance into their sleep. They will open one eye from time to time, and ducks on the edge of the group open the eye that faces outward.

Noticing animals switching in and out of vigilant mode gives us a better sense of what will happen next and is the start of developing an awareness that allows us to come much closer to them than would have been possible before.

The Freeze, Crouch, and Feign

I T WAS MID-MARCH AND THE SUN was rolling up the hill at the end of the day. My walk started in cool shade, but a short, steep stretch of uphill led me back into the sunlight and warm air. There is something menacing about the sight of a great sunset shadow advancing toward you, high on a mountainside: A long, cold, dark blanket is being dragged over you. But it's a treat to chase one up a hill.

I pulled some young brambles away and settled into the litter. There I lay, at the edge of the wood, looking out over fences and pasture. The green woodpeckers had been filling the trees with their raucous laughter all afternoon, but had remained hidden. Then a substantial body landed in front of me, on a fence post barely ten yards away. It was the first really colorful bird bigger than a great tit that I had seen up close for many days. The dull pool-table green of its back was capped by a cheery red on its head. It was plump at one moment and muscular the next.

The woodpecker eyed me and let out a laugh. I knew it to be a territorial call, but still I smiled. Then it turned its back on me, burnishing the red of its head in the low sunlight, before it leaped into an undulating flight and disappeared.

I let the shadow complete its journey. The sun clung to the treetops on the hills to the west for seconds before letting go. The blackbirds' songs soon faded and their chinking began. A pheasant patrolled the open field below, its head and tail poking above the low crop, and the breeze softened. I stood up, shook out my limbs, and walked on.

I pulled myself up into the crook of a beech, turned to face into the light breeze, and locked an arm behind a branch. It was comfortable, and the minutes passed. I sat silent and still, until I became drowsy, my gaze half focused on the thin woods ahead.

The light level dropped further and the pheasants rose to their roosts with much calling and flapping of wings. A quiet filled the woods, and I checked my heavy breathing.

I was roused by the sound of a few loud cracks. They came from within a dense coniferous stand opposite me, about a hundred yards away, beyond the beeches. My instant thoughts were: big deer, fallow. I wondered why I didn't entertain the possibility that it might be some other animal, or perhaps a person.

It was easier to rule out a person. I've walked among those conifers and it's a thankless task, hard going, forbidding even in the middle of the day, not a likely spot by late dusk. There was an intermittent quality to the sound of broken branches that was more an animal's signature. When people move through woods, there is usually a consistency to the noise, often accompanied by voices. No two people would walk through woods so dense and dark without speaking, unless stealth was their aim, and that was made near impossible by dead wood on the ground and the interlocking branches at chest height. Animals can pass through that in "silence with imperfections," but people would fail to. It was the imperfections I was hearing, an occasional misplaced foot breaking something big enough for the crack to travel, followed by more silence. A deer, a large one, and therefore, in these parts, a fallow.

The light was fading more seriously now, colors leaching from the foliage. The wood had become a collection of near monochrome shapes. And then one of the shapes moved. A roe deer was walking from right to left between the beeches. It walked with deliberate, careful steps until it was opposite me, about fifty yards away. At that moment another crack sounded from within the conifers and the deer froze, perfectly still. I felt my breathing halt. A few seconds, maybe three, passed before the roe continued on its journey exactly as before.

Half a minute after it had passed, its mate followed in its footsteps. When it was opposite me, some of the excitement passed without permission into my body and I must have moved. The cotton fibers of my jacket snagged on a rough section of bark and let go a light rasp. The deer stopped suddenly. Both of us were now frozen. There could be no doubt that the animal was alert and aware that something was alive in my direction. A few seconds later it continued, possibly a touch faster than before.

From lizards to woodchucks, many prey animals freeze in response to a perceived threat. It is part of the heightened awareness of induced vigilance and is triggered by a sense of danger: alarming sights, sounds, or smells. There have been times when I've watched a deer pass me downwind and seen it freeze as it picks up my scent.

Some animals freeze determinedly. When the bittern freezes, it can be approached and touched without it breaking its pose. Before it turns into a statue, it improves its odds a little by turning its back toward any threat, displaying the part of its body that most resembles the color of its habitat, the reeds.

Camouflage is one reason why animals freeze. Many have colors, including dots or stripes, that help them to blend in with their background, and some even change their colors to suit their environment. Animals as varied as grey seals and rodents have been found to exhibit a characteristic called "melanism," a darkening of the skin or hair, and the prevalence of this trait is influenced by their surroundings. Studies in the US have found that fox squirrels that inhabit areas prone to forest fires have more black in their fur, and grey squirrels that are light in color are more likely to be found in moist woodland that is fire-resistant.

But camouflage only works if you don't move, hence the freezing. It is a basic attempt to disappear. It also allows an animal to listen more effectively. As a defense strategy, it is a little bit counterintuitive, but it has been proven to be effective, not just by evolution but during scientific observation, too. Raptors and owls that hunt rodents made fewer kills when their prey froze. Ironically, some hunters use the freeze response to their advantage, issuing a short sharp sound to freeze a passing animal where they want it during the few seconds needed for a shot.

Some animals will freeze after a brief burst of activity. Hares will dart for cover before freezing, an effective strategy against some predators, but not intelligent ones. Hunters who grew wise to this ploy have learned to track them down and pick them up. And the francolin, a partridge-like bird found in Africa, suffers from an even worse predictability: On sensing danger it flies up into the air three times, but only three, before freezing. One, two, three, lunch.

One of the best ways for us to induce an animal to hold a freeze is for us to stop still in our own version of a freeze—a proper one; reaching for a camera, tapping a friend on the shoulder, or tilting your head is not a freeze.

I had a gentle breeze on my face during a morning walk a few weeks ago when I surprised a roe deer. It was thirty yards from me when it turned and froze. I instinctively did the same. There we stood, the pair of us, for at least two minutes, frozen and staring at each other. The deer's tongue flicked out a few times, its back arched twice before it relaxed and lowered its haunches a touch. Its ears twitched, then it bounded away. The freeze is an interim measure: An animal is looking for a cue as to whether it needs to escape or return to normal behavior. I believe that a freeze in an animal it considers to be a predator, like us, confuses it slightly, leaving it caught in this limbo state. It creates a wonderful opportunity for longer shared moments close up.

Richard Jefferies came across a flock of northern lapwings while out on a shoot on a bright October morning. "There might perhaps have been fifty birds, all facing one way and all perfectly motionless; . . . They act so much in concert as to seem drilled. So soon as the possibility of danger had gone by each would begin to feed, moving ahead."

The freeze is a simple, powerful sign that tells us an animal has become hyperalert and vigilant and is aware of a possible threat in its environment—a threat that is very often us. Any further cause for alarm, even minor, will send the animal fleeing. If it does not bolt away, the thawing of a freeze indicates that the animal perceives the threat to have diminished.

Crouching is closely related to the habit of freezing. It's another way in which an animal makes itself less conspicuous. We can all remember sneaking around home or garden, peeking around corners from a low-ered position during hide-and-seek-style games. It's rare to see kids look around a corner while standing tall. Crouching is a logical and instinc-tive way to reduce our body size as a visible target, and it works. Gazelle fawns that are pursued by cheetahs stand a better chance of survival if they crouch. It is worth reminding ourselves of how big a difference a few inches can make when you view the world from low down. If you are unconvinced, try marking a tree in open ground with chalk at intervals between one yard and the ground, then look at the tree from a hundred yards away. Next, lower your body slowly until you are prone with your chin on the ground as you watch the chalk marks disappear. Crouching is part of this simple disappearing act. It is clever in another way, too, as it covers any shadow—one of the signs an aerial predator will pick up.

Crouching can be triggered in birds by calls, especially those from the mother. On hearing a parent's alarm call, the young birds will crouch and other invisible responses are also set in motion. When we are frightened our heart rate leaps, but some deer and birds, like ptar-migan, experience a drop in their pulse rate, a response known as "fear bradycardia."

I regularly see songbirds lower into a crouch position as they give their alarm calls, but some intelligent birds tailor their response to the threat. Crows tend to hunker down into a crouch when threatened by a peregrine falcon, but take to the air if a goshawk is closing in.

Crouching is used by predators, too, animal and human. The lowered body position of stalking leopards is so iconic that leopard crawling has been used as the name for the prone advance, sometimes employed by infantry to approach a target. In both cases, it presents the lowest and smallest surface area. Stalking predators will generally keep their heads as low as they can while keeping their prey in sight: the crouch position in motion.

Crouching is a sign that flows both ways, from prey to predator and vice versa. It is worth bearing this in mind when approaching any animals, even in a domesticated setting. Common sense dictates that you shouldn't approach a horse from behind, especially not in a crouch.

Freezing is not the same as feigning death. After they have exhausted other responses, some prey animals will try a final throw of the dice: They play dead. Freezing is common, and you are likely to see some form of it during any extended period outdoors, but feigning death, or thanatosis, is a rare strategy to witness. That said, it can be seen in a very wide collection of animals, including reptiles, chickens, ducks, foxes, squirrels, rats, rabbits, and, most notoriously, opossums. When an opossum plays dead, it does so determinedly. No amount of picking it up or shaking it will convince it to rouse itself from this extreme form of survival sulk.

If freezing appears an odd strategy for a vulnerable animal, then feigning death in the face of a predator is surely insane. Not quite. There is some logic to it. Feigning death is most common in situations when there might be a pause between a predator capturing its prey and killing it. Think of the fox that sneaks into the chicken coop and slaughters all it surveys. Mass killing is the habit of an experienced fox. Less worldly-wise foxes may spot a collection of apparently dead chickens and decide to carry them off to fill the larder, caching them for any lean days ahead. In one study of fifty ducks that feigned death when attacked by a fox, twenty-nine lived to tell the tale. It is easy to imagine those rookie foxes coming back to their larder later and being irked to discover that their dinner has walked off. The next ducks and chickens may not be so lucky. Indeed, the same study found that experienced foxes were more likely either to kill prey that feigned death or, at the very least, to chew their legs off—hence the mayhem in henhouses.

The Flight

THE SUN WAS SETTING BEHIND ME and there was a gentle breeze on my face as I climbed the hill. The fox stepped out of the undergrowth and onto the path. I froze. It cocked its head, turned to face me, then darted back in the direction it had come from.

Minutes later I climbed over a barbed-wire fence into a field, surprising a pheasant that stretched itself into a run. I was still excited by the colors bouncing back in the last of the sun that had caught the coat of the fox. I crossed the field and approached another fence. A wood pigeon took off ahead of me, and a few seconds later another. The sheep looked up and I knew a thousand pairs of eyes would be watching me now. As I climbed back into the woods, there was the familiar flapping eruption as the flock of pigeons took flight.

A robin was perched on the branch of a spindle tree. I took one step forward and it crouched. Its next move was up to me. I took one more step. It flew off.

An animal that senses it is in immediate mortal danger will do one of three things: hunker down, fight, or flee. We've all seen these responses and recognize the animals with preferences. A hedgehog, like other armored animals, like porcupines and tortoises, will pull up the draw-bridge and trust in its defenses. Grazers will run. A cornered lion or tiger will not become passive or flee; these animals fight and have the scars to prove it.

Prey are capable of more aggressive actions, as anyone who has ever been chased by a cow will testify, but they rely on flight more often than either of the other responses. It's important to note that "flight," in this context, is about the action of fleeing from danger. It can include, but is not restricted to, birds flying away. A rodent falling off a twig in blind panic at detecting a weasel nearby is a form, albeit imperfect, of flight behavior.

Flight comes near the end of the chain of reactions we have been look-ing at. Animals will go from foraging and routine vigilance to induced vigilance—the peek—at the slightest hint of danger. Depending on the species, this may lead to or include a freeze or crouch. Now the animal is making a very rapid assessment about what to do next, and it turns out to be about energy economics.

There is a strange military saying that I recall my father using: "Don't run when you can walk, don't walk if you can stand, and don't sit if you can lie." It sounds like a manifesto for laziness, but I believe the point is that if we know we're going to need a lot of energy soon, it's a good idea to conserve it while you can.

Animals don't expend energy whimsically—the ones that did grew exhausted, were outcompeted by more judicious ones, and driven to extinction. Fleeing is effective—most chases are won by the prey, not the predator—but it requires a lot of energy, and it's not a card that can be played every time an animal detects a predator. A small bird will use about thirty times as much energy in a short flight as it would have at rest. Any animal has to weigh whether to save energy or spend it, and it is a daily matter of life or death.

Animals that don't flee may still have to use energy carefully track-ing a predator. If their vigilance is likely to go on for a long period, the balance shifts; it is better to flee for a short time than to lose long minutes, unable to feed, in a state of high alertness around a predator. (This preemptive flight behavior has a nickname: FEAR—Flee Early and Avoid the Rush.)

We all witness this phenomenon when we walk slowly past animals in places where they are habituated to human presence, like parks. As we pass close by, the animals will become vigilant and may freeze, but they don't always take off. If we stop and hang about, they may leave. It's just too much effort to stay in a place where constant high alertness is needed.

Rob, the local ranger, is tasked with keeping deer numbers from rising out of control—the trees, wildflowers, and other animals would suffer without this management. He explained to me that one of his favored hunting methods relies on understanding how vigilance is weighed against flight. "If I carry my rifle over my shoulder and walk at the same speed as a dog walker, then I will catch a deer clocking me from the woods to the side of the path, but it doesn't run off unless I stop. If I continue along the path for a bit, the deer returns to browsing and all I need do is slip the rifle off and it's an easy shot. If I'd paused and then tried to sneak up on that same deer, moving stealthily from one tree to the next, it would be gone."

We know that some animals will run or fly away, but we have lost sensitivity to how it happens and how we can predict the sequence. We may find it strange that we find it easy to get close to lizards near the start of the day, but nowhere near them by lunch. Our starving ancestor, though, knew that a lizard is less likely to flee if it is cold than if it is warm, so the height of the sun in the sky has a direct bearing on the likelihood of getting close to that animal.

Animals are also sensitive to season, hunger, location, experience, and social rank; birds that are lower in the pecking order are slower to flee, as they see an opportunity to feed after the higher-ranked birds have left. If we combine this insight with what we know about vigilance, we can see that a low-ranked hungry, foraging animal is far more likely to stay put, vulnerable to attack, than its superior, which has fed and is now alert. We may not detect all of these things on first looking at a group of animals, but we can spot many with practice. It is likely that our ancestors were aware of these nuances through practiced hunting.

If an attack is suspected, the prey animal attunes to the distance, angle of movement, body language, and speed of any approaching predator. Distance and change in speed are key signs for it. It is the change in speed that is most critical, not the speed itself. Studies have shown that animals are 60 percent more likely to judge that an attack is imminent, and therefore flight is essential, if a predator accelerates.

A situation we encounter daily, whether in the wild or the city, is of birds taking off as we approach them. We all recognize this as flight behavior, but we have become desensitized to the choreography within it. Alarm can spread very quickly through a group, leading to a mass flight by any group of prey animals. The birds can't all afford to take off every time one of their colleagues does so; it would lead to too many false alarms and a lot of wasted energy. Yet taking off is one of the birds' alarm signs. If you watch carefully, you will spot how the first bird taking off sends a signal to the others, triggering a state of induced vigilance— you'll never surprise one after you've caused a single nearby bird to take off.

But the other birds are not set into flight by this single bird taking off. This is where we see energy saving in action: The first bird triggers vigilance in the others, seen in the body language of raised head and broken routine that I described earlier. If one of the other birds picks up a threat, it may take off. The time between the two events is critical; the flock is sensitive to the difference between one and two birds taking off and the gap between them. Once two birds take off in quick succession, it acts as a different, more urgent, sign and triggers the mass takeoff.

The signs that trigger flight do not need to be identical; different ones support each other if they happen in quick succession. At first it is easiest to spot this sequence in the animals that react relatively slowly. I regularly see a pheasant detect me and go into a state of vigilance with a raised head; it will remain in this state, even if it walks slowly away, unless my presence causes a single wood pigeon to fly off. The second sign impels the pheasant to take off. Neither my slow, distant approach nor the single pigeon would have caused the pheasant to go into flight, but the two in quick succession do.

All of the signs of vigilance we have looked at indicate that flight is more likely, as vigilance precedes flight, but there are signs specific to flight preparation, too. Some are rare and grotesque: Herons and pelicans regurgitate their food prior to flight, and elephants experience something known as "flight diarrhea." Edward of Norwich noted something similar in the behavior of hunted wolves in the late Middle Ages: "When the wolf seeth them [the greyhounds], and he be full, he voideth both before and behind all in his running so as to be more light and more swift."

More common and helpful are the minor physical preparations every animal makes. Birds cannot take off without a small leap, so it is logical that they should lower themselves into a crouch before flight—typically they rock forward and lower their head and chest, almost like a push-up. Pheasants signal their level of vigilance all the way to flight by their speed and the shape of their bodies. They will waddle off, heads held high if unalarmed by us, but accelerate into a run with a stretched, elongated body if they are preparing to take off. Both the speed of the pheasant and its shape signify the shift from vigilance to flight preparation.

We saw how a raised head is a sign of vigilance, but it is not an ideal position for any animal to launch into flight. If it lowers its head after vigilance it can mean one of two things: Either the alarm has passed, or flight is imminent. The easiest way to tell the difference is to notice whether or not it has returned to its routine behavior. If songbirds detect anything of concern they stop feeding and hold their heads high or cock them—induced vigilance. Next thing, they either return to feeding or crouch with raised tails and a lowered head. If they do the latter, we know that flight is imminent. Deer behave in a similar way: They browse the undergrowth, lifting their heads from time to time, then lowering them again. If their heads do anything other than return from raised to browsing, flight is likely.

Animals are sensitive to the body language of flight preparedness, and we can see this spreading through groups of geese or ducks. Watch a flock of sheep as you approach and you will see preparedness spread through them.

So far, few surprises: Animals can flee and there are signs that they may be about to do so. But we break new ground when we consider what happens next. Some experienced modern hunters will have focused sufficiently on the habits of their favored species, but outside this small group, it would be considered fanciful to imagine that we can predict what an animal that appears to have panicked and set off will do next. The truth is, within limits, we can.

A robin that is vigilant, left, and then prepared for flight

Each animal's flight pattern is shaped by three things: The cause of their flight, the environment, and that species' ingrained habits. If we spook a fallow deer on a hillside, it will bolt away from us, but it is much more likely to head uphill than down. It will not run downhill out of choice, and if it has to run down into a valley, it will not stay there—it will keep running in a bid to take to higher ground.

There may still be some healthy skepticism that a panicked animal will behave in predictable ways, so let's unpack that. First, I chose the word "panicked" deliberately because it anthropomorphizes the situation; we project our experience of fright onto the animals. It is more likely that this is a simpler, perhaps more automated reaction.

Research has shown that the flight reactions of fish are almost clockwork. Depending on whether an attack comes from the side, head-on, or behind, and having noticed whether the fish is either actively swimming or in a gliding phase, we can predict with confidence what the prey fish will do. Sliding farther down the scale, springtails and mosquito pupae will always escape in a fixed direction relative to the way they are facing. Some birds that have been captured and then released exhibit a bizarre but dependable flight behavior: They fly in the same direction regardless of weather, migration patterns, or local environment. Mallards fly northwest when released.

How does this sort of knowledge help us, though? Here it might be worth a diversion into our personal experience. Who has not enjoyed a game of tag, where one person is It and has to chase, then touch another person, who in turn becomes It? This is a fun game, but it offers a serious insight into how we can shape our skills.

If you watch a group of children playing tag and try to analyze what is going on, there is a temptation to view it as energetic and random mayhem. But think back to the last time you actually *played* the game.

If you play with someone faster than you—typical of many predator/ prey chases—your only hope is anticipation. By learning that certain people double back, others try to sidestep, and some rely only on speed, you can work out how to head for where someone *will be* after you accelerate toward them, not where they currently are. Of course, we don't think like this when playing the game, we just tear around huffing and puffing. But that's the point: We have entered into an unconscious study of the others' "flight responses"—we are sensing what they will do next.

A similar game of brinkmanship is going on when any sportsperson attempts to tackle another. In ball sports, one of the most common tactics a defender will use is to feign an attack, perhaps by lunging, then follow up with a tackle on the anticipated response. In soccer, a foot goes out one way, but quickly changes direction. The sport of fencing and the game of chess rely on this.

There is a reason that these situations are nicknamed "cat and mouse": It all starts with animal flight behavior. And if we ever succumb to thinking of the flight of any animal as random, we need to get out there and play tag again. Anticipating animal flight behavior is the biggest and most beautiful game of tag there will ever be.

We can play the game with animals without giving it a lot of thought. After all, that is what hunters have done for thousands of years: They study their prey and learn to anticipate its next move without slow strategic thought. But the point of this book is to accelerate the process, and for that we need to know some of the building blocks.

If we are shocked into running away from something, we won't take the wind direction into account, but many animals do. Each species will have its habits: White-tailed deer tend to flee into the wind, red deer with it, or, as Edward of Norwich puts it:

> *Therefore he fleeth oft forth with the wind so that he may always hear the hounds come after him. And also that the hounds should not scent nor find him, for his tail is in the wind and not his nose. Also, that when the hounds be nigh him he may wind them and hye him well from them.*

The direction in which an animal flees will be shaped by the urgency of the threat, too. Birds are more likely to fly directly away from a slow attack and perpendicularly away from a fast one. Birds that flee a ground threat will loop back to land on a nearby tree, often higher up, but those fleeing an aerial attack will shoot out and not return to the same area. The angle at which a bird flies away is also shaped by the angle of the attack: Blue tits fly more steeply upward away from attacks that come in from the side than from above.

There is an obvious weakness in flight behavior that is too predictable, and evolution has equipped many species with unpredictability as part of their defense. But, to borrow and bastardize Donald Rumsfeld's lexicon, this is still predictable unpredictability. Many deer species will zigzag away from a threat. It is a beautiful motion to watch, but strangely predictable: bounce, bounce, switch, bounce, bounce, switch. Maybe I'd feel it was more effective if I was at full speed, feeling the anaerobic burn, desperately trying to sink my teeth into a haunch, but from the vantage point of a leisurely walk in the woods, it's almost comically easy to predict the deer's next move. It reminds me of those chase scenes in movies—James Bond driving the car away from the massive machine guns in the helicopter, or dodging the bullets as he slaloms down a ski slope. The bullets always send some snow or grit into the air as they miss, hitting the exact spot where Bond has just turned from. (Over a drink, I teased a friend, who happens to be one of the Bond scriptwriters, suggesting that the baddies anticipate these turns by aiming ahead, anticipating the direction Bond is so obviously about to go in, not the one he is currently heading in. I think Bond will live to zigzag another day.)

Zigzagging is common in some rodents and cattle, and especially common in species that are hunted in open country. In the wide-open landscapes of the tundra, animals as diverse as hare and ptarmigan rely on the same zigzagging pattern. It is also more likely if the predator is heavier than the prey: Sharp turns are trickier for the bigger creature—this is one of the ways in which a gazelle can beat the faster cheetah.

There are variations on the zigzag, such as the stop-start motion of some rodents, like guinea pigs, or different types of jumping. California ground squirrels jump sideways as they go about their escape while African squirrels leap vertically. And birds have their own version of the zigzag. Blue tits that are attacked by a bird of prey will more often than not execute a "roll and loop" immediately after takeoff. The faster the attack, the more likely the loop.

There are enough species out there and enough behavior types that we are tricked into thinking that the way an animal flees is random, but all we have to do is focus on the habits of the species that we see most often or that intrigue us and the patterns will emerge. For now, just pick one or two animals you see regularly and practice watching the stages unfold: feeding with routine vigilance? . . . induced vigilance? . . . flight. Make a mental note of how the animal flees and where it goes. A sense of what is about to happen will creep up on you.

The Refuge

I WALKED INTO A CLEARING IN the woods. There was some holly, a few isolated hazels, one prouder goat willow in the center, and a collection of beech and wild cherry trees on the far side. The squirrel sat up on its haunches, froze, then ran away. It did not go where it wanted to go; it went where I wanted it to go. That last sentence is not true, but it is a true reflection of how it feels when you successfully anticipate the next move of an animal.

The flight key gives us insight into when and how an animal will attempt to escape from a threat. Now we'll look at how we can anticipate its next moves.

We can predict the location of a fish's "rise," the ripples it creates by coming to the surface and taking an insect, by studying the flow of the water, the insects, and the weather. After we've practiced the enjoyable sport of rise-watching a few times, we start to feel as though we're sensing the world like a trout, seeing the waterscape as it does. But this is not some poetical or philosophical foray into the mind and body of another creature; it is a practical exercise. We learn to assess the factors that influence the behavior of any animal, which helps us map and predict them. We get a feel for what they are about to do.

The fish is engaged in a predatory exercise, but we can have equal success when observing prey animals in flight, because there is method in the flurry of an escape. When prey animals run, they head not just away from a threat, but toward a place of safety: a tree, a hole in the ground, a crevice, a thicket, or the sky. Once we know the preferred refuges of the animals we see, prediction becomes straightforward.

Squirrels use trees as their favorite refuge—we've all seen them race up one as we approach. But there are patterns within this simplicity. Squirrels do not like single trees because an isolated tree is a cul-de-sac; predators can wait at the bottom or perhaps climb the tree, leaving the squirrel with nowhere else to go. Squirrels will always choose a group of trees, and their interlocking branches, over a single tree that is equidistant, and will often cover more ground to reach them. The squirrel raced away from me up the cherry tree, along a branch, then hopped onto the branch of a much taller beech. I'd known this would happen; it would never choose the low isolated trees, even though they were closer.

One of the simplest refuge rules is "head for cover," and most prey animals prefer it: woodland, hedges, and thickets are all part of a prey animal's map of its surroundings, and they act as magnets at times of flight. Some plants make better cover than others; if an animal disappears, I try to peer into any blackthorn, as its tough thorns make it a perfect refuge. Deer will race to cover: If you see a deer in open country, but with scattered trees, study where the nearest cover is, and when the deer gets spooked, watch it being pulled into the trees.

Prey animals retain an awareness of the distance to their nearest refuge, and this influences the timing of any flight decision. The farther from refuge, the more likely a threat will trigger flight. It is easy to observe this: Any animals that recognize a predator in a wide-open area, like pasture or wilderness, will flee long before it gets anywhere near them. It's tempting to think this happens only because they find it easier to sense the predator coming, but it's also because the animals are literally more "flighty" when they know they have a long distance to cross to reach cover. We can get within a few feet of prey in the woods, but it's hard to get within a hundred yards of them in wide-open areas. That is why we will sometimes see squirrels happy to watch us walk close by, from the base of a refuge tree in a park, but not in the open areas. Rabbits appear more sluggish near their burrows and twitchy when they have ranged a little farther from home. Interestingly, animals that do not recognize us as predators, like some wild reindeer, will approach humans out of curiosity.

Birds follow their own patterns according to the group they belong to. Songbirds approach trees head-on, and woodpeckers, creepers, and nuthatches flee to the backs of tree trunks. Marsh or grassland species make for bushes, while doves, chickens, gulls, owls, and corvids will take to the air and try to beat the threat there. Prey will often differentiate between a ground-based predator and an aerial one. Field mice head into open country if pursued by a weasel, but into cover if threatened by a kestrel.

Of course, there are nuances to this. Animals have geographical preferences, and we must consider flight habits. As we have seen, animals can take wind direction or gradient into account: fallow deer and hares prefer uphill to downhill, and reindeer flee uphill and upwind at first, but each will turn toward the refuge of cover, if it's available. So, even if a movement starts as a flight *from a threat*, it soon becomes a race *toward a refuge*. If we combine these two stages, we can see that predicting a deer will soon race toward the copse above it is not psychic. It is two keys brought together: the flight, uphill, and the refuge, the copse.

Once an animal has reached a refuge, it has to decide how long to spend in hiding—because, as we know, time spent hidden is time lost to foraging—which depends primarily on how great it judged the initial threat to be. The speed of an attack is critical: The faster a predator approaches and the more acceleration it shows, the longer any prey will remain in hiding.

With squirrels, you will have noticed how, when they flee, they run, then scurry up the far side of the tree, combining flight, refuge, and hiding in one action. You may also have spotted that the squirrel doesn't like to remain hidden for long. If you keep still and the wind is toward you, the animal has no way of working out what you're doing. It doesn't like this, so it returns to vigilant behavior—the peek. It pokes its head out from one side of the tree to check on you, then hides again, then peeks out from the other side. Keep this in mind when you're next out for a walk with a friend. If you see a squirrel, you may be able to make a spooky prediction: "That squirrel we're walking toward is about to sit up, freeze, then run to the cherry tree, climb it, and look at us from halfway up." Vigilance, freeze, flight, refuge, vigilance. "Sorry, I'm not sure which side it'll peek out from, but I'd guess it'll be the left, as the breeze is from the other side."

The Cacophony

A S DUSK APPROACHED, I WAS TUCKED up under a Western red cedar, a book resting on my knees, when the sound of blackbird indignation rolled across the land. The woods ignited with one accelerating rising call, setting off a collection of chinks, chooks, and flapping. I looked up to catch the tawny owl swooping in, appearing in front of me as it dipped below the lowest branches of the cedar. The owl clocked me when it was about ten feet in front and jinked away, then up into the nearby beeches. The blackbirds continued their protest, soon joined by the wrens and other passerines. As I ventured out to investigate, a grey squirrel added a kuk-kuk-kuk-kuk-kraaa to the din.

The outdoors is thick with messaging. Every organism is part of a communication network. Ants pass on information about the best routes to food, and trees tell each other of insect attack; both using pheromones, a type of chemical chatter from which we are excluded. Much of the conversation sits close to but just beyond our possible experience. Elephants can detect a female in heat six miles away through vibrations on the ground; and beneath the ground, mole rats can make sense of vibrations made by other rats fifty feet away. A male robin sings differently when courting a particular female from when he's singing speculatively and alone—this is discernible to the target of his affection, but sadly not to us.

The good news is that a large proportion of animal exchanges are both audible and intelligible. This is not luck or a happy coincidence, but rather evolution's logic and part of the original purpose of our senses. If we needed to understand bat sonar or listen to whale song for our survival, we would be able to do so, but we don't, so they remain interesting, but academic. We can hear all that we need to hear; the only thing that is missing is our historical ability to sense meaning in our luxuriant natural soundscape. We have not lost the biological ability; in a survival situation, many find that these skills return.

Fred Hatfield was a frontiersman who spent decades in the Alaskan wilderness in the middle of the last century. Monitoring sounds of wildlife was critical to his survival, but also for understanding the movements of one other human, too. Klutuk, a murderous psychopath, lived in the same region as Hatfield, and it was often more important for him to know what the other man was up to than what the large mammals were doing. Fortunately, the code was simple to break: a popping sound was a beaver slapping its tail on the lake as it dived; a grunt mapped a moose; a coughlike bellow was a grizzly bear, "upset and angry about something, as they always are." Most alarming, though, was a dog's bark—there were no wild dogs, so a bark meant Klutuk, and Hatfield had time to reach for the rifle.

We do not need to find our lives threatened to regain this ability. Wherever we are in the world, the code exists. We don't struggle to identify a horse's whinny, so why should we be daunted by the change in sound as a great tit shifts from tapping a nut to warning its colleagues it has spotted us approaching?

Animals create sound in four main ways. A few make nasal sounds: blue and Barbary sheep, ibex, chamois, and marmots whistle through the nose. Some use other parts of their bodies: rattlesnakes famously shake their tails, and we have all heard teeth clamping shut, beaks clacking, the shaking of skin and heads, and possibly the rattling of porcupines' quills. The deliberately loud flapping of wood pigeons taking off is the most common example in my local woods, and I rarely go there without hearing it.

Some animals make noises as they interact with objects in their environment—the beaver I mentioned above, for instance, but many waterfowl smack the water with their wings on takeoff. Others, like amphibians and water voles, make a splash or pop as they enter the water. Rabbits thump the ground, using it as a drum, camels and others stomp, and everyone is familiar with the drumroll of a woodpecker.

We ourselves use the first three methods: we snort in disbelief, clap in appreciation, or bang the table in anger. But by far the most common method for us and other animals is vocal. Animals cry out, bark, chirp, squeal, and purr, as do we.

There are differences in the biology—birds don't pant because their lungs allow airflow more complex than ours, which is why birdsong is never breathless in quality—but the aims are similar across the animal world. A mixture of impulses surrounding survival, food, sex, and territory can explain most animal communication—and a fair share of human conversation, too.

While there is complexity within the world of animal sounds—parrots can say everything we can and make many noises we can't—there is a helpful rule of thumb: The more important the message, the simpler it tends to be. Bees perform their celebrated waggle dance, passing information to other workers about the direction of food relative to the sun and the distance. It is complex communication for an insect, but it can afford to be because it is helpful, not urgent. The more urgent messages involve threats to survival and, typically, are short, sharp vocalizations.

Thousands of miles away and hundreds of years earlier than when Fred Hatfield was sensing dog barks to detect danger, the Leco people of Bolivia were warned of the approaching Spanish conquistadors by the extraordinary racket the parrots in the rain forest made. "The cacophony" is the simplest and most striking auditory key. If a group of animals starts making an unusual clamor, there will always be a reason for it. The logic is inescapable, and it comes back to energy. Animals won't waste energy in making a brouhaha for no reason. It will have been caused either by something positive, like a newly discovered food source, or a possible threat. They may be mistaken—a suspected predator turns out to be benign—but the noise won't be without reason.

First, the positive reasons. Many birds have contact calls, short sounds that they use to check in with each other. If a large enough gathering takes place, a chorus of contact calls may build to quite a volume, but the tone will be steady and without urgency. It sounds like what it is: chatter.

Some species advertise new, rich sources of food, which may, as we saw earlier, seem counterintuitive, but there are good reasons for it. It encourages the better vigilance that groups offer, but is also a way of shaking things up to a visitor's advantage. Ravens are territorial, and a dominant pair may occupy an area where an abundant source of food, like a large animal carcass, has been found. If an outsider makes the discovery, loud calling opens the find to others, thereby overcoming the dominant pair. It's like a social media posting about a riot, which draws others in, overwhelming a pair of security guards and triggering mass looting.

When the Prussian naturalist and explorer Alexander von Humboldt was exploring the Llanos and Orinoco region of South America, he experienced a hearty cacophony. During one night, the forest erupted in a loud commotion, waking Humboldt. He decided to analyze the chorus of sounds, seeking signal in the noise. He found it in a chain reaction. The jaguars were chasing tapirs, which took flight. In their escape they roused the monkeys above them, which in turn set off the birds. A simple predator-prey hunt lay beneath the rumpus, and this is the most likely cause of any sudden rise in animal noises. One or more species sense an imminent threat.

If a bird of prey, like a sparrowhawk, passes over songbirds or small mammals, the news will quickly spread, and sounds will ripple across the landscape. The sense that "something's up" often means that something is up there. But our aim is to refine that sense of what the something may be.

The typical cacophony is a collection of alarm calls. Everyone will pick up on it: The sound blares out from the background and draws attention, even in the unwilling. It will quickly trigger a general awareness of a predator in the area. It is occasionally possible to work out which one from the noise, but by the time we're doing this, we will probably have started to sift the cacophony into its component parts.

Most social animals that need to be wary of predators have a way of warning each other of detected danger. Alarm calls are always among the simplest sounds made by each species, as they must be short, available, and intelligible to the youngest. Alarm calls are integral to each species and a key aspect of their behavior—pheasant chicks can be raised by turkey hens because they share a similar alarm call, but not by chickens, as they don't understand it.

Complex song takes time for birds to learn, so it is never a sign of alarm. We're not so different: imagine you are walking with a friend and something spooks you. It's unlikely that your first reaction will be to launch into a poetic monologue about the waft of air stirred by the hornet that flew so close to your face. It's much more likely that you utter a four-letter word rather loudly.

Each animal has its own alarm call, and we will grow familiar with those we experience regularly. It is one of those layers of awareness that is hard to miss once you have tuned in to it and so easy to ignore until you do. A few days ago, I was sitting in a wood with a group of fifteen people on a course. As was normal, the forest quiet was punctuated by the occasional bird alarm call, including on one occasion a wren that was perched close by. My instinct was to look to the alarm call, but I overrode it to study the faces of the group. Out of fifteen, I noticed three whose eyes or faces turned instantly toward the call; the others didn't visibly acknowledge it. If we had been a group of hunter-gatherers, it would probably have been the other way around. The call had been caused by someone returning to the group after leaving it for a pee. They were spotted on their way back by the wren, seconds before any of us.

There are variations in the tone and rhythm of alarm calls across birds, and we can collect a few that we recognize individually, but it helps to know that most songbirds issue a short, repetitive sound, usually between a "tk-tk-tk-tk" sound and that made by stones clacking together—the stonechat gets its name from its alarm call.

A long, gentle, uphill gradient had not been steep enough to warrant a rest or level enough to allow my pulse to settle. It was overcast, warm, and humid, and I sweated. The path broke out of the woods at a junction with a forester's track, and I stood in the middle of it, enjoying a clear view of the flat, grey sky. The humidity and dropping light promised rain.

There was a rustle and a crack. I lowered my head and stared in the direction of the sounds. I was looking for a deer and suspected a roe. After a few seconds, the slightest motion marked it out against the fawn background of the woodland floor. The roe had frozen, giving it a moment of invisibility, but the slightest twitch of its ears revealed it. We stared at each other. It barked and skipped ten feet back before turning to face me and freezing again. I stopped looking at the roe and scanned the woodland to either side of it, waiting for my eyes to lose the sky and regain the wood. I sensed that there must be another deer out there. If this sense was given words, they would have been, "Where are you?"

If we think about the primary purpose of the alarm call—communication within a species—this offers the first added layer of meaning to the simple sound. Alarm calls are not for our benefit, and usually indicate the presence of other members of the same species nearby. Studies of many different species, from tiny birds to large monkeys, have revealed that alarm calls are not wasted; a lone animal is less likely to call than one with company.

The first few times you experience the alarm call of an animal, it's normal to focus attention on that animal, but if you grow familiar with the call in any species, it is only a small step for it to spark an awareness of others. The roe deer's bark was an example of this reaction. Roe deer are solitary for much of their lives, so the sight of one does not automatically suggest the presence of others. But a barking roe deer will often trigger a response in another.

After a few seconds, I began my search for the other deer by the edge of that forester's track, but before I could spot it, I heard the second deer bark in response to the first. The barking continued for several minutes, each ricocheting off the other. Deer are joined by other cloven-hoofed animals, such as sheep, goats, and antelopes, in uttering short, harsh calls in response to a threat. Once we grow used to listening for the response, we can sense the other, invisible, animal nearby.

(It's worth noting that an alarm call is not an emotional response. It's not driven by fear. It is an effective method of reducing the risk of predation that has evolved across many species. Some animals occasionally issue a fear call, but it is rarer. The fear or distress call is a near-final act of an animal when it is about to succumb to a predator—it may serve to shock its attacker, alert others of the same species, or invite rival predators, thereby creating pandemonium and allowing escape.

These explanations stand up to scrutiny within an evolutionary context, but it is hard not to anthropomorphize the situation and wonder whether the poor creature might be screaming because it is plain terrified. Prior to distress calls, some animals will also make defense calls—carnivores that are cornered by a predator usually growl or hiss. Rabbits and hares sometimes do this, too—it may be mimicry. The full sequence of calls might be alarm, defense, distress, but this is uncommon, and our focus should remain on the ubiquitous alarm call.)

There are times when one animal needs to convey the nature of the danger to others in a way that prompts a reaction that is not only fast, but also tailored to the specific danger. Green monkeys issue different calls to distinguish between a lion and an eagle. A monkey that responded against a lion attack might endanger itself further if an eagle was preparing to swoop. Green monkeys react to a lion by scampering up a tree, but to the eagle's call by looking up. Differentiating between ground and air alarm calls is repeated in many species, from chickens to raccoons. And we can tune in to it.

An alarm call common to songbirds indicates an aerial threat and is known as the "seet" or "hawk" call. You need look up consciously only a few times when you hear it before the upward glance is automatic.

It's interesting to consider how instinctive the alarm call and response are. It's difficult for us to imagine it, because trying to imagine something is a conscious effort, and we're discussing an unconscious pairing of events. But if we spend a moment with Niko Tinbergen, one of the real heroes in the field of animal-behavior research, we'll have a better idea of how this works.

Tinbergen, a Dutch Nobel Prize–winning biologist, was studying the behavior of a family of herring gulls from a concealed spot when he moved and accidentally startled one of the adults. It reacted predictably: It scuttled away and issued an alarm call. Gull chicks interpret this in a way we might think of as "Take cover!" However, the call on its own offers no more detail than that. It doesn't specify an aerial or ground threat and gives no information about the direction the threat is coming from.

The chicks heard the alarm call and reacted instantly by running with heads out and elongated necks toward shelter (flight? . . . refuge). It just so happened that the nearest shelter was the hideaway where Tinbergen was standing; his startling of the parent gull set off a chain reaction that led the chicks to run headlong toward him and gather at his feet.

It's a cute story on one level, but instructive on another because it gives us such a clear view of how signs work in nature. When scientists play recordings of lion alarm calls to green monkeys, the monkeys dart up the trees. And this is the vital point: They do this even if there isn't a lion or another monkey within a mile. They sense and respond to the sign, not the threat, and the sign, an alarm call, is key, not the nearby animals or their behavior. The idea that the animals interpret signs, not animals, is quite a radical departure from the popular view of animal behavior, so it may seem strange until we grow used to it. In fact, it is unlikely to sit comfortably with us until we experience it for ourselves.

Our chances of doing so are helped by two things: First, animals are generous with their calls; and second, information is shared, not wasted. Animals will make use of the alarm calls of other species as well as their own. Most ecosystems have a form of neighborhood-watch scheme, where the vigilant animals' alarm calls raise the level of vigilance in other prey.

And we're not talking about species that are necessarily even similar; alarm calls give warning to a wide range of other animals. Vervet monkeys react to starlings, mongooses to hornbills, squirrels to black-birds—the full list would probably run to the end of this book. In southern Africa, the grey go-away bird will issue an alarm call upon spotting a lion, which triggers a response in any local gazelles. It also warns of approaching humans, much to the chagrin of gazelle hunters.

But what at one moment is a hindrance can at another be a help: For millennia, hunters have known that their target's target can be a friend. Anyone who wants to maintain an awareness of where a bird of prey is can map their movements from the sounds and motions all around. In the past, falconers relied upon a small, carnivorous, butchering bird called the shrike. In 1883, the English naturalist James Harting wrote: "This elegant little bird is used, not to attract the hawk as might be supposed, but to give notice of its approach. Its power of vision is perfectly marvelous, for it will detect and announce the presence of a hawk in the air long before the latter is discernible by human eye."

The shrike is a fascinating bird: It kills prey by impaling it on small spikes, like long thorns or even barbed wire. Of more relevance here is the theory that the name "shrike" is onomatopoeic, giving us a clue to its high, shrill call.

If the call can help us sense the characters out there, the next level of awareness is sensing the story within the sounds. Some birds' alarm calls vary according to the urgency of the situation—one style when they sense potential danger and another for a surprise attack.

A call that is regular is unlikely to be a sign of urgent danger and is probably a general warning, until it accelerates or gets noticeably higher. The black-capped chickadee, a small North American songbird (another with a name based on its call), adds extra "dees" as a predator draws closer—"chickadee" builds to "chickadee-dee-dee-dee." Its neighbors tune in and make use of it.

The common blackbird has seven calls and most are easy to identify without much practice. Its flight alarm call, which it issues when startled, sounds to me almost like the world's tiniest engine starting up. It accelerates and gets higher very quickly; you will hear it if you walk through any woodland with blackbirds. It's a sound we might enjoy hearing the first few times we recognize it, until we realize we're triggering it. As it rings through the surrounding countryside, it alerts all to our approach, making surprise sightings less likely—birds, rabbits, foxes, and deer all depart or grow vigilant.

Similar things happen in mammals. Rodents, including squirrels, tend to accelerate their alarm call as danger increases. Many squirrels have separate calls for aerial and ground threats. Each squirrel will have its own calls, but there is a tendency for aerial predators to trigger a whistle or two, while a threat on the ground elicits a chattering or churring sound. Vervet monkeys have different calls for the threat of a snake, a leopard, and an eagle, each triggering an appropriate response—the snake call prompts them to stand high on their hind legs and inspect the grass.

Animals are not always honest. Great tits that find a quarrel of sparrows all bunched around a food source have been known to issue a false alarm call, scattering the sparrows and giving themselves an opening to a mischievous snack.

We know that primates and corvids communicate with a richness and complexity that we are yet to unravel. And there are doubtless levels of communication throughout the animal kingdom that we are not yet aware of. But we can learn to decipher much of the meaning we have been missing by first noticing the sounds, then pairing them with events in our environment. The moment that our unconscious does the pairing, noise becomes signal.

The Track

THE WEB BARRED MY PATH AND cheered me on. There was enough light from an overcast sky for me to catch the dewdrops on the spider's silk and the silvery scaffold, which was stretched between two privet bushes.

When I head out early in the morning, I dread the arrival of dog walkers. This is unfair: I have no more right to the land than they do and am a dog walker myself at times, but the virgin quality of the woods at dawn is tarnished by their shouts and the barking. The web reassured me that nobody had come that way.

Tracking, the art of reading a story in marks on nature, is a universal ancient skill because for most of our history it was essential for survival. It is one of the ways in which our superior intelligence overcame the handicaps of slow-footedness and weakness relative to many other animals. To this day its use is widespread among indigenous societies, although perhaps less keenly so than in earlier times. In the 1850s, Thomas Magarey, the Irish pioneer of Australia, encountered Aboriginal mothers putting lizards in front of their infants to give them a quarry to track and pursue.

Louis Liebenberg has argued convincingly in *The Art of Tracking: The Origin of Science* that tracking was the first science. It was one of the first outdoor skills in which intuition was superseded by conscious analysis of evidence—that is, slow thinking. By measuring the marks we find in the ground and the distances between them, then comparing them to a remembered or written record, we can accurately identify species and gauge their behavior in a way that is hard to do by sight alone. If you subscribe to Liebenberg's premise, and I do, this is an approach that led to the science-forged world we now live in.

The expert tracker is expected to slow their thinking and follow a methodical approach. Inuit rejoice in spotting fresh tracks and learn to locate them within the complexity of their environment. A polar bear's prints may run parallel to a pressure ridge on the sea ice, the downwind side, because seals like to loiter among the ridges. The bears know this, and so do the Inuit.

The intuitive outdoors person can enjoy looking for the signs that give insight without analysis. Many leap out as changes in shape, color, and shade. We all recognize a horse's hoofprint, not least because we have given them shoes with a shape that stands out as unnatural in the mud.

All animals, birds included, leave their own footprints, and familiarity breeds instant recognition—just as we may recognize the footprints of our own family on the beach, but not those of others. A fast identification is often imperfect: We spot the track of a bird without hesitation, but cannot recognize the exact species, which is fine.

Whenever animals or humans move through a landscape, they force changes and create fresh patterns and anomalies. Things stand out when they jar the stasis of the surroundings. Think how quickly your eyes light upon litter in nature. The glaring silver and orange of the abandoned drink can is impossible to ignore, not because there isn't much litter, but because nature doesn't make things with that shape or color. Perfectly straight lines are rare, and indigenous tribespeople might go for a week without seeing a right angle. The bicycle track in the mud stands out, as do the drag marks of a predator carrying prey over wet ground.

It takes no training or analysis to sense the passing of animals in the line of bent grasses or a series of broken bracken fronds; the changed shapes and colors stick out. The stone that has been rolled out of its mud socket or the leaves that have been turned by passing feet to reveal a lighter side are conspicuous, too. The more we look, the quicker we are to spot a shine or scuff on a log and the faster we recognize it on the next; the badger's highway becomes luminous.

Acceleration and deceleration or an animal's sudden change in direction become obvious to us. Dirt is thrown in the opposite direction of any sudden switch, and a lip is forced up on a track if an animal comes to a sudden halt. At first animal trails that run across a main path are invisible to most, then obvious once our eyes are accustomed to looking for them and, soon after, unmissable, even in low light.

I have had the good fortune to work with John Rhyder, one of the foremost wildlife trackers in northern Europe. We live and work not far from each other and enjoy exchanging information and observations about natural navigation and tracking. After spending time tracking with John, I notice four things. First, tracks that I would have had to look for become obvious; and second, I gain a more intuitive feel for the speed at which an animal has been moving. Third, individual paws become easily recognizable—two badger prints that looked near identical at the start of our walk are now easy to separate into left and right. The badger's outside toe (the little toe in humans) is more distinctive in the ground. This is true of many birds, too. Fourth, I sense, from the color of the tracks, how long it has been since the animal passed through. In rough terms, the compression of an animal's foot changes the color of mud, and as time passes, the color gradually reverts to that of the surrounding earth.

In some ways, this reverses the science of tracking; careful analysis has confirmed that the pattern and shape of prints in the ground reveal the identity, speed, and gait of an animal—whether it was walking, trotting, or galloping. If the hind legs of a deer land behind its forelegs, for example, it is at the slower end of its speed range. If the hind legs then move forward of the forelegs, it is probably picking up speed. Hooves also splay more when the animal is traveling fast. When you've been looking at the same species for long enough, the gap acts like a speedometer. If you're following an animal at a distance and notice from its tracks that it has accelerated, it has probably become aware of you—a prompt for you to slow down and proceed more cautiously.

Larger animals cannot help but leave traces of their resting places or homes; a mound of stark white chalk reveals a badger's recent excavations, and compressed undergrowth marks the bed of a large stag. When you practice noticing these changes in color and shape, they soon become vivid.

One of the most satisfying areas to sense quickly in the tracking story is time. Trampling-tolerant plants, like self-heal, tell us that a path has been well used over long periods. The browning of a broken branch says that whatever passed did so long ago. But a dark line of missing dew whispers that something has been through very recently. And then, a little farther ahead, the steam rising off its droppings makes us quicken our pace. All of this is possible without lying on our belly to ponder the slower clues. The analytical tracker can stop to consider whether, now that the sun has passed behind the fir tree, a trampled blade of grass may be taking longer to rise back up. But we're gone, on to the next pattern.

The land is becoming untrampled. If you come across a vehicle track in a wild area, its shape will stand out, but if the plants between the ruts have reached above knee height, you will know that it is used, but not regularly. Plants rising in the ruts instantly suggest abandonment. Every change in an environment will lead to tracks becoming more or less desirable for people or animals. A housing development will lead to plants reclaiming animal tracks all around it, just as the closure of a rural pub will lead to a footpath becoming overgrown.

The Circling

THE JANUARY COLD RELENTED A LITTLE overnight and the birds were busy on the softening earth. The ground rolled away to the south, broken with a rebellious bump at Halnaker Hill. The windmill's decorative sails had been removed for maintenance and it looked naked, just a dark nub against the whitest light of the horizon. Many years ago, those sails worked in the wind to mill grain, but now this proud, unnatural shape at the top of the hill acts as a perfect landmark—conspicuous, yet elegant. I have given it bit parts in navigation courses and on trips to and from my children's school. "Look, kids, the windmill!"

"We know, Dad."

There is a common view that the brightest days are cloudless, but that's not true. On a day of broken cloud, some places are brighter still, as the direct sun teams up with reflections from the clouds, creating a dazzling array of light. That day, the low winter sun bounced off the clouds and the reflections came back hard.

There was motion among the oaks. A pair of crows were restless, hopping and fidgeting, uncomfortable. Then a tiny flash as the sun caught one of their beaks. I watched them, hoping it would happen again, but it didn't. Continuing uphill, I felt my heart working. No day is complete without that feeling, the raised pulse of contentment.

Pheasant feathers lay by the fence. A fox must have followed its line, as it likes to do. Tiny dewdrops scattered the sunlight, adding to the dead cock's color. The breeze carried the rich scent of excrement. I faced into it, looking across the fertilized fields to the southwest.

There was a rippled signal in the faces of the sheep as I passed their fields. At first only a few black faces were visible, but as I got closer, their walking and browsing stopped and a growing number of dark shapes confronted me. Gentle motion and off-white colors would mean that they hadn't sensed me or that I was of little concern; stillness and spreading black faces told me that they had clocked me. The path led me closer to the flock and they bolted. Two sheep triggered the exodus, the others following almost instantly, one jumping before running.

I reached my perch and nestled into the corner, a small recess between two hawthorns. After a cup of tea from my Thermos I settled in earnest. I kept silent and still, my eyes hopping along the landscape to the west. There was a short commotion as some corvids bounced a pair of buzzards off their patch near the woods. A robin hopped onto a fencepost about thirty yards from me. It faced one way, then another, never still, its red breast only visible to me when it caught the sunlight.

A solitary oak stood in the nearest field, and many birds took turns there. The ground wore a mustard tinge, the stubble of last year's crop, and drew little life. But the farmer had plowed the field beyond and the gulls had made it their own, patrolling it with vigor, marching toward any others that dared land, then launching aerial persuasions if necessary. The gulls had my attention. I watched their maneuvers with unusual interest.

They are so common on the fields near our home that I can fall into the trap of associating familiarity with a lack of value. But not that day: as the minutes passed, I sensed that small corner had accepted me.

The long-tailed tits told me I was now part of the scenery by gathering all around and uncommonly close. There were about half a dozen that I could see without moving my head, but many others I could hear behind. They came closer still, two within touching distance. Keeping perfectly still ceased to be natural and became a conscious effort. My neck wanted me to move, but I didn't want to lose these friends, with their fluffy black-and-white faces. I succumbed: A gentle turn of my head, a single alarm call, and one flew off, then another, and then they were gone.

The gulls flew low over the soil, scanning for food. When they saw something they liked, they had a small problem: They were flying too fast to stop instantly. They solved their dilemma by performing a short turn, a full but tight circle, then threw out their wings and landed on the spot they fancied. I watched them flying and circling to a stop for half an hour, when their motions were happily familiar. The circle meant they were stopping for food; it's easy to read from hundreds of yards away. Soon I could see it before it was traced, in the banking of the wings. Gulls have brake lights, banking white wings that signal a small circle and stop.

Later, I saw the same pair of buzzards. They rose slowly in long sweeps on a thermal above a coniferous forest. More circles in the sky. Another sign. The sun had visited the dark woodland beneath and warm air was rising. The circles and the conifers were connected.

All shapes in nature have meaning. A circle is economical: It is the shape with the greatest area-to-circumference ratio—if you want to use the least fence for an acre of field, it needs to be a circular field. And if you want to build a nest without wasting effort or materials, make it round. A circle is also the shape formed when anything turns at a constant rate. When deprived of external reference, humans walk in circles because we drift constantly off a straight line; the radius of the circle varies from person to person, but the shape is predictable. This is partly why so many people who get lost find themselves back where they started.

A circle is also the shape formed when any creature wants to keep moving while remaining at the same distance from something. It is this last attribute that gives meaning to the circling we are most likely to see. At the center of the circle there is something of keen interest to that animal. The buzzards felt the lift from the thermals and wanted to stay on that ride; the gulls were drawn to some juicy specimen in the freshly turned soil. There is another type of gull circle, a much more impressive one, and it points to an often invisible tractor. A telltale gathering of gulls in their hundreds forms a whirling band, a circle that creeps over the land in one direction and then, if I watch long enough, back again.

Anyone spending long periods outdoors will come to know the circlers in their patch. The English travel writer Bruce Chatwin's companion was incensed by the black-and-white plovers that circled above them in Patagonia. The birds were shrieking as they wheeled, signaling to the world that there were humans at the center.

A circle in the sky can be underlined by sounds from below. A circling crow with a raucous blackbird beneath it might suggest a fox in the wood. And many predators, like wolves, will circle animals, including humans, as part of their investigation. Even with hungry predators, the circle should not be read as a sign of intent; it reflects a law of nature—there is no other way to inspect something from all angles at a safe distance.

The circling of a predator can create circles of another kind—a defensive shape. Grazing animals are prey, and one of their evolved responses to circling predators is to bunch together and face outward, creating a circular or pinwheel shape. It is a habit that continues to be observed close to home and in the wild, from wildebeests in Tanzania to musk oxen in the Arctic. Circling by prey is a sign that points out from the circle instead of toward the center.

Dogs circle before going to bed for the night. This behavior stems from the days when they had to make their own beds, by leveling grass or undergrowth. It also helped to drive out snakes and other undesirables.

Returning to the birds, some species, like the grosbeak, will try to preempt defense and form a circle while feeding on the ground; it is an efficient form of group vigilance. Perhaps the most famous of circlers is the vulture, a scavenger. A vulture can tell from thirteen thousand feet above the ground whether an animal is asleep or dead, and others value its perception. Their circling is a sign of fresh meat, which other scavengers, like hyenas, understand. Human hunters who have wounded an animal will use this sign in the sky as confirmation that the animal has died and will hurry to the spot. They will most likely have to ward off other carnivores that have also spotted the circle in the sky and zeroed in on it, beating them to its center.

If an animal has been killed by a predator, we can tell if the predator is still feeding from what happens after the circling sign: A vulture that circles, then lands on a tree, indicates that a kill has been made and the predator is still at the scene.

The Stotting

*B*OING, BOING, BOING.

The bouncing roe disappeared between the hazels and its two messages were clear.

A few signs in nature feel counterintuitive until we grow used to them. Two that we are most likely to see have overlapping aims. The first is used by prey to tell predators they have been seen, and the second is to make attack less attractive.

Predators know that a successful hunt is likely only if they manage to close within a certain distance before their target detects them. If a prey animal spots a predator at a safe distance, it may send a sign to the predator that the element of surprise is gone and a chase would be a waste of effort; as we have seen, some squirrels and deer flag their tails, and lizards wag them.

Occasionally the animals make these signs when they strongly suspect a predator is lurking nearby but before they have spotted it. Prey constantly monitor their environment for clues to trouble ahead, like mammals stampeding, cracking sticks, or birds taking off with flight calls. But they must sense the risk to be very real or this sign is counterproductive;

they reveal their whereabouts to predators that were otherwise oblivious to them.

The second of these signs has a similar aim—to make a lethal chase less likely—but through a slightly different mechanism. Most predators fail in most of their hunts. They don't need to succeed in many: One good meal a day or, in the case of some of the larger cats, almost a week may be enough. But nobody likes to work hard for nothing, and prey have evolved a way of reminding predators of this. It is called a "pursuit-deterrence signal."

When skylarks are being pursued by merlins, they have to work hard as they climb to escape, but they have an elegant way of telling their pursuer that there's lots more gas in the tank: They sing a boisterous song. Ungulates such as deer and gazelle have a cheeky habit of reminding predators that they are not just lithe but fit and swift, and that a chase

will not end well for them. On detecting the predator, they jump in the air using all four legs, a strange maneuver called "stotting" or sometimes "pronking." The subtext is: "I'm so full of energy, I can't stand still. I've got to bounce up and down! Please chase me—I'm just itching to outrun you!"

A less common and totally counterintuitive strategy prey uses when it detects a predator is to approach it. Fish and gazelles are both known to do this, to inspect the threat, then return to their group. This strategy may teach the group more about the predator's location and intent, or it may be more selfish. The exact logic behind it is not known, but studies have shown that it is effective. The gazelle that does the inspecting is less likely to be attacked by a cheetah, so it could be a form of pursuit deterrence.

I knew the second I saw the roe bouncing between the hazels what it was telling me: "I've seen you and you won't catch me."

The Guide

THE BEDOUIN PRIZE SECRECY. IT CAN be seen in their proverbs:

Katm as-sirr min kunuz al-barr
Guarding secrets is one of the desert's treasures.

Man dall katal'
He who guides kills.

Historically, the Bedouin lifestyle has been one of desert survival, moving from one scant pasture to another across the harshest landscapes, while contending with internecine rivalries and conflicts. Their culture combines immense hospitality with fierce protectiveness—you're either in or out—and has bred a tradition of brutal laws and customs: Blood vengeance—seeking out and killing those who have transgressed—is expected. But it is also understood that the killer must find their victim: No one may lead anyone to a human quarry in the desert.

I don't know the full cultural history for this tradition, but I imagine that the toughest of lifestyles was manageable if you felt that life was all about your small group and the desert. In this context, the desert is both your challenge and your savior; you can find the sustenance you need to survive and you can shield yourself from external harm with the cloak of the desert's barren anonymity. But if you feel your movements and habits are being shared with friends and foes alike, it's a matter of time before you're surprised and killed. The Bedouin expert Clinton Bailey explains, "Every Bedouin child is therefore instructed that, if asked by a stranger about a neighbor, he must deny knowledge of his whereabouts and even of his existence."

For wildlife, awareness of another animal's whereabouts is an opportunity, and any creature that reveals too much is endangering itself. In this sense, the animals are Bedouin. They won't show us things deliberately, but anything we can sense, which adds to our picture, is of value.

Like so many signs, much of this is common sense in hindsight, yet strangely invisible. The bird with a twig in its beak is flying to its nest. So simple, so obvious. Today, though, many people seeing a bird flying to a tree with a twig would consider it difficult to point out ten minutes later the direction of the bird's nest. The senses are offering the information, but the brain no longer registers it. At sea, a bird with something in its mouth is guiding us toward land, but any animal with something in its mouth is an unwitting guide and, however simple, it's a layer worth adding.

Gamekeepers keen to control the numbers of stoats or weasels on a property might see one of these animals with a rabbit or mouse in its mouth and decide not to go for a fast kill, but to stalk it. The stoat leads the keeper to its young and the whole family is killed, a savage reality that the Bedouin would recognize.

While out hunting, the Alaskan ethnobiologist Richard Nelson learned to take note when a raven somersaulted in the sky ahead of him. It proved a reliable guide to the location of prey, and Nelson kept his side of the deal, allowing the bird to share the meal.

Not all guiding drips with blood. As we have seen, gulls and many other birds become active whenever a farmer breaks the soil. We can learn to see the activity on the ground, before we see the land, mapped in the bird behavior in the sky. The southern African honeyguide bird calls to let the honey badger know where it will find a newly discovered beehive. The badger breaks open the hive and the bird gets its prize, the wax. It is a behavior that has been adopted by the Bushmen of the area, who mimic the calls of the badger. And in many places, from city centers to the Arctic, the roles are reversed: The birds follow us, knowing we turn up food wherever we go.

During hard times of frozen ground, foraging birds may follow any creature that digs, scrapes, or scratches at the surface. A robin will follow a badger, pheasant, wild boar, mole, or human breaking through the frost.

The Squall Squawk

THE HAWTHORN BUSH LET OUT ANXIOUS chatter. The rest of the hedgerow and woods beyond joined in. It was time to seek shelter.

We have seen how changes in the wind and sky warn of worsening weather, but there are myriad other signs. Scarlet pimpernels, wood anemones, and many more wildflowers react to deteriorating weather by closing their petals, but in truth they are better at reflecting what is happening than predicting it.

Another sign that gives a fast sense of bad weather is the "squall squawk." A squall is a localized area of very bad weather, a dark cell that passes through rambunctiously but quickly. Because they are so localized, they are one of the hardest weather phenomena to predict precisely and, believe me, I've tried. I once spent weeks on end being buffeted by them on the ocean and never managed to give myself more than half an hour's warning, even though I had radar to help. Squalls are most likely to take you by surprise on an otherwise fine day, particularly if you are somewhere with poor views of the surrounding area, like a city, a steep valley, or woodland. Otherwise you can see them forming and approaching—moody blobs, growing, darkening, the heavy rain often visible as streaks below.

Squalls on land give us a chance to familiarize ourselves with the "squall squawk," the sudden change in bird sounds and behavior. It is a rolling chorus, but unlike the dawn chorus in that song is replaced by a collection of sharper, edgier, less harmonious notes. There is an urgency to its sound, even to our ears. I regularly hear the crows, thrushes, blackbirds, nuthatches robins, tits, chickens, and many others kick off at the sudden approach of bad weather. During a squall, they also shrink into shelter, abandoning open spaces, like fields, and move into the trees.

Similar effects have been noted all over the world in birds and a wide variety of very different species. Sharks will flee the area a hurricane is about to pass through days before it arrives, and elephants pick up thunder a hundred miles away through their feet. The legendary naturalist Gilbert White learned to forecast the weather by observing the behavior of his tortoise, and on the other side of the world, cockroaches have given warning on the Pacific Islands. Arthur Grimble, the twentieth-century colonial administrator and author, wrote, "We did learn later to accept cockroaches as domestic pets (or almost) for, in the Gilbert Islands, whenever foul weather threatened, whole rustling clouds of them would come flying into the house for refuge."

Part IV
Signs of Wisdom: Advanced Keys

Flock, Bubble, and Burst

L OOKING OUT ACROSS THREE LARGE FIELDS to the hill on the far side, I sensed that the distant sheep were sleeping.

Our neighboring farmer's sheep graze on the hillside fields I can see from home. I don't know them individually in the way many shepherds do, but I've come to know the flock. It has been illuminating to remember how these animals grew from being an anonymous lump to a flock with character and meaning. There are now some simple behaviors that I enjoy sensing instantly.

I normally see the sheep in the distance, and often they're too far away for me to tell which way they're facing. Yet their group behavior reveals their mood and plans; there is a message in the shapes they form.

In general, groups of prey animals will gather closer to each other in open areas where they feel exposed and are more likely to spread if they're in familiar sheltered areas, like light woodland. Animals at the periphery of any group are at greater risk, and if they're anxious, we can watch them trying to avoid being on the edge. Frogs will hop into gaps to get away from it, and experienced birds prefer not to nest at the extremes of any colony, as those nests suffer the greatest predation.

If sheep appear widely scattered with no clear pattern, they are settled and grazing. But if they are in a tight central, rounded clump, something is troubling them.

My favorite pattern is actually the looser, rounded shape of a flock asleep. It will be set in from any edges, and there is an even spread to the animals, neither bunched up tight nor spread wide. Sheep need a lot less sleep than we do, so I tend to see this pattern only if I catch them early on a midsummer morning.

If there is a denser collection of several sheep at one edge of the flock, it acts like an arrowhead, revealing the direction of travel well before any motion is detectable. At the opposite side of the flock, at the trailing edge, the sheep are more spread out and fewer, often with one or two lagging considerably. A flock on the move may walk in long, straight lines, visible from a long way off, each individual obediently traipsing after the one in front. There are familiar trails on the hillside, a visible trace in the grass, a darker straight line that runs before and after the procession.

Sheep are not credited with great intelligence or initiative, but shepherds know that some animals lead, others follow, and many more tend toward the center of a flock. In wilder regions, the leaders were traditionally spared slaughter, as they were helpful to the shepherd for their proven ability to guide the others.

Fascinatingly, competition and vanity appear to be involved. Sheep that see themselves as leaders do not like to find themselves led and jostle for position, surging toward the head of the flock as they fall behind. There is no competition to be seen as a follower, so it is this jockeying for position that creates density at the front of the flock, readable from a distance.

After I'd watched this for a few years, it dawned on me that the shape of sheep on the move is analogous to that of trees exposed to the wind. Trees form dense, sculpted, rounded shapes on the exposed side and are looser, with bigger gaps between branches, downwind. And just as there are lone straggling sheep, there are solitary branches on the downwind sides.

Derek Scrimgeour, a successful competitor in sheep-herding competitions, has raised the art of communicating with his animals to the highest levels. For this shepherd, the reading of the signs is part of a "conversation or a dance." So what is actually going on? Let's examine some simple signs to see how the dance plays out.

The relationship between the dog and the flock will be expressed on many levels, but the two key areas are the positions of the animals relative to each other and their body language. The shepherd remains attuned to both in their dogs and sheep. The distance between the dog and the nearest sheep is critical—it's part of the language between them: A sheep will not let the dog closer than a distance determined by routine and its familiarity with that particular dog. If the dog gets too close it will induce a flight response in the sheep. If a sheep registers the dog and becomes wary, it will turn away from it. Humans turn to face perceived threats, so this may appear counterintuitive behavior, but sheep have evolved to keep their vulnerable neck area away from predators and expose their more robust rump.

If the dog lowers its head, ears, and tail, this is a sign of aggressive intent—the crouch—and a shepherd will spot it. If it displays this body language from a great distance, it is of no concern to sheep or shepherd, but if it accompanies its venturing too close to a sheep, the signs suggest that the dog is weighing its responsibilities with its predatory instincts. The shepherd will summon it with a well-rehearsed call.

A satisfying sign to note within flocks is the "bubble." As we have seen, if a flock of sheep or other group of prey feel seriously threatened, they will clump together. This is an instinctive response that makes it harder for a predator to isolate an individual from the pack. If the group is alert but not yet alarmed, individuals at the perimeter will try to keep a safe distance from anything that arouses concern.

The classic example of this is the flock being herded by the sheepdog they know. This ancient relationship works because sheep's ingrained terror of canine predators has been softened by the familiarity of the farmer's dog. The fear is inherent, the sheep keep their distance, but if the dog behaves in its normal way, it does not create panic. Instead, the nearest sheep will keep a close watch on the dog and continuously maneuver so that they maintain a safe distance from it. This creates a radius of space around the dog, and as it moves toward the animals, a bubble appears within the body of the flock, pressing in from the edge and growing as the dog draws nearer.

The most satisfying observation to make is when we see a bubble in a group of sheep and sense the likely location of its cause before spotting the threat. It is easiest to see when sheep are following a fence that borders a path or other public land. Watch for long enough and a strange dog will create a bulging bubble in the group. We'll sense where the culprit is, even if it remains invisible.

If you'd like to enjoy an urban version of the bubble, try walking slowly toward a large flock of city pigeons. If you get the speed right and don't trigger flight, you will see a bubble appear and spread among the birds. The size of your bubble will be influenced by your speed, but also your size, body language, clothing, and whether you have any food on you. You may also spot bubbles within flocks triggered by birds of the same species. Some birds have a literal pecking order; a dominant corvid entering a group with lower status will cause the other birds to stand aside, forming their own small bubble.

If you are looking to kill time in town, try sitting on a bench in an area with lots of pigeons and studying the bubbles created by others. You may sense someone walking toward your bench from behind when a bubble opens ahead—a moment to be savored by urban bubble connoisseurs.

Breaking out of the woods and climbing still, I felt the cold breeze had more authority now. I stopped, sat on the lee side of a grass mound, brought my feet and hands close to my body, and hunched my shoulders. There was a busy sound to the hills, unusual for winter. It had been cold for several days, and perhaps the animals felt they could no longer wait it out, but must get busy. A lone rabbit hopped along a fence line. There was a large flock of wood pigeons on the opposite hill, close to the woods, and among them a solitary fallow deer, with her head down.

About twenty minutes passed and then there was an eruption. The pigeons, hundreds of them, burst away from the field and flew low over the woods, disappearing down into them. The deer looked up and around, but did not move her legs. Seconds later, she thought better of it and sauntered into the woods. I scanned the field and the trees for some clue to this disturbance. I was limited to a very general feeling: Something was definitely out there, and it wasn't me—I was too far away and hadn't moved. Besides, that would have looked different—the deer would have fled before the pigeons.

My mind clicked into its slower mode: An aerial predator seemed the most likely. It would spook pigeons while leaving the deer untroubled. I scanned the sky just above the tree line, but spotted nothing. A full minute later, a fox walked along the field, parallel to the woods but twenty yards out into the field. It had a dark object, a large bird, in its mouth. It was a full load for the fox—its trot slowed, then it paused. It began again, but the rests grew more frequent. I sensed that it was physically exhausted, but could only guess at the preceding scenes. A prolonged chase for any bird is unlikely; these are smash-and-grab raids—the fox will either win or lose in a second. It must have been the weight of the bird that had tired it, and although it was too far away for me to see clearly, that suggested a pheasant.

The fox turned and headed through a musit into some gorse at the woodland edge. It emerged seconds later, without the bird, and bounced back the way it had come.

One of the key benefits to animals of forming groups is described formally as the "herd defense" or, in less formal circles, the "many eyes" theory. If it takes only one in the gang to spot potential trouble and they have a way to pass on the message quickly, it is an efficient way of improving vigilance.

Increased vigilance is not just about the scary things in life, but about the good things, too. Animals can learn and make discoveries more efficiently in a group—scatter some bread crumbs on a lawn and you will likely see one, two, four, nine birds arrive in quick succession. Not all of these birds saw the bread, but the message got out.

This begs the question: Why don't all animals form large groups? For some species, there isn't enough food for more than a small number in a region. Think of the mammals in tough environments—leopards in the savanna or foxes in the Arctic. If an animal can hunt and defend itself effectively on its own, it won't share resources; there is little benefit to a badger in traveling among a large group, and they are notoriously unsocial foragers.

From a sign perspective, we don't need to know why some animals are social and others not; we just need to become familiar with these patterns. Very quickly we come to associate the sight of one animal with the probability of another.

If you're bitten by a midge or buzzed by a wasp, you know they're not alone. A single crow's mate may be close by, but possibly no others. An elephant indicates others nearby, but a rhinoceros may stand alone. Every animal on Earth has its own pattern of gregariousness, a sign of the likelihood of others nearby. The more satisfaction we take in spotting these trends, the sooner our brain registers them. It can then quickly anticipate the next animal we will see.

In 1981 a pair of researchers, J. E. Treherne and W. A. Foster, published an academic paper about the behavior of a marine insect, an ocean skater called *Halobates robustus Barber*. Nearly two centuries earlier, Nelson became aware that the French and Spanish fleets were heading out of Cádiz and that battle was imminent. These two events would have no connection but for the parallel the academics drew in the signaling that took place in each case.

Treherne and Foster were focused on group behavior and had noticed how the insects at the periphery of the group became aware of a threat and transmitted the information via a signal. The signal passed through the group and, critically, moved faster than the threat. Insects at the far edge of the group became aware of danger before their senses were capable of detecting it. Nelson was aware of what the enemy was up to before he could see them, because the British fleet signaled with flags.

The information conveyed by the flags moved much faster than the enemy's ships. This allowed Nelson time to signal back some practical information to his colleagues, then add, "England expects that every man will do his duty." Treherne and Foster named the behavior in animals as the "Trafalgar effect."

The Trafalgar effect explains not just the "burst" of wood pigeons above, but the widespread bursts of many animals. It is what we mean when we say, "The herd was spooked." A herd cannot be spooked, but individuals within it are, and this spreads rapidly to the others. In slow motion, the eruption can be seen to spread like a ripple through the group as each animal receives the signal and takes off, their response passing the signal to the next animal in turn, and so on. Sometimes it is possible to see which side of the group responds first, which gives us a clue to the direction that the perceived threat comes from. At other times, we will just sense that something is not right.

A few days later I lay at the edge of a field on top of a hill, staring out over land as it rolled with bumps down toward the south and the sea. A flock of gulls took off from the field, then peeled away over the dark conifers on its far side, before rolling back toward me. The flock appeared to have purpose at one moment and none the next. It swelled and turned to smoke, constricted into knots, then grew again. It had substance and then none, a body, then a ghost. A great thick knot appeared in the flock, and I scanned the sky for the threat.

"Allelomimesis" describes how any large group of animals can appear as an individual organism. Bird flocks offer the best-known examples, and the murmurations of starlings get the most attention. But there are hundreds of animal collectives that qualify, from shoals of fish to gangs of buffalo and cauldrons of bats.

There is a type of animal identification that relies on group characteristics, instead of the more common method of studying individuals. As distance increases, birds become harder to identify. But birds flying in flocks have group characteristics entirely separate from their own as individuals. There are the famous V formations of cranes or geese, but all flocks have a character. Some birds follow a clear leader, while others fly in loose or tighter groups. In distant treetops, I often recognize finches in flocks from their undulating flights between the trees long before I work out the exact species. From a distance, the individual is as hard to recognize as the group is easy.

For thousands of years, no one knew how vast numbers of fast-moving animals could keep in sync with the whole, but recent studies have cracked the secret. The birds don't see the flock; they see and imitate only their neighbors. They are capable of monitoring the actions of up to seven. This is similar to the way aerobatic display teams maintain order: A pilot will follow a leader on their wing, without giving too much thought to the shape the team as a whole creates. Provided that each pilot or bird follows effectively, we will see a large group perform extraordinary synchronized rituals in the air.

Some swelling and contraction within any group is normal—the animals don't maintain a rigid distance from each other, and gentle fluctuations in their spacing are constant. However, a dramatic and sharp contraction is unusual. When I saw the gulls condense into a tight knot, I sensed a predator in the area. I had not seen that behavior in gulls before and did not spot a predator on that occasion, although the sense that one was in the area remained strong. I have witnessed it before, in starlings, which come together if a falcon is looming, and it has been noted in other common species, like ducks.

It is thought that they do this because it helps to sow confusion in and increase risk to fast predators. A peregrine falcon will attack at such great speeds, up to two hundred miles per hour, that it has to be certain of making a clean strike. If it accidentally hits something, like the wrong bird, at that speed it will likely kill the victim and itself. When a large flock of starlings contracts rapidly, it increases the chances of an accidental collision and makes the prospect less attractive to the falcon.

The Retreat and Rebound

THE WIND HAD BLOWN ALL NIGHT and woken me every hour. Now the rain joined in, but without the same commitment, showers whipping in and abating. I thought of gökotta, the Swedish act of rising early to take in the joys of the morning in nature. It eluded me and I dozed off again, urging the weather to follow one course or the other. It heard me and cleared. The winds faded and the sun made its way between clouds that held some of their speed.

Later, emerging from a copse of conifers, I followed a track uphill to the north. At a corner, a robin announced its displeasure from the high branches of an elder tree. As I slowly approached, it hopped to the top. I continued, it waited, then let out a call and flitted to a second elder behind the first. I ducked beneath the first and watched the bird; its alarm calls grew louder. It flew off again, this time landing a short distance away, on a fence post a few yards behind the elders. I carried on toward the bird. It hopped along the fence, first a few yards, then a little farther. I stepped slowly toward it. I had no intention of harming or catching it, but it didn't know that. It hopped along another yard, its calls ratcheting up.

As I lifted my foot to step forward, I thought, I know what you're going to do next, Mr. Robin. And he did.

Many animals, including squirrels, badgers, and many birds, are territorial. They claim a patch of land for food, mating or nesting, then defend it against intrusion, particularly by animals of the same species. Some animals, including deer, become noticeably more territorial during certain seasons, including the rut. But the behavior of all territorial animals will be strongly influenced by whether we find them on their own patch or outside it.

The pattern I experienced when stepping toward the robin was classic for an animal in its home territory: It retreated, but only so far. As the retreating distance shortens, even as we advance steadily, it is a strong sign that the bird is nearing the edge of its territory. The next action is for the bird to fly up and over or around us, landing back nearer the heart of its territory, which was what that robin did.

Once you are used to seeing this happen, you start to sense the invisible elastic that tethers the bird to its territory; we can push against it, but only so far. Ping! The bird takes off and flies over us.

If an animal is outside its territory, it has an inherent sense of trespass and behaves differently; it is quicker to retreat and will do so for greater distances, often vacating the area altogether. It is also less likely to be vocal.

Sometimes we will sense the elastic in the apparent courage or tameness of, or in the awkward lines taken by, a wild animal. Whenever I surprise a deer that is close, I freeze. As soon as I move I expect it to flee, but if it doesn't, even after I have made some obvious movements, I sense I have surprised it at the edge of its territory and I am standing in the most logical route back to its comfort zone.

The effect is greatest when there are limited options for escape and the deer is faced with a dilemma: Does it head toward the area it associates with security, even though that means passing me, or run in the opposite direction, away from its home? Often they choose to run by me, even if that means passing very close. If the deer is at the edge of a territory and the ground is open, it will shoot out to the side, then work its way back.

Territories are established with other animals of the same species in mind; magpies do not allow other magpies any freedom to explore in their nesting area. But the territory of one species can be a sanctuary for another, provided there is no rivalry, and this can explain some counter-intuitive behavior between predators and prey. Raptors tend not to hunt in the immediate area of their nest, which protects against accidental attacks on their own young. Songbirds can be safer very close to the nest of a bird of prey than farther away. It may look perilous, but it offers a double layer of safety: The raptor doesn't attack it there, and keeps other birds of prey at a distance.

The Jink

THE DEER BOLTED. AND TURNED. I knew instantly that something unusual lay ahead.

It is as though there are two worlds outdoors—motion and stillness—and it is easier to look from one into the other. When we are still we can see all that moves and all that is still, but as soon as we begin to move, parts of the still world will hide.

The deer I surprised used that one-way window against me. I was moving slowly through dense undergrowth of spurge and bramble, trying to keep the noise down. But the two fallow had frozen by the time I picked them out against a green background. I froze, too, but a twig snapped under my foot and the deer bolted. They ran, zigzagging away from me, eleven o'clock, one o'clock, eleven o'clock, one o'clock, between a yew and an ash. I expected this to continue until I lost sight of them, but it didn't.

The deer were about seventy-five yards away when they took a sudden turn, half back toward me. They would have passed close to my right side, but took another, gentler turn and disappeared. I knew instantly that there was something ahead. I continued in the direction I had been walking, the direction in which the deer had first chosen to flee, and was surprised to see some wood pigeons take off ahead of me.

Many biologists, particularly those made overexcitable by evolution, view life as one big sex-and-energy experiment—every behavior can be explained as part of a strategy that improves the odds of successful reproduction. I don't dispute the science and find it very helpful, but I rebel against the idea that evolution can prune all whimsy out of life. That said, the science is powerful, and strong insights come from the basic premise that animal behavior is mainly dictated by survival and procreation. Put another way, if we spot a wild animal doing something energetic and odd, there will be a good reason for it. One common example is a key called "the jink."

We grow familiar with animals' patterns of motion. A dog meanders while sniffing the ground to pick up a scent, but runs in a straight line when in pursuit. Rabbits will graze, pause, and hop along a woodland edge. And each bird has its signature patterns of flight and feeding.

Animals tend to travel in the most efficient way, which favors straight lines. When we use expressions like "make a beeline" or "as the crow flies," we are acknowledging that the direct route is often the best for animals. Every time an animal deviates from a straight line, it is interesting to consider why.

Some creatures have trademark inefficient styles of getting around. As I write this, a speckled wood butterfly is flying erratically outside the window. It changes direction every couple of seconds. This does not appear odd because it is a typical flight pattern for a butterfly; it's an insect that does not have many defenses against predators other than evasion (poisonous butterflies are less erratic than delicious ones). Butterflies have evolved a technique to change direction more sharply by using the turbulence their own wings create, and monarchs are able to pull a hand-brake turn, changing their heading by 90 degrees in under a body length. The curious thing about butterflies in flight is that we can often discern their general direction of travel, but not the exact route they will take. This makes it easier to predict where they will be in five seconds than in two.

The erraticism of butterflies and the zigzagging of the deer are strategies for evading predators. They come at a cost in terms of energy expended, but in evolutionary terms it is a price worth paying for not getting eaten.

The more familiar we become with each animal's signature pattern of moving, the more likely we will instantly detect any sharp deviation from the norm. A jink in a butterfly's flight may be meaningless, but if we think of many common birds that fly in straight lines for a period, like pigeons and crows, something must trigger any sudden alteration in course—a jink. It is uncharacteristic.

Birds' jinking is a sign poachers used to detect trouble. A gamekeeper might be well camouflaged in rural attire and lying in wait. But the poacher, a student of animal behavior, would study the birds as they flew over the land and spot the jink of a pigeon as it went over the hiding place of the gamekeeper. Wily poachers could change course themselves in time to avoid getting apprehended.

But the good gamekeeper is no fool and will use the same tactic, spotting the jink in the air and using it as a map to set a trap to catch the poacher. The laws of nature are the same for these two adversaries as for animals in the wild: The predator needs to get lucky just once, the prey needs to be lucky every time, and luck favors the aware. The gamekeeper may choose to notice the jinks, but the poacher can't afford to miss them.

You can study the jink of a pigeon or crow quite easily. If you are walking along a path or track with a good view of the sky that also has some cover to either side—a hedgerow that is taller than you is ideal—then the ground is set for a concocted jink. The birds flying overhead will get little warning of your presence, as you are hidden by the hedge, but you retain a good view of the sky. Watch a few birds fly over and look for the jink as they spot you. If they are flying low, you may see a jink in their flight unprompted, but if you are in a popular area, then it is likely they are high enough initially not to be alarmed. Now peer through a gap in the hedge and choose your bird, one that is low enough. Just as it is about to pass directly over you, raise your hands above your head suddenly and give a loud clap. Watch the jink in action.

From the perspective of somebody a few hundred yards away, the jink you created would be visible, but you would not. And yet they would find it easy to pinpoint your position; the jink would reveal your presence as clearly as a red dot on a map.

If you spend time motionless outdoors, you can surprise wildlife. A badger, rabbit, fox, or squirrel will saunter past, only to change direction upon detecting you. In the past week, I've spooked both a buzzard and a great spotted woodpecker in this way. The buzzard was farther from me and arced away with some grace, but the woodpecker was passing from one bush at the edge of the forest to another farther down, only to find me lodged between them. There followed an inelegant maneuver, all flapping and harsh turn, reminiscent of those displays in air shows where a fighter jet is pushed to its limit in a turn, accompanied by the roar of strained engines. It was a chance to enjoy the cream-and-crimson of the bird's underbelly.

It may help to think of the jink as a force field or repellent. Whatever the cause, something is forcibly sending an animal in a new direction. Many will defend territory, and occasionally a jink is a sign that a bird is trespassing. When a hen robin is making a new home with a cock and learning her new territory, she will at first occasionally stray beyond the invisible boundary of his domain. This will trigger attacks from her neighbor. Once the hen learns the invisible fence in the air she is less likely to stray beyond it, but until then she may find herself vocally repelled by the irate neighbor, or even by the memory of an attack. She will show this with a sharp change in direction. The principle is identical to all other jinks: There is something out there that the animal feels threatened by.

The jink is most commonly triggered by sight, but it applies to almost all animals and senses. It may be triggered by scent. If you think of the wind carrying yours downwind in a steady stream, it will prompt either a freeze or a jink if it passes the nose of any prey on the move.

Bats don't see us, and in the dark we struggle to see them, but they often make their presence felt when they jink away from us. They might fly past us in a straight line and remain undetected, but if a bat is fly-ing straight at us, it may detect us, using echolocation, quite late in its approach. This results in an audible jink away: We hear the close, faint flap of the bat on maneuvers.

Gamekeepers and hunters have long used the jink to herd animals in the direction that suits them. In the Middle Ages a deer might be dissuaded from heading in a particular direction by a "blencher," some-one or something placed in its likely path to steer it away and toward a favored destination.

This brings us back to the fallow deer that zigzagged away from me before doubling back, then slipping to the side. The zigzag is part of a normal pattern—it was only a sign that the deer were in flight mode. The jink was more interesting; there was certainly something ahead that had spooked them for a second time and forced them back almost toward me. As I continued, threading my way over and between the thriving clumps of brambles, I contemplated the wood pigeons that were sent into flight ahead. The jink was an instant sign and the wood pigeons would have been another, but they didn't marry perfectly. If something ahead had forced the deer back, perhaps a dog walker, it was highly likely that the pigeons would have been put to flight before my arrival. Two contrasting signs triggered some slower thought, but I couldn't unravel the mystery before the solution appeared ahead.

There was a pair of parked forester's trucks, one red and one white, and they clashed with the dominant green of the woods. I looked for their owners but saw nobody, and suddenly the puzzle was solved. It was the weekend; the foresters had left their trucks and would not be back until Monday. The garish vehicles had been enough to jink the deer back toward me, and the fact that they were temporarily abandoned explained why the wood pigeons had been unperturbed until my arrival. The pigeons had grown accustomed to them, in a way that the deer hadn't; if there had been foresters at work, the pigeons and the deer would have sought a more tranquil part of the wood long before I came stepping through.

The Shimmy

T HERE WAS A MOTION HIGH IN the bushy ivy on the south side of the beech that I knew without looking to be a pigeon. Moments later I passed a fluttering of bramble leaves. I waited for the invisible wren to hop again and it obliged, darting to the neighboring clump of brambles with a short alarm call.

Later that day a silence was broken by the springing of a branch above my head. I strained to peer between the foliage of the canopy, catching slices of sky until the expected buzzard silhouette crossed one. Toward the end of the day a squirrel jumped from goat willow to yew, then to another yew. It was invisible and visible at the same time.

Every animal has weight, so every time it rests on anything that yields, it creates a motion. I call it "the shimmy." Each shimmy has a signature determined by the weight of the animal, the way it moves, and the character of the object it rests on.

Whenever we are outdoors, we will detect lots of motion. Our brain prioritizes motion over many other things we sense because in evolutionary terms, motion is always important—it may be a threat or an opportunity. There are three types of motion that we will see: animal movement; inanimate objects being moved by other inanimate objects, like the wind blowing leaves or clouds; and inanimate objects being moved by animals. It is the last category that we're interested in here.

As we have seen, context is part of the pattern: We can sense an animal by combining the type of motion with the place and time at which it happens. From experience, I know that a small amount of motion in the green leaves of nearby undergrowth is very likely to have been caused by a wren. I identified the wren I mentioned from its shimmy and also from its habitat. Birds of prey, like the buzzard, perch much higher in the trees—they're keen on a good vantage point—and stamp silence onto the woods around them. They also launch silently when disturbed, unlike the wood pigeon, which likes to make a clatter. So, if there's no wind, a substantial high branch bouncing is the signature of a recent bird of prey launch—a scan will usually find the culprit. A repeated substantial shimmy in one part of high, thick ivy is nearly always a wood pigeon, while a line of motion in it is more likely to be a squirrel.

Like so much of what we look at in nature, the physics is basic, but the possibilities are extraordinary. An animal cannot come to rest on something that is too weak to support it, so the size of the branch will rule out animals of a certain size straight away—mammals don't usually attempt to rest on ivy, but birds often do. The character of the shimmy is determined by the nature of the greenery and the size and typical behavior of the animal. Mammals give branches more of a stuttering motion than birds, and each plant species reacts differently. You will discover how different branches react when you watch animals flit from one species to another. The squirrel we met earlier in this chapter set the thin, floppy goat-willow branches dancing, but I detected only the faintest of vibrations in the leaves once the animal had leaped into the sturdier-branched yew.

The place we see the motion is also part of the signature. A bouncing branch at the edge of a tree is a clear sign of a departure, but a circular shape of motion emanating from a bush means the animal is still there. The direction of travel is a clue, too. Nuthatches are the rare bird that climbs down trees headfirst as well as up.

We can't always identify an animal precisely, but some notion is always possible. In our garden, there are several laurel bushes and a shimmy in them is the mark of the thrush family. From the motion of the leaves alone, I can't tell instantly if the bush is hiding a blackbird, song thrush, or mistle thrush, but I can be confident it is one of them.

Once we've detected the shimmy, our brain will automatically add more filters. That is what experience offers. The habitat, season, weather, sounds, previous sightings—all are filed in the database part of our brain (and the more time we spend outdoors, the better the database) and serve to turn a random motion into the signature of one animal. A shimmy is often accompanied by a bird call. The one I encounter most frequently is a branch wobbling to the liquid sound of a blackbird's flight call.

It is not just about spending more time outdoors, but also caring about the meaning of what we are seeing. Our brain will only start to do the clever bit if we take an interest. The trick is never to let a motion that you sense was created by an animal go without interrogation. What was that? It's a question our brain is used to and likes.

We spend our lives adding meaning to motion in other contexts: Ask someone how an exam went, and if they hold out their hand horizontally with the palm down and rock it, we recognize instantly that they are saying "so-so"—not great, but not terrible. It is a motion we have come to know without thinking about it. The only real challenge to finding meaning in motion outdoors is interest: We have to want to banish randomness from our view.

Ripples in the water are a form of shimmy. A fish taking an insect at the surface creates a "rise" pattern, and something similar happens with creatures that live above water. In a stream I pass regularly, I often see the shimmies of invisible water voles, semicircular ripples that fan out from the bank. A particular pattern forms in a pond when a swift swoops to take a drink in flight. By midsummer I recognize it instantly, but not always the first time I see it each year. Some senses need refreshing with the seasons.

Much harder to spot, but satisfying when we do, the opposite of the shimmy is the "no shimmy." Unless you're sensitive to the shimmy and vigilant for it, its rarer sibling is a sign you can go a lifetime without spotting. The first time I recognized it I was walking along a path lined on either side by waist-high bracken. There was a good breeze and the bracken was oscillating gently with a steady rhythm. The motion was consistent, except for one frond that stayed still. It stood as high as its neighbors, as open to the wind as the rest, yet it didn't move. I stepped in to investigate the cause . . . and the wren flew off. It was at least another week before I sensed a wren in a still patch of brambles, but the satisfaction was well worth the focus.

Any animal that is resting on a small branch will dampen its motion, changing the way that foliage behaves in response to the wind or even other animals. I remember once I was tracing the passage of a squirrel along some hazels by watching the shimmy move away from me when one branch didn't respond as I'd expected. It turned out the first squirrel had joined a friend.

One of the principles of our approach is that every plant and animal is part of a map of our surroundings. Each organism is telling us something about our environment, however seemingly trivial—a slithering snake reflects the rising temperature on a late spring day. The shimmy allows us to take this principle a step further, because the outdoors is filled with motion created by animals that are invisible to us. Once we learn to recognize the signature of the motion, we start to sense animals without seeing them. Knowing their habitat helps us to bring the pieces together. The rustle of a bush can become part of a map, because sounds can give us a feel for the animal and plant simultaneously—the rustle of a squirrel running up ivy is one I know well. It is a sign of being near a woodland edge, where ivy grows thickly up the trees. The parting and wafting of long grasses that indicate a pheasant running are signs that there must be water and trees nearby, as pheasants will not travel far from either.

The Ignore and Mistake

I STEPPED CAREFULLY TO AVOID THE LAST bluebells
of spring, as the ground prepared for summer. A raven croaked
overhead, and there was the steady cycle of a chaffinch's lowering notes. I must have surprised a grey squirrel that didn't bother to
freeze—it darted to a beech and shot up the other side. There was the
pause, then a peek, and then it did something I wasn't expecting. The
squirrel took a few quick steps along a horizontal southern branch and
jumped down at least six yards, landing noisily among the leaf litter
before scampering off again. It was a rare and intriguing example of a
flight to refuge gone wrong. I felt that there was some other creature of
concern to that squirrel very close by, possibly in that tree, but it did not
reveal itself.

The beeches were sparse now, and I paused to graze on the leaves of
a hawthorn. I sniffed its flowers and they were fragrant. It was another
sign that spring still had a hold; when summer arrived, the flowers would
take on a less pleasant scent. Passing a solitary spindle and then a field
maple, I broke out of the woods into a clearing. In front of me, behind
the scrambling brambles, was the great rusting circle of an abandoned
charcoal kiln. The air was warmer now, and I wondered for a mad
moment whether some ghost of a fire was still burning in the kiln, then

came to my senses: It was the clearing. The sun was breaking through high cloud at times and warming the ground in the clearings, leaving the woods cool. A second later I picked up the scent of the warmed ground, a dusty verdant smell. Then it happened, all very quickly.

I heard the crack, then saw a fallow doe emerge from the undergrowth about thirty yards in front of me, just to one side of the kiln. It was at a full gallop and heading toward me, aiming for a spot about five yards to my left. I was standing in the open and wearing clothes that would not have blended in well. It had to see me. I fully expected it to jink—to spot me and alter course abruptly away. But it didn't. It held its line and our eyes met. Still no change. It continued running straight and sped past me, disappearing down a dip and behind a bank of brambles. My gut told me exactly what was about to happen next. Two seconds later it did: The dog appeared out of the same undergrowth that the deer had emerged from. It, too, was running fast, but it paused in the middle of the clearing, nostrils up, head moving from side to side. It saw me and picked its route: the wrong one. The deer had given it the slip, and I was happy about that.

Any prey animal will react to a threat or predator in the ways we have been exploring. If it ignores an obvious threat, the most likely explanation is that a more pressing danger is out there somewhere. It's a cue to expect a predator to appear very soon. "The ignore" is not a complex sign, but we are likely to pick it up too late the first few times. As we get used to it our reading of it speeds up and we start to sense what is about to happen, instead of working it out after the event.

It's not always as physical as a dog chasing a deer. A more common and subtler version of the ignore happens when we feel we've done quite well to sneak up particularly close to an animal. A songbird that has allowed us to get much closer than normal is not oblivious to our presence, but focused on something more important. If it is silent and not foraging, there may be a bird of prey overhead.

A variation of the ignore applies to predators, too. If you have lost your dog during a walk and been puzzled as to why it fails to respond to your calls, it's probably because dogs and other predators can experience a type of deafness—psychological, not physical—when in pursuit. The owners of the dog chasing the deer could have called all they liked, but until the chase calmed or was given up, the dog was unlikely to respond. In the dangerous heat of a hunt, prey and predator screen out the rest of the world until it ends.

A variation of the ignore is "the mistake." You will see it when an animal does something uncharacteristically rash, stupid, or clumsy, like the squirrel jumping from a height or birds flying into windows. In these cases, the animal is focused on a threat to the exclusion of even its own environment. Mistakes are much more likely to occur during the urgency created by a chase. Our noticing a mistake or clumsiness in an animal helps us to sense a closing predator.

The Eddy

I FELT THE WIND ON ONE EAR, then the other. I sensed the animals were gone.

We can feel the wind on our face or body and can see and hear trees being harassed. Emily Brontë described it elegantly: "One may guess the power of the north wind blowing over the edge, by the excessive slant of a few stunted firs at the end of the house; and by a range of gaunt thorns all stretching their limbs one way, as if craving alms of the sun." We can see the wind imprinted on distant clouds, and there are closer clues, too. Leaves, twigs, or dust might be carried along in front of us on a strong breeze.

At certain times and in certain places the wind direction we experience is more variable than we perhaps expect. I'm not referring to the general wind direction over a broad area, but to the winds we experience in an exact spot within a landscape.

As we saw earlier, the broader wind direction will be fairly constant until there is an imminent weather change. But when this wind encounters the land and the many obstacles on it, its flow is disrupted. This can lead to significant variations in wind direction over short distances because all fluids are thrown into circular patterns, eddies, when passing an obstruction. Draw your hand through water in a bath and you'll see patterns form. If the eddies are minor, perhaps the wind passing over a distant hawthorn, we experience gentle fluctuations in the breeze we feel. But sometimes the shape of a landscape conspires to form more substantial eddies, which can give the wind direction a much more volatile character.

If we take note of whether we are experiencing a breeze from a steady direction or are in a place where the wind appears to come unpredictably from different directions, we can assess whether we are experiencing a major wind eddy. It's important to remember that both eddies and steady breezes occur in the same location at different times because the wind will arrive from different directions on different days, passing different obstacles on the way. A landscape may be subject to eddies when the wind blows from the west but not the east. A steady wind direction is fairly obvious, but one sign that confirms a steady rhythm is the fluctuations of leaves; they oscillate or wobble with a constant frequency when wind direction and strength stay fairly constant. The next time you feel a steady breeze, study the leaves and you'll spot the rhythm.

Understanding whether we are experiencing a steady wind or are in a major eddy is critical to gaining an intuitive sense of whether you will encounter animals. One is a gift, the other a handicap: A steady breeze allows us to walk into it and denies animals their ability to smell us approaching. If we are in an eddy, our scent is announcing our presence to any animal with a nose.

It is possible to get up close to many wild animals when walking stealthily into a constant breeze, but in eddies they have mysteriously disappeared. Along with many of the other keys, tuning in to this will help you sense how likely you are to spot rabbits, foxes, badgers, and deer—it is part of what many consider to be luck.

The Crook

L AST YEAR'S BEECH LEAVES WERE CRISP underfoot as I climbed a chalk hill in early May. It had been dry and warm for days, and dust was whirling in the breeze for the first time that spring. Venturing off the scoured white of the path, I picked my way between the stretching arms of coppiced hazel and took uncomfortably long steps over clumps of brambles.

The wood was filled with the territorial wrangling of the birds—it's a crowding noise that falls more easily into pockets of friendly sound when we stop moving. I set my pack down and sat on the ground. I saw a chaffinch ahead, its fast descending notes urging the forest to accept its claim to that spot. Behind me, and a way off, I heard the more calming sound of a stock dove. Between the branches of the beeches, I could see a grassy field rolling down and away. The air was now more humid than it had been earlier in the day, and my knuckles ran over the dampness on the back of my shirt. I lay down.

Half an hour passed before a pair of wood pigeons flapped urgently overhead. Then, two minutes later, predictably, a walker and her dog appeared from the same direction. Happy that I had the setting I wanted, a mixture of light woodland and breaks in the canopy that allowed a good view of the sky, I decided to settle for the evening. I rolled out a mat, slowly accepting the place as my bed for the night and hoping it would accept me. It didn't.

Something was wrong, not in a pulse-quickening way, but I sensed I had picked a bad spot. I rolled up the mat and made my way back over the brambles, returning to the path the way I had come.

The next day, I returned, determined to grasp the cause of my earlier unease. I sat in the same spot for a little more than three hours, not convinced that the answer would present itself but keen, curious, and stubborn in equal measure. Then it appeared before me.

There was a subtle kink in the trunks of the beech, ash, and maples that I could see. I bounded around the trees, a bloodhound with a scent, and the mystery was solved. I had picked a spot with ground that was not steadfast, a place that was unusually vulnerable to storm damage. The slight bends in the tree trunks signified that the earth had shifted at some earlier point, perhaps a decade ago, judging from the uniform height of "the crook" in the trunks. Trees that had been growing vertically had been tipped a few degrees and had resumed growing at an altered angle. Behind them I saw evidence that some young trees had come down at about the same time. The new humidity in the air had been the missing piece in the jigsaw: the weather had been deteriorating, isolated storms were possible, and I had chosen a place that offered little resistance to either heavy rain or strong winds. I had sensed there might be a serious problem if storms broke around me, long before I understood why.

Nature's Coat

"THIS IS RIDICULOUS!"

I remember chastising myself many years ago for a lamentable journey. I had just driven six hours to the Lake District, in North West England, given a one-hour talk in a dark auditorium, and driven six hours home. Appalling planning meant that I had gone to the trouble of traveling all the way from England's south coast to the beauty of the Lake District and back, without standing before anything that could generously be termed a landscape. I had gained no memorable outdoor experience at all. It was a shambolic way to go about things, and I vowed never to let it happen again.

Soon enough I was on the road again, this time to a talk at a festival in the surreal surroundings of Portmeirion—a north Welsh village designed by an Englishman to look Italian, and the setting of the cult 1960s British TV show *The Prisoner.* But this time there was a little white space in the digital diary. I parked the car near a village called Church Stretton in Shropshire and walked out into the landscape. The village had earned the nickname "Little Switzerland" a century ago, which I thought boded well for a natural-navigation walk among the hills. There were high broken clouds and sun—a day of warm, milky light. Dust hung in the air, and I could smell the harvest. After locking the Land Rover, I walked uphill for ten minutes, then surveyed my surroundings. Within seconds a gong was sounding in my head, a joyous alarm: The shape of the hills in the middle distance resonated strongly. Long, thin hills, higher at the far end, tapering down, smooth, rounded . . . I was looking at drumlins! I had once detoured for an hour to catch a glimpse of drumlins on the west coast of Ireland, but here some magnificent specimens were popping up in front of me without introduction.

Drumlins are one of the rare, esoteric superstars of natural navigation. They are aligned with the flow of the long-departed glacial ice and form vast compasses, visible from miles around. They can be found in much of the northern US from Maine to the Puget Sound region. The drumlins I saw, like so many others, were aligned north-south.

I walked across a saddle and climbed again as the sun began its late-afternoon descent. Sitting in a hollow among sheep droppings, I felt a chill for the first time. I crawled out, nosed through some bilberry leaves and watched a bellflower bob in the wind. Most of the hill was grass, heather, or bracken, and the blue of the flower marked it out. The land was exposed; the light wind I had felt in the valley where I had parked the car was here a force that gripped the hillside. It held it so tightly that on the southeast side it appeared to come from the southwest, while on the northeast side it blew in from the northwest. Only at the top of the hill could I feel the true west-southwesterly wind.

On my way down, something struck me as curious. I had found the heather more beautiful and alluring on my walk up the hill, but now as I descended it had lost its appeal and I was drawn more to the bracken. This was strange, not least because bracken has few devotees. It is neither a pretty plant nor much loved by naturalists, and has never been a favorite of mine. And yet I was feeling its pull. Myriad paths threaded across the hills, sheep tracks mainly, and at each fork on the way up I had leaned toward the track that ran through heather. On the way down the opposite was true and I went with the bracken. It must have been the different light levels and angles making one plant more attractive to me than the other, I thought.

In the last light of the day I looked at the areas of heather and those of bracken; they were clearly delineated. There were none where the two mingled successfully. The heather would dominate all the way up to a ridgeline and on the opposite side the bracken ruled. But it was not all about aspect or even altitude: bracken was being displaced in large swathes in areas where it was otherwise doing well. It was as though a giant had taken his enormous paintbrush, dipped it in heather-colored ink, and swept it across broad parts of the hillsides and valleys. It clearly had nothing to do with water, soils, or geology. It was a beautiful, confusing, and intriguing pattern. Then the penny dropped.

I was walking in an exposed area, above the tree line, and few plants can thrive there. Bracken was on the edge of its survivable zone, and where the land was especially open to the elements, like on the southwestern, windward sides of the ridges, it gave up and the hardier heather thrived. Such zoning is common on all mountains, but here there was an added beauty: The saddle between the hills was funneling the winds down into a valley, repelling the bracken from some areas but allowing it to thrive in others. The bracken was forming a map of shelter; the heather marked areas of exposure. The land was color-coded.

On the way up the hill, my legs had been working hard during the last warmth of the day and I was seeking cooler areas. On the way down, there was the chill of less exercise and a disappearing sun. Without realizing it, I had been using nature as a thermostat, the heather showing me the paths that offered a cooling breeze and the bracken the routes that would keep a coat on me.

Two Frosts

A LIGHT BREEZE CAME IN FROM THE northeast as the sun rose well south of it. It was winter and the ground was hard. Without a blanket of clouds, heat had risen out of the ground all night.

I walked into the breeze, and the patterns of frost suggested some new code. There were areas of strong white and many more of churned dark mud and flint. Pockets of air had formed concentric rings in frozen puddles and I struggled in my search for meaning in them, but then I relaxed; these icy rings may just be beautiful.

This was the third cycle of cold days and night frosts, and on the south side of the path, tucked in and shaded by the brown undergrowth of the verge, there were strips of grass that the midday sun could not reach. In these areas, there lay a crystalline white covering, half an inch thick in places, looking more like snow than frost. These are the places where frost reigns, wearing a new layer after each clear, cold night. They will not thaw until the air temperature rises. And there is a silence, the deep one that Richard Jefferies knew: "A great frost is always quiet, profoundly quiet."

The frost on the path varied in width, too, broadening one minute and thin the next. Ahead it swelled like a snake that has gorged on a plump rodent. Over only fifty yards a slim white ribbon, no wider than my shoulders, grew until it was twenty yards wide or more, then narrowed again. Further along the track it did the same, and its curves mesmerized me. I saw the cause of the undulations: At first the trees were close to the path, then set back, and where they were in retreat the heat had escaped, leaving hard frost. This observation was so obvious, yet no less delightful for that. Most obvious things will go unnoticed and un-enjoyed.

I amused myself with the thought that one day I would find meaning in the tiny jagged patterns of frost crystals, the ones that hung from a burdened bramble leaf by my side.

The sun had read the script and its light ran perfectly toward me, filling the white path to the southeast. Late in the day we find frost where there is shade, tucked in by the foliage on the south side of east-west tracks and to the north side of taller obstacles, like buildings or trees. Frost compasses become intrinsic quickly; they bed down and feel neat, logical, sensible, comfortable, even. It is no wonder, then, that the frost compasses sprinkled all around me made me uneasy. They were *wrong*.

Scattered among the well-grazed grass there were countless tufts, bumps, and mounds—the ground was far from level. And next to each of these protrusions there was a small patch of frost, about as long as each bump was tall. But it was on the *wrong* side. Each white smudge was consistently on the southwest side. There was no mistaking it, and at first no liking it, either. It unsettled me. Analytical thought took over.

Of course. At some point the air temperature had risen above freezing and warmer air was being carried over the ground by the northeasterly breeze. Everything the breeze touched was thawing fast, but where it couldn't reach, the frost lingered. I was looking at wind-thaw—not sun-thaw—compasses.

As is so often the case, this simple observation was reflected in great nature poetry. A few weeks later, re-reading Coleridge's "Frost at Midnight," I was struck by the opening lines:

> *The Frost performs its secret ministry,*
> *Unhelped by any wind.*

I walked for about ten minutes among those rebellious splotches, focusing on little else, before they felt natural to me. And it took my brain the rest of the morning to learn to identify the two frost compasses automatically—but it got there. Intuition reigned again. There remained a few stubborn patches, where perhaps wind and sun had worked together to confuse the picture, which prompted more careful thought. But, on the whole, a wrong had been righted. Out of the corner of my eye I saw the white on a tree stump twinkle north.

I turned for home. My left cheek chilled and my right cheek warmed.

The Clepsydra

THE GOATSBEARD WAS YET TO OPEN as we slid from blackcap to the first chaffinch. There had been clear skies since Aldebaran (a star in the Taurus constellation) rising, and there were just three puddles left from the rain as I entered the ancient wood. It could only be one outstretched-knuckle-length to the dew lifting off the track, and I looked forward to casting my shortest shadow of the year. I felt the painful tickle of summer in my nostrils.

The common view among naturalists today is that a sense of time in nature is a largely aesthetic joy—we appreciate the dawn chorus in the way we might enjoy a concert. I don't wish to detract from this perspective, but that emphasis overlooks another layer: the practical.

Fortunately, it is not a choice of one or the other. I regularly return to the principle that understanding meaning in nature and the practical value it adds *enhances* the aesthetic. Contrary to Keats's concerns, once we know that a rainbow always appears opposite the sun, a rainbow gives us weather forecasts, helps us navigate, and tells the time without losing any of its beauty. And knowing this makes us more likely to stop and look properly, thereby enhancing the aesthetic experience. A sense of wonder is more likely when we learn to read nature, allowing a practical understanding to be twinned with aesthetic pleasure.

A clepsydra is a clock, an ancient device that used a regulated flow of water to measure and display time. Egg timers, with sand, have better survived the test of time, but the principle is the same: Something flows through a gap at a predictable rate, allowing a volume of collected sand or water to be read as time passes. I haven't chosen that word as a chapter title to show off, but because I'd like us to look at time outdoors in a different way. Alternatives might have been "The Seasons," "Calendar," or "Clock," but they all suggest patterns of thought that I want us to break away from.

Take the word "seasons." It's so familiar in the context of nature that it's near impossible not to think of them: spring, summer, autumn, winter. But that is already a blunting of our awareness: There is a huge difference between early summer and late. The Anishinaabe of Canada see six seasons and, more critically, each is tied not only to the solar calendar, but also to its pairing with environmental events; *tagwaagin* marks the autumnal color change and becomes *oshkibiboon* when the leaves have fallen. The English poet John Clare twinned mistle-thrush song with the arrival of hazel catkins and expected to hear the blackcap as willow catkins turned from white to yellow. But even these are broad brushes. The St. John's wort flowers a few yards from me look different than they did at this time yesterday.

What is the practical view of time outdoors? When we looked at "the edge," we learned to appreciate how activity outdoors is not spread evenly, even in wild areas, but is heavily focused in certain places and along certain lines. The same is true with regard to time: Activity is not evenly spread across the year or the day. We are accustomed to certain peaks—the dawn chorus, spring flowers blossoming—and our particular interests may sharpen that awareness in one or two areas. Lepidopterists are as sensitive to fluctuations in June weather as mycologists are to October twists. Fly-fishers know that their fly may hatch on one particular day—the St. Mark's fly earning its name for its habit of emerging on or near that saint's day, April 25.

The key to gaining an extra sense with time is a greater awareness of the changes and a rekindling of our relationship with the lost pairings. The sun, moon, stars, weather, plants, and animals are all joined by their relationship with time. The lichens on a church reveal its age, but will look more lustrous in the months when the gravestones cast their shortest shadows. This is also when we will find butterflies among them and Scorpius in the night sky.

We cannot be expected to sense the swelling of a crow's testes as they respond to changes in daylight length, but there are many connections that we can feel. Wild cherry and bluebells put on a magnificent show of blossom, high and low, at the same time of year that we see the Lyrid meteors peppering the northeastern night sky, and birdsong fills the air.

We see the birds on the lawn each January morning because the sun has passed the rooftop, thawed the ground, and allowed feeding to begin. The next day, sunrise is a minute earlier, but the gathering may be ten minutes earlier, if there was a little cloud cover during the night; and half an hour earlier if the wind backs to the west. The robins are first, followed by the blackbirds, then the song thrushes.

We may find ourselves part of a time pairing. Why are there more birds on the lawn this morning than usual, and why are they staying later? Last night we were out and didn't feed the cats until eleven PM. Feeling guilty, we gave them more than usual, and they, too, are enjoying sleeping in; they haven't ventured out yet this morning. The bird congregation clock was adjusted by our meeting friends for a drink and staying later than planned.

Let us return to the idea of a water clock to witness a sensitivity we have lost. After it rains, we see that puddles have formed and rivers rise. But in some parts of the world a clock starts, and its ticking can be heard in the language used. Among the Fulani people of the Sahel, who tend their cattle in Burkina Faso, the water features mark time for practical reasons. A *hokuluuru* is a small pond that will contain water for up to a month after rainfall; a *deeku'yal* pond will hold water for a few days; and a *cutorgol* is a watering hole that dries very quickly. A *gedeeru* is a spring that runs dry in the summer, but a *mamasiiru* will flow throughout the year.

It's tempting to think that awareness of the relationship between water and time is driven entirely by the climate and geography of this part of Africa, but that's not true. It is a sensitivity that is necessary for a pastoralist lifestyle. And we can prove this by looking closer to home. "Bourne" is an Old English word for a stream, stemming from Anglo-Saxon, typically one flowing from a spring in a chalk or limestone landscape; a "winterbourne" will not flow during the summer. Many retain a fondness for our old landscape terms, but it was not so long ago that a shepherd who led their flock on a hot day to a dry creek would have viewed things differently. They were unlikely to find themselves in that situation, though; the shepherd would have remained sensitive to the streams that were reliable, not just by the calendar with numbers, but by the one that is reset each time it rains.

There is a track I pass regularly that is lined with puddles on the southern side after heavy rain. After a serious downpour, there will be a string of six in a row, but after two dry days only three remain. It takes a dry fortnight in summer for the last to fade away. Over the past few years I have learned that it is not just the number of dry days that determines the surface water in the land, but the humidity, too. Puddles last longer and ponds lower more slowly during humid spells. The puddle clock runs slower when the air is damp, much like some antique grandfather clocks. As we saw earlier, distant landmarks fade to white in humid air, so the color of a faraway hill can reveal the likelihood of finding water in the pond around the corner.

Eons and Moments

If we look at some signs of time, zooming in from long to short, from eons to moments, we can also look at a few of the pairings our ancestors may have sensed. There are clues to events many millions of years ago in the shape of the land—the more rounded a mountaintop appears, the older it is likely to be. Conical mountains are the youngest—they have not been exposed to the millions of years of erosion that give a softer, more domed appearance. The most perfectly pointed ones may even have been created within the memory of a civilization, in which case they will appear more robustly within the lore of that society. The Hawaiian islands are recent formations, in geological terms at least, and myth relates how Pele, the goddess of fire, formed them. (Her face was spotted, apparently, in a photo of an ash cloud above the Kilauea volcano as recently as 2017.)

Every layer of the ground holds time and stories. In 1995, at Eartham Pit near England's southern shore, archaeologists found human fossil remains dating back half a million years, the earliest human fossils ever to be discovered in the UK. They were found there because at that time it was an ideal site for hunter-gatherers; there was a small cliff overlooking a coastal plain, complete with a watering hole. Hundreds of ax flints were found alongside bones, complete with butchery marks. They may appear to have little bearing on our contemporary outdoors experience, but nothing is random. To this day, if you find evidence of human activity in a hunter-gatherer region, you will see signs of water, animals, hunting, and butchery nearby, too; for centuries explorers have relied upon this truth for their own survival.

Every landscape—its forests, parks, boundaries, overall character—is shaped by its history. The longer a landscape has been left alone, the likelier it is you'll find it rich with historical clues, such as in its ancient trees. A great old oak, for example, has three phases of life, each lasting about three hundred years. It grows, stagnates, then goes into decline:

> For three hundred years, the oak grows and grows,
> For three hundred more, it enjoys repose;
> For three hundred now it downward flows.

Oaks, like many trees, hollow out and begin to collapse in the tertiary stage of life. Each tree species has its life span and so is a marker of time, in the way that every rock is, too. Peach trees are entering old age at 30, but there are yews I sit under regularly that are 2,000 years old. Some pines will live beyond 5,000, and there is one spruce in Sweden that is reputedly 9,500 years old.

Early in this chapter I mentioned walking into an ancient woodland. Many species of plant reveal the age of a woodland. Some reproduce in a way that means it takes them a long time to colonize anywhere. The billions of seeds that may be airborne at any one time may germinate where they land, but the hay-scented woodruff forms slowly expanding mats and can't leap from one place to another. Its presence, along with other ancient-woodland indicators, including wild garlic, yellow archangel, wood sorrel, wood anemone, and moschatel, all indicate woodland that has been established for many hundreds of years. With practice, we quickly sense when we pass into or out of these areas.

Hedges yield their age through their diversity. Hooper's rule argues that you can date a hedge by multiplying the number of woody plant species you count in a thirty-yard stretch by 110 to give its age in years. Hedge hegemons will debate the validity of this method for the rest of time, but it's interesting here for two reasons. First, it does work to some degree: the more species we count, the older the hedge is likely to be; and second, it's a good example of slow versus fast thinking. If you are passionate about hedges, you will start by using this rule, diligently counting species and doing the simple sum. But there will come a time, sooner than you might have guessed, when your brain decides to take the shortcut and a hedge you have only just set eyes on announces its age before you can begin counting. The same process is happening with all that we see outdoors, governed by our interests and experience. The shape of a church, its architecture, will give an instant sense of age to an enthusiast; the shape of the yew in the churchyard will give a sense of age to a tree lover.

The girth of a living tree is the most dependable way of gauging its age. Again, there are slow ways of doing this: divide the circumference in centimeters of a tree growing in open country by 2.5, or that of one in woodland by 1.25, and you have an estimated age. But our eyes give us an intuitive sense of age, and if we remember to be more impressed by girth in woodland, a few notable specimens will stand out that may not have otherwise. Bark ages in a way that is reminiscent of our skin; the smoother the bark, the younger the tree. Rough bark grows upward from the ground.

When trees are cut down we find one of the most familiar time signatures in their rings. It is well known that each ring marks a year of a tree's life and that the width of each ring gives us some insight into the climatic conditions of the year in question: The lighter, larger part of each ring represents the larger cells and faster growth of the spring; the darker lines reflect the smaller cells and slower growth of summer. It is less well known that these annual time stamps are widespread: Hunters in the north know that you can age a seal or polar bear by looking at the rings in their claws—easier after rather than during a hunt, I suspect.

Closer to home, there are myriad signs within plants and animals that mark the difference between youth and maturity. Ivy leaves that have several lobes and points are immature; those with a single point are mature. Blackbirds with a yellow beak are displaying a sign of maturity; in their first year it is duller. Once you are used to spotting this, you may also notice a yellow ring around the mature bird's eye, but not around the youngster's. And, as with humans, we can expect substantial differences in behavior between young and mature animals, one common difference being their savvy: Youngsters are more curious and even reckless. The animals that learn the dangers become cautious adults; the others don't make it. We sense that the blackbird with the dull beak is more likely to take the food at our feet; the one with the yellow eye ring will keep its distance.

Felled wood has its own clock. Alder and cherry oxidize and quickly turn a vibrant orange before fading. Ash turns from pink to orange to almost white, while the heartwood turns almost black. We could continue with details of the age of trees and the timing of their felling, but what we are really interested in is the connection and therefore insight that these give us.

The longer a tree has lived and the longer the time since it was felled give us a sense of what to expect in the more modest life around it. As we saw in "the celebration," every plant and animal is sensitive to levels of light, nutrients, wind, and water, and any tree that dominates a patch of land will shape them. But a tree that has come down will trigger a new eruption of life, as each of these variables changes dramatically.

What may once have appeared as merely a pair of random tree stumps can offer a richer story. One was from an ancient tree that came down a few years ago, another a younger tree that fell recently. The life you will see around the first, from plants to insects, will be very different from that around the second: In the case of the ancient tree, a seismic change has taken place in that small environment, and enough time has passed to reflect that. In the case of the younger tree, the change has been more modest and nature has had little time to display it.

The foresters in my local wood are busy clearing a stand of Norway spruce. I was fond of the spruces and will miss them—they offered Nordic allure to one area of the beechwood. But I am also excited to witness the change with each walk over the next few years—the wildflowers that previously would not have stood a chance and the butterflies they will invite in. Soon the girth of the stumps, the number of rings, and the color of the wood will tally with the colors of the flowers, the lichens, and the activity of the insects.

The trees, light, and lichens form three parts of the same slow timepiece. Trees throw shade, which inhibits lichens, and the lichens that grow mark time. Walk alongside any light-colored stone wall (which is more likely to be alkaline and therefore lichen-friendly than a dark one), look for scattered trees growing along its southern side, and you will see a colorful clock painted on that wall. To sharpen your innate sense in this area, notice the places where lichens are now struggling due to new plant growth—the vibrancy of their color may have faded—and where there is a "lichen shadow," an area in which you would expect lichens but none are visible, a tree has recently been removed.

There is a tradition for using plants and animals to predict the future, but most methods that offer long-term forecasts are of dubious value. Nature reacts constantly to changes in the environment, but rarely foretells them. Trees respond to the previous seasons, forming buds in those conditions, but they cannot anticipate unusually hot, cold, wet, or dry weather. In spring, plants judge when to act based on two main triggers: the length of night and the temperature. The variability in seasonal timings from one year to the next comes from fluctuations in seasonal temperatures, since night length decreases in a regular and predictable way. One warm day does not a spring make, and scientists have discovered that trees are capable of counting the number of warm days. But they are not infallible, and all plants and animals remain vulnerable to an early warm spell.

This is another difference between the ancient/indigenous/farming perception and the modern urban one: A warm spell in early spring will prompt very different gut reactions. An unseasonably warm early-spring day that allows the coats to come off will be welcomed by many, but sets alarm bells ringing for others. It is a critical period for farming—"Better a wolf in the field than a fine February," and as the Bedouin say, "March sustains the crop or March destroys the crop." Equally, a later than normal cold snap will wreak havoc. Where I live in South East England, the south-facing land is increasingly being turned over to grapevines; in the past ten years the area devoted to vineyards in England and Wales has more than doubled. There was a vicious late frost in 2017, which killed off three-quarters of the crop in some areas. Everything is paired, one cold morning with the price of wine years later.

A colder than normal winter will lead tree leaves to unfurl earlier the following spring. But one of the best ways to spot early signs and precursors of spring is to look low down. Close to the ground, the temperature is higher on average in spring than higher up, and this, combined with less exposure to harsh winds, gives the smaller trees a head start, bringing them into leaf about two weeks before the taller ones.

The arrow of time for plant signs is usually backward—they reflect past conditions and remain ignorant about what lies ahead—but there is one very widespread indication of what the future holds that is often overlooked. When we see a large, proud tree, we expect it to be there the following year and, barring freak storms, for many years to come. But all the lower plants are sending a message within their own life cycle. Once we know whether each plant is an annual, biennial, or perennial, we are being offered a small insight into what the future holds. Annuals complete their full life cycle within a year and die. Biennials live for two years, typically flowering and producing seeds in the second. Perennials grow for several years. Horticulturalists are familiar with this way of looking at nature—it is key to garden planning—but in a wilder context, we think mostly of the plants we see as perennials: We expect to see the same thing the following year. Most ferns and members of the aster family, including the daisy, are perennial and will be back. But annuals have no right to that spot the following year, unless they win the competition for it all over again, so they are most sensitive to the change indicated by a felled tree. Biennials are perhaps the most interesting, as we can usually tell which year of their life cycle we're looking at and get an instant sense of what will follow. A foxglove with no flowers one summer promises many the next, and that will be its last. So, we can see now how the color of the felled stump and the lack of flowers on the foxglove are linked; when the stump has another twelve months' color, the land around it will resonate with the rich purples of the foxgloves.

Seasonal changes are familiar to most of us—they're hard to miss altogether. But modern life has little time for the pairings that once leaped out and get lost now in the general commotion. The V formations of geese skeins heading north in April no longer remind us to look east for the V of the constellation Virgo. In cold climates, any mental map must be redrawn as landmarks disappear under heavy snow, but as the stranglehold of winter yields to spring, we might sense the sap rising in the dark holes that grow around the trees. The spring sun heats the tree, the warming trunk thaws the snow, and the snow retreats. The growing hole in the snow is a cue to tap the sap.

The Bedouin know to sow crops when the Pleiades appear in the night sky. When Canopus appears, there is a risk of floods, and they must not camp in the wadis—low-lying desert areas—but when "Sirius hangs over Canopus like a bucket rope," winter is yielding to spring. The winter rains associated with the orange giant star in Taurus, Aldebaran, may support life low down, even as higher areas remain arid:

> *O happy valley flowing with Aldebaran's showers*
> *The highlands are in drought, while it is rich in flowers.*

The Inuit know that the appearance of Aajuuk, the Two Sunbeams (stars in our constellation Aquila), signals that it will be only a week until the sun rolls a touch above the southern horizon again, ending the oppressive period of dark daytime. These are the shapes of time.

Time and Behavior

We have not lost our senses altogether and still cherish any nature prepared to stick its head above the parapet, the early-leafers like gooseberry, honeysuckle, and lords-and-ladies. And we must salute those flowers that jump the gun—blackthorn's impatience sprays hedges with white flowers before its leaves are out. At the end of the year we can admire the foolhardiness of ivy flowering well into winter and the insects that flock to it—bees rejoice in its resilience.

The passage of time is marked in our senses of taste and touch. I love the spring shoots of spruce: They have a cleansing scent when crushed between the fingers, and it is sanitizing to nibble them. They are better suited to making tea than eating raw, and my ten-year-old's face is something else when he chews an acerbic one. Spruce shoots have a friendly softness to them at this time, almost rubbery and with no harshness yet in the needles. I knew we had left spring and found summer when I plucked one from the tree the other day and brought it to my nose, only to flinch as the now firmer, sharper needles pricked my nostril. Many other leaves show a marked softness early in the year—beech, another favorite, is like the most delicate papyrus in its first weeks.

Songbirds that were bashful in late summer are ready to approach come December, head cocked one way and then the other. All living organisms have clocks that determine not only what we will see, but also their behavior. Robins are early risers. We hear their song near the start of the dawn chorus, but they are also early feeders and more belligerent as day begins.

Most animals are busier and more mobile at the start and end of the day, and this is when we are most likely to spot them. In the middle of the day, there is a reticence or lethargy in wildlife that can be frustrating if we are not expecting it.

Once we are familiar with this simple pattern, it leads to ingrained levels of expectation. A walk in the countryside as the sun rises is accompanied by keen anticipation, but when the sun is high in the sky I go out more in hope. I see evidence of badgers near me all day, but I expect to set eyes on them only near dusk.

I fondly remember showing my family the shy *Mimosa pudica* plant, a common weed in Thailand, during a holiday walk. Its leaves recoil visibly when you touch it, and plants that move are guaranteed to entertain. Mimosas earned their place in the history of our understanding of nature for a related but different habit: the way their leaves open and close at the start and end of each day. One of Alexander the Great's admirals, Androsthenes, noted that tamarind leaves open during the day and close at night; this is our earliest written record of "nyctinasty," plant reactions to the nightly drop in light levels. Goatsbeard has many other colloquial names, including Jack-go-to-bed-at-noon; its flowers close by midday. Rather wonderfully, although we have been spotting this effect for thousands of years, scientists are still not agreed on why it happens.

Jean-Jacques d'Ortous de Mairan was endowed with a great name and even better job description: He was a pioneering chronobiologist. As we have seen, before the eighteenth century it was widely known that plants react to the day-night cycle—even the common daisy (its name is a corruption of "day's eye") opens and closes each day—but it was assumed that varying levels of light explained all. In 1729 Mairan performed the simplest of experiments, which proved that something a little more significant was going on. He kept a mimosa plant in the dark. The plant continued to open and close its leaves in sync with the daily cycle. Strange. Mairan didn't provide all the answers, but his simple demonstration lit the fuse of curiosity that led to our understanding of the daily cycles of nature: the circadian rhythms. We now know that animals have more than one internal clock and several ingenious ways of keeping them synchronized.

The mimosa plant was able to open and close its leaves on time for a few days in the dark, but not forever. Steadily it started to lose time, opening at night and closing during the day. The same is true for all plants and animals: We are all capable of tracking time without external reference for a while, but steadily we lose track. It wasn't until the second half of the twentieth century that we started to understand how nature keeps time, and the picture is still developing.

It turns out that light is critical, particularly blue light, but not because it is the clock itself, but because it is a key *zeitgeber*, or time giver, for many organisms. Blue light helps keep the clocks in sync with the day, but proteins are responsible for the timekeeping itself. We don't need to delve too deeply into the microbiology to grasp this, not least because we may have personal experience of it: We will feel sleepy in the middle of the day if we fly to the other side of the world, until the light zeitgeber has had a chance to reset our protein clocks.

Time, Patterns, and Pairs

At this point you would be justified in thinking, This is all good stuff, but how does it impact on our practical experience of the outdoors? Once we are attuned to nature's clocks, we will begin to sense what's coming. Until that point, it's like being at a railway station without information boards or clocks: Trains arrive and leave, but it's hard to know what will be along next.

The dawn chorus has earned this title because we find it easier to lump the birds together in a choir, but there is a rolling sequence. In my part of the world, robins, blackbirds, and wrens precede song thrushes, blackcaps, and chiffchaffs, which in turn come before chaffinches. But even if we aren't familiar with the exact species, we can get a good sense of what will come next because birdsong fills sound niches. If you hear two or three birds singing, the next to join in will sound different and probably fill the obvious gap. The same is true of insects, like cicadas, and frogs (in the tropics you may notice how the frogs grow quiet at dawn, a reversal of the temperate trend for noise levels to ramp up with the sun). Sensing this sequencing and gap filling allows an intuitive feel for what comes next, but the real insight comes from pairings.

Recall that there is a part of our brain that monitors the things it thinks we want or need to be aware of. In a café it might be gossip, but out in the wild we can shift this alert system back from whence it came. We do this by returning to making pairs.

One of my favorite habits is to daydream in the forest at dusk on a fine day. I've noticed that many animal noises do not rouse me from this lack-adaisical state, but others do. The chink-chinking of the bedward-bound blackbirds doesn't stir me, but the roosting squawk of pheasants does. It's not the brash volume of the sounds, but that it often coincides with the earliest patrols of crepuscular mammals. It is uncanny how often I am reclining against a tree, eyelids heavy, when a flapping, vocal pheasant signals its bedtime. I remain still but open my eyes to watch a fox amble past. The joy of pairings!

The dawn chorus is a daily beating of the bounds, a reestablishment of territory. It's the putting of a coat on a favorite library chair each morning. Dawn is a good time for the chorus because the cooler air allows the sounds to travel farther and it is not a prime time for feeding. Knowing this helps to explain how hard it is to surprise animals at this time of day: the cool air close to the ground transmits the sound of our footsteps farther—the dawn chorus becomes the sound of skittishness in the forest.

Animals are creatures of habit, and their routines are governed by the zeitgeber sun. They often follow the same commute each day, a walk or flight from home in the trees to water, food, and back. I see the same buzzard patrolling the same tree line at the same time each morning. We might expect to notice this in birds and mammals, but the same is true for all creatures. There are so many steady patterns that we experience but don't fully click with.

Perhaps swimming in the sea on holiday we are stung by a jellyfish before lunch three days in a row, but our friend who prefers to swim before supper never is: Jellyfish go to sleep at about four PM, sinking to the ocean floor and remaining there until dawn the following day. The wasps always spoil your picnic because they have learned where and *when* you like to eat. We don't yet know that for certain, but it seems logical since we *do* know that bees learn to time their visits to certain flowers to arrive when the nectar is most available; it varies not just with the season, but also the time of day.

Experiments have proved that bees, birds, and many other animals have a dependable inner clock that allows them to use the sun as a reliable compass. Time and direction are two sides of the same sun coin for bees, birds, humans, and all other creatures; if you know one, the sun will offer the other. If you know it is the middle of the day, the sun will be due south. If you know the sun is due south, you can deduce that it is the middle of the day. If you know it is midsummer, you know that the sun will rise in the northeast; if you see the sun rise in the northeast, you can deduce that it is midsummer.

We are more likely to notice animal habits if they support our own. For many years agricultural laborers were sensitive to the signs in nature that meant the sweat and toil were nearing their end. The streaming dark lines of roosting rooks rang a bell in the sky to end the shift. And we are more likely to appreciate any plants and animals that buck the trend and offer us stimulation after the sun has set. The scent of honeysuckle or the calls of owls in the early evening are common favorites.

The sleepiness of animals shapes their visibility. You may be in the right place to see a certain animal and there may be a lot of that species about, but if it's asleep, it will be hard to spot. The amount of sleep animals needs varies hugely: Horses can get by with as little as two hours per day, but bats need twenty.

It is not only living organisms that mark time over the day. Shadows shrink in the morning, reach their shortest in the middle of the day, and grow toward infinity in the late afternoon. This effect is painting all that we see outdoors: A furrowed field will look dramatically different at the start and end of the day compared to its appearance when the sun is high. Animal tracks stand out better near dawn and dusk—the lower the sun, the longer the shadow, and the more dramatic the small wrinkles in the land that appear.

As we saw in "the browse," a bite taken out of a leaf might tell us which animal has passed by, but saliva still on the leaf screams that it is only a few minutes ahead of us. Every lump of dung reveals something about its former owner and the time since they passed. Steam rising from it on a cool morning tells us that the horse is still close by, but as the clock ticks, the dung stops glistening as it dries—more quickly on its southern side. The white pillars of pilobolus mold congregate to mark the several days that have passed. This fungus gives rise, too, to one of nature's more marvelous compasses. The mold grows on a stalk, which orients itself toward the morning light—the stalks tend to point southeast.

Pilobolus is also known as the "hat-thrower" fungus because it launches its spores a couple of yards away from the dung it is growing on. It does this to escape the "zone of repugnance." The fungi's life cycle depends on it being eaten by another grass grazer, which won't happen if it starts life too close to its home dung—grazers avoid the grass near dung. The dark spores escape in a tiny exploding sac of liquid, traveling with the greatest acceleration of anything known in nature. Racing drivers may occasionally experience forces of 5g; the pilobolus spore is launched with 20,000g. But however explosive the start of its aerial voyage, the spore must also avoid any tall grasses that are growing next to the dung, and there are likely to be some because of the zone of repugnance. They do this by launching from a stalk that has grown toward the light. It is a phenomenon, albeit on a much smaller scale, that we see in any opening in a woodland: Green plants, such as nettles, lean toward the opening in the canopy.

The habits of this delightful organism underline a broader important point: We derive meaning from nature by understanding it on its own terms, not by layering our needs on to it. The fungus can give us a sense of time and compass direction, but it does not care about days, hours, minutes, or north, south, east, or west; it responds to light, which happens to come more abundantly from the southeast in the morning. Remembering this improves our approach to all natural navigation techniques and indeed all nature deduction. In practical terms, this means that the fungus stalks will point close to southeast, all other things being equal, but they will point north if there happens to be an opening in a dense woodland canopy only on that side.

Many periodic events refuse to be governed by the sun's daily or annual patterns. Conifers reproduce annually, but deciduous trees, like beech and oak, flood the market with their nuts and acorns every few years. It is evolution's trick for beating the hungry boar and deer. There is not enough food each year for animal numbers to remain constantly high, so they drop until a "mast year," when the ground is saturated with more than the animals can hope to polish off in one season. The uneaten seeds start life as saplings. Boar and deer numbers shoot up and the cycle begins again.

The same cycles of rising and dropping numbers can be seen in the populations of predator and prey; in an area with few foxes, the rabbit population explodes, the foxes feast, and their numbers shoot up, too; the extra foxes whittle down the rabbits until the foxes begin to starve and the cycle begins again.

The moon's cycle lasting 29.5 days makes it a good anchor for many of the annual events that don't fit with the sun's rhythms. The Maple Sugar Moon follows the Hard Crust on Snow Moon for the Potawatomi of North America, but these pairings stem from observation, not causality; the moon is not the driving force behind them. In fact, on land, surprisingly few cycles are governed by the moon; the tides being the best known.

In Agiuppiniq Island, in northern Canada, the locals are tuned to a relationship between the ice and the moon's phases. A full moon leads to faster currents, which pull apart a particular crack in the ice, making fishing possible. Farther south in Canada, a Cree Indian guide called Noah, from Kawartha Lakes, near the border with the US, was able to guarantee good fishing for his clients. He relied on a guiding force he referred to as the Great Spirit, and those who used his services were certain he sensed things they couldn't. A witness to his skills wrote afterward, "These big fish couldn't talk, but their actions and the type of interaction held messages and instructions to those who could interpret them. . . . His presence practically guaranteed success for everyone;

there was no doubt Noah 'knew.'" Interestingly, the closest that the angler got to reproducing the Cree guide's skills was by following tables that showed the moon phases.

We know that animals that have gone into hiding will reappear at some point, and that this clock will be shaped by the trigger for their hiding. But biology sets a more insistent clock in some places—the Inuit know that a seal that has gone below must resurface within five minutes. And beyond our senses, regular changes are taking place on fast and slow cycles—humpback whales change their song every five years or so.

In some communities, the layers of time come together to create a definite moment. The Ávila Runa of the Amazonian Ecuador know to expect the flying leafcutter ants to take to the wing around August, but they need to predict the precise moment as the ants are an important food source. The critical day follows a period of storms, when dry weather has returned. And the exact time that they will fly is always immediately predawn (5:10 AM, according to one researcher!). We know that dawn and dusk are times of fervent activity for animals, so one tactic prey employs to throw off predators is to emerge in great numbers just before dawn. It has the added advantage of avoiding most of the nocturnal predators, like bats, too. By tuning to the season and the weather, and by studying the activity at the nest, looking for guard ants clearing the holes, the locals can pinpoint the exact moment that the ants will fly.

We return to the moschatel wildflower. Its nickname, "town hall clock," would seem fitting, but actually refers to its shape. It does mark time, when it flowers in early spring, and acknowledges nightfall by emitting a musky scent. If the plant is bruised by the trampling of an animal, it loses its scent. We sense time passing in the scent of a flower and the passage of an animal in its fading scent, just as we sense both in the lost gleam of dung.

There is a daunting richness in the way nature marks time, but as always, we can keep it simple by observing pairs. We notice that rabbits are especially active when the ragwort they avoid blossoms among the shorn grass. We learn to expect the blossom when we see Taurus race ahead of sunrise. The shape in the predawn sky and the color yellow give us a sense of the animals around the corner.

PART V

A World of Signs: Digging Deeper

Labels That Come to Life

*C*ARDAMINE PRATENSIS, TO GIVE THE cuckooflower, or "lady's smock," its formal name, is a favorite of mine, because it is a strong personal reminder of the way we can learn to see nature again. For many years I was used to seeing this pretty pale pink flower growing in damp meadows near the River Arun, but I rarely spotted it elsewhere. Early on I learned to call it the cuckooflower, but each winter I tended to forget that name, along with a generous selection of other sporadic seasonal sights.

Then one spring many years ago I saw the flower and instantly thought of the river. At that moment, and not for the first time, I couldn't recall the flower's name. After thumbing through a guide, I was reminded of it and learned something new: that *pratensis* is Latin for "meadow." But somewhere deeper, I already knew what the plant was telling me: that when I found it, I was approaching a damp meadow and a river. It is the plant or animal that contains the sign, not the words we attach to them.

When Alexander von Humboldt traveled in the Orinoco region of South America, he was deeply impressed by the ability of the indigenous people he met to find their way through dense jungle and to identify the plants they encountered. Humboldt reported that they could identify trees just by tasting the bark. When Humboldt tried it, he failed: All fifteen trees he sampled tasted the same to him. There may not appear to be much that links these two observations—how the locals could find their way and recognize species—but the connection is fundamental.

Academics sometimes use the number of wild plants and animals we can identify as a means of gauging outdoor wisdom, and those seeking a way of reconnecting with nature may feel, regrettably, that it is largely about identification. This is probably a hangover from the smash, grab, and label era of natural history. But to believe that identification is the goal is to miss the point.

Identification is never more than half the challenge, and on its own never represents wisdom or insight. There is little or no value in being able to summon names if they lead nowhere. The modern view is that habitat can help us to identify a species, but the ancient view was the other way round: Identification was of little value without it being an indication of danger, use, or habitat.

In the 1950s the British-American anthropologist Colin Turnbull lived with an isolated group of Pygmies for three years in a region that is now part of the Democratic Republic of the Congo. During his time deep in the forest, he observed in detail how the Pygmies related to each other and their environment. In his classic book *The Forest People*, we glimpse not just the lifestyle of those people but a reflection of our own, too. Most importantly, we're given a clue to the bridge we need to cross to regain some of our lost wisdom.

When a girl called Amina traveled into the forest from a nearby village to stay with the Pygmies, it was clear that she wouldn't last long. "She did not even know . . . which vines to follow to find the delicacies hidden in the ground by their roots. She belonged to another world." Amina lived close to the Pygmies, yet she had lost the ability to recognize plants and what they indicated. For the Pygmies, this created a great gulf between her and their way of life.

We find similar perspectives throughout indigenous communities. In the Amazon the wisest are called "vegetalistas"—those who possess the greatest insight into the plants that surround their communities. Among the Bedouin, someone who is unhelpful might be called "more worthless than tamarisk," an insult that would be used only in a community where plant wisdom is widespread. It wouldn't work in Westernized societies, although tamarisk is widespread, because our practical relationship with this plant has withered. Tamarisk burns quickly to ash, so it has no value to the Bedouin as fuel for fires. The purpose of identification is to unlock the meaning and value of the plants and animals. But how do we relearn this?

With time spent outdoors we will all learn to identify a growing number of animals and plants. We have evolved and were born to do this—all our ancestors could do it. It starts in childhood, when we recognize a few familiar shapes and colors; after spotting the things that can hurt us—wasps, nettles, and brambles—we learn the more distinctive shapes and colors, the lobes of an oak leaf, the magnificent form of a swan, or the white-spotted bright-red dome of the fly agaric fungus. The more time we spend outdoors, the more our collection grows.

I see coal tits, blue tits, and great tits regularly. There are size and color differences that make separating them fairly straightforward, but we shouldn't expect to be able to do it on first encountering them. More typically we learn certain markers: The great tit is larger than the coal tit and has a black vertical line down its breast. The "blue tit has a blue hat" and a black line through its eye. We can learn and recall the differences when getting to know the birds. If we apply them a few times over a few weeks, our brain will take over and create the shortcut.

If we maintain an interest, we learn to identify some things without always being able to articulate how we did it. Every bird has its own shape and colors, but it also has its own signature habits and flight pattern. And this is where things become more interesting psychologically. We can quickly learn to identify an animal or plant by broad category, without necessarily being able to pinpoint the species or name. We cannot confuse the steep descent of a hawk with the flight of a similar-sized pigeon, even out of the corner of our eye.

It is this simple ability, available to us all, that ironically makes some people feel they were born without it; they see others using fast recognition, but don't know how they got there. Those with a rural upbringing will doubtless remember parents or grandparents pointing out these things—the last vestiges of important rites of passage in wilder indigenous communities. Time that was once dedicated to differentiating between edible and poisonous roots in the woods is now given to warnings about communicating with strangers online.

The ability to identify birds without understanding how we are doing it even has its own name: it's called knowing the "jizz" of a bird. (This may be a corruption of GISS—General Impression, Size, and Shape; the etymology of the word is uncertain, but its meaning is clear, and it's useful for our purposes.) If we come to know the general appearance, behavior, and habits of a bird, then we know its "jizz," which allows us to identify a bird quickly, without recourse to sifting through our database consciously. It offers good insight into the difference between slow and fast thinking outdoors.

I once found myself among reed beds in the RSPB nature reserve in South West England. A group of us were there to broadcast, explain, and elaborate on the dawn chorus. It was a bizarre job that felt even stranger as sleep deprivation kicked in. At about four AM, I quizzed the local RSPB warden, Steve Hughes, off air. We enjoyed listening to reed warblers, coots, and the unbelievable booming bitterns. As we listened to a faint new sound in the pitch darkness, Steve explained something intriguing: "It really shocked me the first time I tried to identify bird sounds in the dark. It was so much harder than I expected. I couldn't understand why it was a struggle, until I realized that it was much easier to identify a bird if you can see the area the sound is coming from, *even when you can't see the bird*. The microhabitat suggests the likely suspect, and then the bird responsible becomes obvious much more quickly than when we can't see its surroundings. There are loads of subliminal cues that our eyes pick up that make identifying birds from their calls easier, even if we think we are doing it just by listening."

Fast thinking takes the context into account automatically, as part of the pattern.

Our collection of telltales grows to reflect our interests and environment. Those who live near deciduous woods learn that beeches have signature torpedo-shaped buds. Ash trees have branches with ends that curve upward in their trademark way. Wild cherry trees have distinctive reddish-brown bark, with horizontal "stripes" (or "lenticels," open pores that allow gas exchange).

We learn tricks for spotting broader groups: As a rule, moths have feathered antennae, butterflies don't; centipedes have one pair of legs per segment, millipedes have two. And we learn to recognize sex, too. It's important to forest rangers to be able to tell the sex of any deer they see. They know that a female roe deer can be easily identified, even as a silhouette in fading light, by her "anal tush," a patch of hair that hangs from her rear and is sometimes mistaken for a tail. Berries mark any holly tree as female.

Identification patterns go beyond the visual. The acrid musk of fox scat marches far on a breeze, and there are patterns that help with sounds like birdsong. Song thrushes have a wide variety of songs, but habitually repeat them twice before changing tune.

Once we know the telltales, species greet us instantly, like a handshake; walking through the woods becomes an experience rich with automatic recognition as we pass old friends. The next step is to appreciate that every species has meaning, and this is the point where the signs start to become attached in our memories. For example, beeches mean dry ground, so the torpedo bud and dry ground become paired.

To keep things simple, the aim is:

1. To learn to recognize the things we see in nature, with or without a name.

2. To remember that each one is a sign and learn what that sign is. If a name helps with this, then it has some purpose. Otherwise it is dispensable.

3. To practice making the association until it becomes automatic.

What does that look like in practice?

We are unlikely to confuse deciduous trees and conifers, but refining our ability to recognize a tree and remembering its meaning gives us the sign. Unlike many other conifers, pine trees lose their lower branches and can be identified by the shape this creates from a distance. To my eyes, the pines' habit of keeping upper branches makes them appear to be reaching out with arms. Pines need lots of light, so they are more common on the southern side of forests than on the north. The shapes of the trees we see and the aspect of a wood in the distance are connected in a way that can, with practice, become a familiar pattern. We see south reach out to us.

The comma butterfly is recognizable by its distinctive jagged outline. Its preferred habitat is woodland edges. It can be a struggle to remember this sort of detail at first, but associations help. I spent a while remembering that woodland edges are often jagged lines, which kept the association in my mind until the fast-thinking part of my brain adopted it. Now I see a jagged woodland edge in the outline of the butterfly, sometimes before I remember its name.

Some of the best plants to befriend early on are those that are instantly identifiable and carry a simple, dependable sign. Ferns are just such a widespread group. They are an interesting collection of plants, with neither seeds nor flowers, but most carry the message: moisture. There are at least ten thousand known kinds of ferns, but we can recognize members of the family from their familiar fronds; we are most likely to encounter those that thrive in moist sites. Moisture is a sign of shade, and shade can indicate a northern aspect. Soon, instead of scrambling to identify the name of the species, we sense recognition and a sign. We sense north in the pattern of fern fronds without knowing their name.

Three Luminaries

THE GWI, A HUNTER-GATHERER PEOPLE OF southern Africa, can sense water at a distance by observing the flight patterns of birds, and can work out where to find mammals by watching cattle egrets and oxpeckers. They know the animals in their environment have typical behaviors: physical customs they call *kxodzi*, and language, *kxwisa*. When hunting, the Gwi identify eighteen different categories of behavior in the animals they observe.

Agriculture led to specialization of knowledge, and for that wisdom to be focused in fewer people. The traditional hunter-gatherer would have been able to identify more plants and animals than those living in an agricultural society. But farmers can produce more food from a small number of crops in a smaller area than the hunter-gatherer covered. This is not a better-worse argument; it highlights how outdoor wisdom became more narrowly focused. Then, as the technology that accompanied the Industrial Revolution allowed the few, the farmers, to become ever more productive, ignorance about outdoor ways blossomed in the many.

The good news is that science nurtured a problem, but also offered a solution, which developed from ancient times and accelerated over the past five hundred years. In the fourth century BCE, Aristotle studied animals and their behavior and wrote down his observations. That may not sound dramatic, but consider the direction of travel over the past millennia and its importance can be seen.

Outdoors wisdom was passed on by oral tradition. After the agricultural revolution of around ten thousand years ago, the wisdom about the outdoors was held in a perilously small group of people, and the only thread passing it on to future generations was lore. And this was happening just as that rural wisdom became culturally less important—the desire for stories about wild roots and rodents withers when you're confident that you will not starve. For millennia, the wisdom has been held by a shrinking number, a trend that continued with only minor reversals until the small renaissance over the past few decades. Stories have their place, as we will see, but they are less vulnerable to time when the wisdom they contain is also written down.

Aristotle's scientific and academic approach has proved the bulwark against the uncertain transmission of knowledge by oral tradition. Once it's written down, future generations have a choice as to whether or not to rekindle an interest in it. Even if there has been no enthusiasm in an area for centuries, the savvy is still there, frozen in time on the page—ancient library fires and other calamities allowing.

Aristotle proved the method, but it was a slow start. Some of his classical descendants, Roman authors like Cato the Elder, codified knowledge about outdoor methods, but they added little insight of their own. And, perhaps understandably, they focused on agriculture rather than wilder matters. Then, in the early seventeenth century, things took a leap forward.

In 1623 Charles Butler, a beekeeper, studied the behavior of his bees and wrote a seminal work, *The Feminine Monarchie, or the Historie of Bees*. It continues to be read by the keenest apiarists to this day. Butler established the queen bee on her throne and made many other pioneering observations, including a few forgivable errors, but what really sets his work apart were his motive and method. Butler was recording his observations of the social behavior of an animal in a systematic way so that others could refer to and disseminate his knowledge. For the first time, someone from another place, another era, someone who had never met Butler or perhaps even seen a beehive, could learn a great deal about bees. And where Butler and his bees first went, thousands of observers and their species have followed. Butler showed the way for the lesser Darwins of this world. And the modern outdoors person who is keen to relearn rare skills is indebted to them all. We can draw inspiration and knowledge not only from indigenous communities, but also from the ever-growing academic field of nature study and the pioneers within it.

I have benefited from such wisdom on thousands of occasions, often accelerating my understanding of patterns and associations I have noticed. Only yesterday I was able to confirm that the wildflower yellow archangel, which I had seen on damp, north-facing banks in my local chalk wood, has been studied and found to like alkaline soil, high moisture, and low light levels. The work of those who have gone before turned a suspicion into confidence and accelerated my intuitive sense of place and direction from this plant.

Indigenous wisdom and scientific research are our first two luminaries, which speed our rekindling of these skills. The third is close to home: domestic animals. Pet owners will be familiar with the signs that their animals use to convey restlessness, hunger, irritation, or anger. But we get a step closer to the wild with animals that are given more space, like horses.

Like most animals, horses display some signs that we can read without much experience and others that are less intuitive at first. If we see a horse with its head down, a hanging bottom lip, and a slumped hip, we may instantly sense it is asleep. However, if a horse lifts its head, exposes its teeth, and makes a strange face, something between a smirk and a grimace, we are witnessing the "flehmen response." This peculiar contortion is named after the German word for baring the upper teeth, and it helps the animal to smell more acutely by allowing odors to reach the sensitive nostrils. To the inexperienced it may appear to be a sign of anger, irritation, or distress, whereas in fact the horse has picked up an intriguing scent, perhaps feces, urine, or a possible mate.

The ears and head are flags to the horseperson, revealing attention and mood. If the ears are forward, the horse is paying positive attention to something in front; if they are back, the horse is focusing on something behind, but quite possibly with anxiety. If the ears are pinned back, the horse is angry and we need to take care, as it may bite or kick. Ears out to the side indicate a relaxed, sleeping, or oblivious horse; they are not attentive to their immediate surroundings and may be spooked by any surprises close by. A horse with a lowered head is relaxed, and one with a raised head is alert to something in the distance. If the head is only slightly down and is snaking from side to side, the horse is in an agitated, combative mood.

As we learn to recognize and then familiarize ourselves with these signs, we can enjoy noticing the moment at which our brain takes a useful shortcut. What starts as a plod—"Oh, the head is down and ears are out. The horse is relaxed"—will quickly become a sense of a relaxed horse. This is our bridge, and our observation of domesticated animals is as much about proving to ourselves that the method works as anything else.

At first, we will want to keep things as simple as possible, but it is important to remember that no animal sign can be viewed in isolation; they are part of their environment. Adam Shereston has specialized in training horses by communicating with them—many people call it "horse whispering." When we met, he told me that he tailors his work according to the time of day. Horses, like all prey animals, have to be warier of predators at dawn and dusk, when their biorhythms make them more alert, sensitive, and responsive. Adam explained, "If I have a horse who is in 'dull out mode'—that is they've started to lose their sensitivity through the over-domestication of stable life—I will try to work with them at dawn and dusk. This is when I'll get a better, more natural response out of them. But if I have a horse that has been frightened and has become nervous and too flighty, then the middle of the day is the best time. The horse will naturally be more sedate then."

They are also sensitive to wind direction, and Adam prefers any nervous horse to have the wind behind them, providing a more relaxed setting. Even prey animals with great peripheral vision, like horses, will have blind spots directly behind them, and if they can smell what is behind them, it makes them less nervous. High winds make horses edgy, and Adam believes this is because they make the grasses flex, so the horse finds it harder to detect any animal motion.

Physical space is also very important. Horses are flight animals; they will choose to run away from disturbing situations rather than confront them. If they are confined and escape is impossible, flight animals fight back, kicking, biting, and striking out with their front feet in the case of horses. Adam has brought around countless difficult horses over the years, but never yet been hurt by them.

In my conversations with him, I've also been struck by how important he considers his own frame of mind. This is not a one-way street. He pressed his fingers to either side of his head: "I have to get this out of the way." He doesn't want conditioned thoughts and preconceived notions to cloud his reading of an animal. And he is convinced that our emotional state plays a key part in any animal's response to us. He has even experimented with a wasp nest, noticing that a calm mind leads to no stings even as the occupants crawl over his face. "If we are angry or tense, we are at that moment in a defensive fight state. A wasp will sense this, feel threatened, and possibly sting us. If we are still, relaxed, and in a state of peace inside, a wasp has nothing to fight/flight or defend against. The same applies with horses."

Adam uses some terms that I'm not yet sure how to work with—animals "vibrating on the same frequency" and "energy fields," for example. But we are united in a belief that we were all once capable of reading animal behavior in an intuitive way and that this is something we can rekindle. My approach is slightly more mechanical in the early stages than Adam's may be, but I believe we are sensing many of the same things and trying to reach the same place.

Wolves and dogs give us a good idea of the differences between wild and domesticated behavior. Dogs will gaze directly into a human's eyes; a wolf will not. Dogs will "point" with their bodies to communicate direction with humans; wolves do not. And dogs are sensitive to "pointing" in humans—human gestures and body language that indicate direction; wolves are not. The biggest difference is in the way a dog actively seeks human company and attention; a wolf does not. On this emotional level, there is a gulf: Wolf cubs and dog pups that have both been raised by humans will align their affections very differently. Given the choice between an adult dog and a human, the dog puppy will choose the human, the wolf cub the dog.

Some behaviors differ when we turn our attention from a domestic setting to a wilder one, but the method doesn't; it remains about observing patterns. Noticing that wood pigeons have a habit of flying up steeply, clapping their wings, then descending steeply—the male's display flight—allows us to sense a bird's territory. But it is also an introduction to an important part of sensing: prediction. Familiarizing ourselves with patterns of behavior means that the early part of a routine reveals the latter. We come to know that the wood pigeon flying steeply up means that it is about to descend sharply; the first behavior is a sign that offers an instant sense of what will come next. We can notice how each bird—and indeed, animal—shows such sequential behaviors. Corvids and blackbirds have different styles of flying over hedges: Corvids go up and then down, while blackbirds take a lower, flatter route. As we watch these birds approach a hedge, we are able to sense what will happen next. Partridges duck behind hedges and disappear, giving the impression they have landed where they vanished. But before landing, they have a habit of making a sudden turn and continuing flight out of sight. Sneak up to the hedge and peer over or around it and the bird is long gone, but once we know this pattern, we will not expect to see it where others may. We have a sense of an animal's movements, even when it is out of sight.

Some animals yield faster than others, but they'll all surrender in the end. Lions are much easier to read than tigers or leopards, but no animals are a closed book. And we have a great advantage over indigenous tribespeople and our ancestors; thanks to Aristotle, Butler, Darwin, and company, we can borrow knowledge from those who have spent long years studying a species. If we find our task challenging, we can take a step back and remember that the three luminaries are there to support us. Hunter-gatherers offer inspiration, scholars add to our wisdom, and the animals close to home remind us that we can still do this.

A Noble Pursuit

T HE !XO, ANOTHER AFRICAN hunter-gatherer people, are aware of the communication network between animals and their place in this web. If an injured antelope escapes during a hunt, then the black-faced babbler, a grey-brown songbird, will guide the tribespeople to the place where the animal died. But the information flows both ways: As the hunters try to sneak up on their prey, small birds perched on trees make sounds that give the game away. They warn the antelopes of the hunters' presence, and the !xo feel the birds are laughing at them.

We were all hunters and gatherers until about twelve thousand years ago, when we began to settle. Women were integral to food-finding, and children were brought into the fold with games. The domestication of plants and animals led to a revolutionary lifestyle change. Until then, gathering, which we would now call foraging, predominated, but both skills were essential to our survival as a species. Foraging requires knowledge, but hunting requires knowledge and high levels of skill—to hunt in an era of low technology meant knowing how to outwit another creature and mastering the skill. But foraging and hunting share something vital: They require an ability to recognize patterns.

In genetic terms, we are still hunter-gatherers. There has been no significant change to our genes, only to our way of life. This is encouraging because it means that our only disadvantage, in comparison to our ancestors, is cultural. We can witness the cultural clash between a contemporary Western lifestyle and that of our ancestors in obesity. It is hard to get fat by foraging—how many obese grazing animals have you seen?

A more typical dietary pattern for our ancestors would have been lean days of foraging, occasional serious hunger, topped up and made possible by the rich energy supplement of a kill during a hunt. If you spend days at a time getting slightly less energy than you need from nuts, berries, and leaves, it makes good sense to gorge on fatty meat when the opportunity arises. It makes less sense to gobble a Saturday steak after a week of pasta. But we sometimes feel the urge to do so, and if we feel guilty afterward, we can remind ourselves that we did it because we are hunter-gatherers.

One of humanity's little tricks is to associate technological progress with wisdom. This is an invented law of sophistication—the more efficient the tools, the more civilized we are and the better the lifestyle, or so the theory goes. In the seventeenth century, the political philosopher Thomas Hobbes famously characterized nature as "solitary, poor, nasty, brutish, and short." The sentiment hadn't changed much a hundred years later, when hunter-gatherers of past and present were depicted as hairy, naked savages. More recently, the Bedouin looked down their noses at the Solubba hunters of northern Arabia, regarding them as barely human—while fearing their mystical abilities in the desert.

One modern consensus is patronizing in different ways. According to this view, hunter-gatherer societies have always been wise in the ways that don't matter anymore—plant and animal behavior—but they paid a terrible price for this in terms of hardship. However, recent research suggests things aren't quite so simple. The Israeli historian Yuval Noah Harari points out that contemporary hunter-gatherers in the Kalahari work ten hours fewer per week than we do. And these societies exist today in an unusually tough environment only because they have been displaced from more verdant, productive regions. It's likely that this lifestyle in less barren areas would afford even more free time.

In short, farmers worked harder and longer than foragers and were rewarded with a less interesting and less varied diet. Harari offers the radical notion that, far from agricultural and industrial revolutions bringing us more leisure, they have almost completely destroyed it. Other academics have gone further, claiming that hunter-gatherers are "the most leisured people in the world." There was more infant mortality before those revolutions, but there were no car deaths. There was also less domestic drudgery—you can't wash, iron, or vacuum things that don't exist. Or, in the words of Bruce Chatwin, "The Golden Age ended when men stopped hunting, settled in houses, and began the daily grind."

Intriguing though this lifestyle and leisure theory is, it is not the main reason for our interest in hunting here, which is to understand how it can assist the deepest understanding of animal behavior. To do that, we must sideline one other mistaken perception of hunting: that it is a gratuitous sport indulged in only by gun-happy sadists. I'm no fan of shooting defenseless animals as entertainment, but I do see where a love of hunting has come from, and it is a beautiful part of our shared history, which has been overshadowed of late.

There have been cultural fluctuations in our relationship with hunting, but we can see how a gulf grew between historical necessity and contemporary leisure for the affluent, in the words of the twenty-sixth president of the United States, Theodore Roosevelt:

> *The Romans, unlike the Greeks, and still more unlike those mighty hunters of old, the Assyrians, cared little for the chase; but the white-skinned, fair-haired, blue-eyed barbarians, who, out of the wreck of the Roman Empire, carved the States from*

which sprang modern Europe, were passionately devoted to hunting. Game of many kinds then swarmed in the cold, wet forests which covered so large a portion of Europe. The kings and nobles, and the freemen generally, of the regions which now make France and Germany, followed not only the wolf, boar and stag—the last named favorite quarry of the hunter of the Middle Ages—but the bear, the bison—which still lingers in the Caucasus and in one Lithuanian preserve of the Czar—and the aurochs, the huge wild ox—the Urus *of Caesar—which has now vanished from the world.*

Hunting became the preserve of the wealthy and greatly contributed to the demise of the larger mammals. It's easy to see how hunting became anathema to many who loved either nature or egalitarianism. But this pastime should not be confused with hunting for survival, an activity that all our ancestors were involved in and one that required the greatest insight into an environment. We can learn a lot from those who managed so well with so little for fifty thousand years.

If an animal is faster, stronger, fitter, and endowed with more finely tuned senses than we are, it follows that we must use our one advantage, intelligence, to great effect. We glimpse this skill in the abilities of modern-day hunter-gatherers. Hunters know that their prey feed on certain plants at certain times of day, and that certain animals have dependable habits in the way they move. Feeding antelopes move from bush to bush, following a zigzag pattern into the wind, which means that a hunter can anticipate each turn and follow a straighter course. The Kutchin of North America understand the moose in a way that allows hunting with wisdom and elegance far beyond those basics.

Imagine accompanying the Kutchin on a hunt, after an earlier initial sighting of a moose. The hunters may not have seen the animal for a long period, but continue to lead you as they pursue a series of chaotic-seeming twists and turns, still with no sight of the animal. It appears a crazy way to go about things. Then, when you are bewildered, exhausted, and convinced that the moose is nowhere to be found, the animal is suddenly pointed out, lying down in front of you, easily within bow-and-arrow range. The assumption might be of mystic ability or sixth sense, but if we look at the diagram below, we can see that it is nothing of the sort. It is a deep knowledge of one animal's habits.

The moose is sensitive to wind direction and finishes any grazing line by doubling back on itself on the downwind side, before coming to rest. This gives it the best chance of picking up the scent of any predator following it. It's a tactic that outwits many animals, but not the Kutchin, who follow it in a series of loops that come back to the animal's trail, but always remain on the downwind side of it. When a loop goes past the point where tracks would be expected without any being found, the hunter knows that their prey has doubled back on the windward side. It is time to change tack, looping in the other direction, before catching the moose at rest and unaware.

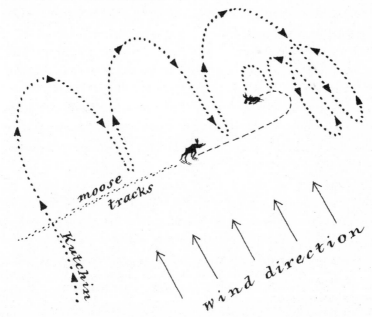

The hunter and hunted are caught in a perpetual awareness arms race. No species can survive unless its awareness of the habits of the other can prevail when needed. This wisdom allows the hunter to sense what will happen next. It is about recognizing patterns of behavior. The inexperienced hunter that wounds an animal will chase madly after it, sending it off at speed and making capture less likely. The experienced hunter knows that a wounded animal will choose to lie down nearby if it is not pursued. They bide their time, then walk slowly to find the animal.

For the hunter motivated by the need to live off the land, no animal is an isolated object; it is one piece of the nature network that the hunter is also part of. Each plant and animal is a clue to the whereabouts of others, but also part of a fuller picture. Aboriginal peoples learned to map water by taking an interest in whether any slain animal had drunk recently. Tick birds in Africa could lead a hunter to prey, but only if they were attuned to the elements. Seeing the birds and walking toward them downwind would prove useless, but approaching the birds with the wind on your face would reveal a dozing beast in the bush.

The hunter becomes aware of their world in all its dimensions. If we are sharing our space with creatures whose sense of smell is a thousand times greater than our own, it pays to know that we can step into a parallel world by climbing a tree and lifting our scent above their noses. We see the latest incarnation of this concept in the "high seats" dotted about in woods with managed deer or boar populations. The ranger uses a tall wooden chair, usually prebuilt against a tree, to wait for the prey to pass by.

The senses are heightened, the hunter looks, listens, and sniffs actively, keeps to the shadows, and makes use of the shape of the land to conceal their approach. They wrap themselves in sound cover, moving when the trees rustle or the wind rakes the leaves across the ground. They are aware that their shape and motion send signals—rare is the hunter whose arms swing.

Like the animals they hunt, the hunter does not think of yesterday or tomorrow; it is the moment that counts for all. They sense the components but do not break the world into them. The sounds, breeze, light, and flickering silhouettes are part of that landscape at that moment.

From our remove, we may have to bring the pieces back together one by one. We will see the joints of the jigsaw. It is only when we have done this enough times that we see the hunter's picture. It is a scene that unites humanity: We share that single purpose and full reading of the landscape with our ancestors. It transcends cultural and physical barriers. Immersed in the moment, the hunter communicates easily with fellow hunters in gestures and silence. Before and after the hunt, they discuss the behavior of the animals for hours. Physical sightings mix with stories, myth, and lore. We can mourn the loss of a large mammal, as true hunters do, but the art of the hunt is wondrous and to be celebrated.

There is a difference between hunting and killing. Hunting knows failure better than success and can be a tedious test of patience, which the overstimulated modern mind may find harder to overcome than the ancient. Our more distant relations know it, too: Chimpanzees have been observed following prey stealthily for more than an hour. Patience is a virtue, and it is not the only one that the hunter has always valued. Hunting literature of the Middle Ages refers to the abhorrence of idleness, the need for industry, a calm mind, and even the importance of getting a good night's sleep. This is where survival and aristocracy become the strangest of bedfellows. The subsistent hunter and the nobility shared the greatest respect for the skills needed to understand a creature and its environment well enough to pursue it successfully. (The etymology of the word "nobility" is the clue: It comes from the fourteenth-century French *nobilité*, meaning "high rank; dignity, grace, great deed." Hunting was seen as a great deed, one requiring the highest skill, and became associated with the elevated rank of the aristocracy.) But it is the universal acknowledgement by societies of opposing political and social values, communities separated by thousands of miles and years, that hunting is a rarefied skill requiring the highest standards of its practitioners that is fascinating. It could be argued that it is one of the highest art forms, however unfashionable that may be in certain circles today. It also brings us to the extraordinary world of venery.

"Venery" came to mean the pursuit of sexual indulgence, eventually disappearing from common use, but before that it was used in reference to medieval hunting skills (from the Latin *venari*, to hunt). In the Middle Ages, it became fashionable to know and use the correct terms for the various signs in hunting, which is where many of our collective nouns for animals stem from, such as "an ostentation of peacocks" and "a murmuration of starlings."

Venery was a way of blending knowledge and exclusivity to create a linguistic badge of belonging. A hunter who did not know the correct word for a deer's droppings, "fumes," marked themselves out as not part of this club. The terms of venery allow us to peer into the richness of the world of those hunters; we cannot see through their eyes literally, but we can linguistically. Some sources list as many as seventy-two such signs, including the slot—the track of the deer; the gait—the pattern of the tracks; the fraying-post—a tree a deer has rubbed its antlers against; and the entry—the place where a deer took refuge. Those people were clearly passionate about reading their environment.

If the whiff of arrogance and pretension comes through from the Middle Ages and can still be picked up in some Western hunting traditions, a very different air is apparent in the indigenous communities. The medieval hunter was directed to be, in the words of Edward Norwich, "well advised of his speech and of his terms, and ever glad to learn and that he be no boaster nor jangler"—in other words, he or she should be wise, sharp, and humble. But evidence of true humility among hunters comes more convincingly from other quarters.

The San people of the northern Kalahari are expected to shun arrogant behavior. If successful in a hunt they may pretend to have failed, leaving the animal at the edge of the village for others to find. Humility and respect are expected within the group, but also toward the landscape and the prey.

Common among indigenous communities is a sense that the environment is generous and benevolent and is to be regarded with gratitude, not aggression. Hunter-gatherers are not driven by bloodlust. This is common sense: If your survival depends on hunting certain animals, their long-term sustainability is vital—gratuitous killing would lead to self-defeat.

The wilderness is a friend, not an enemy to be overcome. This philosophy is rare now in the West, but not lost altogether. Colin Elford, a modern English ranger, writes, "The experiences I share with the deer in weather and places like these leave me with feelings of great respect and also a form of regret, and yet all these feelings combine to enforce a love for the whole system. I talk, sleep, and eat deer—we are joined, a pair!"

The most interesting aspect of hunting is never the kill. A dead animal is a meal to those who need one and proof of success, validation, to others. But it is not the true prize for either; the zenith of hunting is the moment when senses, experience, and wisdom come together to allow true insight. However, we do not need to kill to aspire to this level. Many wildlife photographers are hunters who seek the thrill of the chase and the insight that makes it possible, but take their prize home without harming the animal.

I am lucky that I have no desire to kill animals, but I share the craving for the sensation that the greatest hunters throughout our history have known, when our mind and senses weave weather, time, landscape, and animal character into a meaningful pattern and we come to know our prey's own mind. It is a moment of total, intoxicating insight.

Tomorrow's Hunter

L AST WEEK I HELD A SEMINAR for a group of military intelligence analysts. We were in a theater at the headquarters of the British Army Intelligence Corps in Bedfordshire, about fifty miles north of London. I gave some instruction in natural navigation techniques, using examples demonstrated through projected photos, and explained how I analyzed those images. Then I set the group some challenges based on a new set of photos. The overall aim was for the analysts, who worked primarily within the field of image intelligence, to enjoy a different way of exploring imagery. The session culminated with a picture of a house in the English countryside. I said to the assembled group, "There are over two-dozen ways of telling direction in this picture. But we'll come back to that. For now I'd like you to think of a coastal city." I asked a few to shout out their choice.

"Sydney."

"Vancouver."

"Rio."

The answers came steadily.

"OK. Now I want you to look at this picture of a rural house and tell me what the tide was doing at your chosen city when the picture was taken." There was an audible mixture of chuckling and sighing. The picture contained no view of any water and no view of the moon.

A rich collection of clues made it possible to work out aspect easily. Then it was possible to deduce that the low sun was setting, not rising. So far so simple, but the next step was trickier. It was crucial to gain some idea of what the moon was doing, even though it wasn't visible. There was a faint shadow on some grass, cast on the same side of the tree as the low sun. Some light was catching the side of the house, on the opposite side from the sun. Assuming that the moon was casting these shadows, it must have been on the opposite side of the sky to the sun—in other words, it was rising as the sun was setting. This meant that it was a full moon, which in turn meant that all over the world the tide ranges would be nearing maximum—spring tides.

Those gathered appeared to enjoy the session. It is not for me to say whether it added anything to their own hunt for and analyses of tank formations from airborne and satellite imagery. But over coffee, their commanding officer enthused about the strange similarities in the way we both depended on developing an intuitive ability to spot patterns. He explained how his analysts would go from a slow, methodical approach, which involved identifying equipment by comparing shapes in images with reference material—they could check the shape of an aircraft's wings in a manual to confirm identification—to a point where they stopped using the reference materials but were able to identify the aircraft without conscious thought.

"There, look, T-72 tanks," an experienced analyst might say, to the bemusement of the rookie who was struggling to find any shapes, let alone make sense of them. I asked if this was partly as a result of understanding context.

"Yes. Our brain will filter out the least likely objects very quickly, leaving a much shorter list to choose from. Context and experience then make a quick selection using the information in the image. It becomes automatic."

That morning, before the seminar, I had woken early—military establishments seem to have a penchant for translucent curtains, perhaps because staying asleep after sunrise, even in June, is considered the height of indolence. After an excellent breakfast in the officers' mess, I explored the elegant and impressive grounds. I passed a roaring weir, then found an open area of grass scattered with grazing rabbits.

I brought together all I knew to walk toward a rabbit. With the wind on my face I sensed it move through levels of grazing and vigilance, each one tweaking my approach speed. There were whole minutes of stillness. Advancing again, one deliberate foot at a time, I saw the other rabbits dart for cover, and each of their movements checked my target rabbit's and my own again. I paused, then continued until my chosen rabbit rose on its haunches six feet in front of me. I waited for it to return to grazing and took a step forward, reaching out with my right arm, very slowly. As my fingers closed the gap to less than three feet, the rabbit bolted for the bush that sheltered its friends. To me, this was a successful hunt. I had captured the moment I was looking for, sensing what the rabbit would do next, tailoring my movements until I could almost touch it.

Sensing and recognizing patterns in the rabbit's behavior made a close approach possible, just as recognizing blobs in an image makes tank recognition possible for the intelligence experts. In truth, all work and play is enhanced by experience, another name for pattern recognition. Whatever our chosen area, it is practice that leads to familiarity with patterns and then to expertise. It is the hunter in us that makes this possible and satisfying.

The most important, intriguing, and fun hunt of all is also the most terrifying. In this pursuit, the hunter has to work out whether they are also the hunted. When we are attracted to someone and feel we'd like to form a relationship, we rely on picking up signals in this scariest of landscapes.

More Than Machines

THE SONG THRUSH DID NOT MOVE from the lawn. I stepped closer. Still nothing. I clapped. Nothing. Eventually, when I was only ten feet from it, its hopping became more energetic, and then it took off. I had come to expect a certain insouciance from this individual.

Whenever we identify a wall that separates us from the rest of the animal kingdom, it soon crumbles. Language is clearly not our preserve, if birds can repeat what we say. Ivory Coast chimpanzees use a stick to dip for water in narrow tree holes, but it's not only primates that are comfortable using tools; even some insects are at it. The female digger wasp seals her burrow by using a pebble to knock the earth shut around the hole.

Animals also learn. There are nesting peregrine falcons in Chichester Cathedral a few miles from where I live. They evolved to inhabit areas with rock cliffs and ledges, but our cathedrals serve their purposes well enough, and they have adapted well to the new circumstances. Mice have learned sequences of movements through a maze to find food, then remembered them up to eight weeks later. We all know how quickly dogs learn, and with each passing year we are subjected to ever more ridiculous charming displays of this in TV talent shows. (The owner/trainer is often more interesting to watch in these displays since he or she is giving the signs that prompt the action. As with ventriloquism, the acts are more impressive if our gaze is kept on the animal rather than the human, and with animals, this means keeping the triggering signs surreptitious. Through hours of training and rewards, the dog may learn that a small movement of one hand means it's time to run up and over the seesaw.)

And in a teasingly arcane example of animal learning, researchers at the University of Queensland, Australia, have taught honeybees how to tell the difference between a Picasso and a Monet. As you will probably have guessed, it was actually standard research paired with a good nose for public relations; the bees are sensitive to shape and color, so the brushstrokes and palette choices of artists are well within their competence.

But what has animal learning got to do with our aims of sensing the outdoors more intuitively? And if animals speak, use tools, and learn, is it fair to view them so simply as the givers and receivers of signs? To begin to answer these questions, we need to spend a moment with a couple of the greatest thinkers to have lived.

René Descartes, the French seventeenth-century philosopher, in his *Discourse on the Method of Rightly Conducting One's Reason, and Seeking Truth in the Sciences* (1637), asserted that animals are like machines, containing all the mechanical parts necessary for life and even making sounds, but lacking the certain something that gives us reason, knowledge, and the ability to make ourselves understood. Animals are, in short, like "machines without a soul." He compared their cries to the "squeaking parts in an unfeeling machine."

In the following century another French philosopher, Voltaire, disagreed: "What a pitiful, what a sorry thing to have said that animals are machines bereft of understanding and feeling, which perform their operations always in the same way, which learn nothing, perfect nothing, etc.!"

Today I think most people would quickly side with Voltaire, but these are just two strong views in an age-old debate that rumbles on. There are clearly differences between humans and other animals, just as there are between the animals, but to avoid getting lost in discussing such matters as souls or suffocating ourselves in the philosophy, we must return to the science.

We are a long way from knowing exactly what animals know, but we can be confident of certain areas of their cognition. We know, for example, that some animal actions are directed and others are reflexes, and this may lead to something like a sliding scale of cognition. The German biologist Jakob von Uexküll sums up this idea succinctly: "When a dog runs, the animal moves its legs. When a sea urchin runs, its legs move the animal." And it may be that every animal, including us, is living somewhere on this scale, perhaps sliding up and down it.

We can be confident that animals possess character and experience moods. Character is different from aptitude. Pigeons are brilliant at navigating and poor, relative to crows, at working out rules for solving problems. The two species have different aptitudes. But take two male dogs of the same breed (all pet dogs are the same species, *Canis familiaris*) passing a solitary tree at the entrance to a park and we may observe differences in character. We know that male dogs urinate in prominent places to mark territory with their scent, which means that most trees, walls, fences, and posts in urban parks have been urinated on. But when one male dog encounters the scent marking of another dog, it has to choose whether to move on or put its marker on top of the previous dog's, known as "over-scenting." This is where character comes in: a bold dog will over-scent, but a timid one will keep walking. Humans are similar: Some will protest if another "takes their space"; others will move on.

Within groups of animals of the same species, there may be a division of tasks. Some may be adept at seeking out new sources of food while others are usually late to a discovery and rely on leftovers or stealing from the discoverer. Observation of these differences led to the "producer-scrounger" view of animal social groups. Why do producers tolerate it? Because there are benefits to living in a group, and in any group not everyone is of the same character: Some will always be better than others at finding food, being vigilant, or defending against attackers. The sharing that follows is the cost the producers pay for the benefit of living within a group. Perhaps a little like taxes.

Animals are born with some fearfulness and also learn to be fearful. Prey animals will adjust their behavior if they detect a large number of predators in the area—they learn to be fearful—but within a population there will always be variety in fearfulness because of genetics. The "open field" test has been used to assess this. As we have seen, prey animals do not like the exposure of open areas, unless protected by darkness; they prefer to keep cover or hug the edges. But other animals venture out into the open more because they are bolder, and this is genetic. This research has led some to consider whether some humans are born to be anxious.

The same variation is observed at the aggressive end of the spectrum. Earlier we saw how robins attacked a model bird in their territory, but the researchers also noted how some robins displayed half-hearted aggression and others went in for a no-pecks-barred assault.

If a predator approaches prey, not all animals within that species will choose the same moment to flee. Some are off at the first sign of trouble; others wait until danger levels are higher. By studying the distance at which flight from a predator is triggered, scientists have found that there are timid and bold individuals; those that are bold in one situation are likely to be bold in others, and vice versa. There are dependable character traits.

As in war; so, too, in love . . . People marry for reasons other than love, sexual attraction, and companionship, and animals may be no different—there appear to be social climbers in the animal kingdom. Within many animal groups, individuals have a social ranking—jackdaws know not to antagonize stronger birds. But in 1931 the Austrian ethologist Konrad Lorenz discovered that female jackdaws of a lowly status could elevate themselves instantly by mating with a male of higher standing.

On top of variability in character, each animal is capable of moodiness. If you really dislike rats, then this may not fill you with disgust. In 1978 some laboratory rats were confronted with a swimming task. Rats can swim, so that in itself doesn't sound too cruel, but this particular exercise was specially designed to be hopeless. There was no way for the rats to win, however hard they swam or tried to climb out of the water. There was no escape. After a while the rats stopped trying and even stopped moving. This was diagnosed as analogous to depression in humans.

The rats were given antidepressants and electroconvulsive therapy. They started to become active again. I feel uncomfortable with this experiment and its findings, but that is not important here. This research was a stepping-stone, a depressingly wet and electric one, but a significant hop toward understanding animal mental states. Subsequent research has confirmed that elephants mourn, bees become pessimistic, and many other animals experience states that we would consider evidence of emotions and moods when observed in humans.

Once we appreciate that animals learn, have character, and experience moods and emotions, it means that our view of them must be subtler than as simple "sign machines." This doesn't invalidate our approach, but it does mean that there will be some variability in an individual's behavior at different times. A tired and depressed squirrel will not behave in the same way as another that is fresh and elated after discovering a hoard of hazelnuts. And the euphoric squirrel will not behave in the same way ten minutes later, when it returns to find that its hoard has been stolen.

We are now at the more challenging end of animal observation. We can view animal experience, individual character, and mental state as adding more layers for us to enjoy observing. Each can feed into our intuitive feel of what will happen next because they influence the probability of certain behaviors. But the signs we see retain their meaning. I have met and held the gaze of one particular roe deer only twenty yards away for the past four evenings because it is bolder than most of its species. I have learned something of its character—I know it is unlikely to flee just because it sets eyes on me. Its ears still twitch prior to flight; the sign is the same.

The time this deer and I have spent in a mutual freeze appears to have grown over those four encounters, which may be because it is learning that I have no intention of killing it. If it happens many more times, I'll worry that I'm teaching it bad habits. Hunters have traditionally used a sense of an animal's experience to improve their chances. In the Kalahari, if an animal has been shot with poison, its character and personality feature in assessments about how far it will run. Australian Aboriginal peoples can tell whether an animal is tame by the tracks it leaves.

During the Middle Ages, hunters would use an animal's tracks as clues to its character, but they also gained insight into its age, experience, and character from the sounds it made. Edward of Norwich explains how this worked with the calls of the stags:

> *The harts bellow in divers manners, according as*
> *they be old or young, and according whether they*
> *be in a country where they have not heard the*
> *hounds, or where they have heard them. Some*
> *of them bellow with a full open mouth and often*
> *cast up their heads. And these be those that have*
> *heard the hounds only a little in the season, and*
> *that are well heated and swelled. And sometimes*
> *about high noon they bellow as before is said.*
> *The others bellow low and great and stooping with*

the head, and the muzzle towards the earth, and
that is a token of a great hart, and an old and a
malicious, or that he hath heard the hounds, and
therefore dare not bellow or only a few times in
the day, unless if it be in the dawning. And the
other belloweth with his muzzle straight out before
him, bolking and rattling in the throat, and also
that is a token of a great and old hart that is assured
and firm in his rut.

So, our ability to read signs in no way reduces the status or complexity of the animals we observe—they remain characters and, indeed, fuller ones as we take the time to learn their language. One excellent way to remind ourselves that we are not observing automatons is to practice noticing that signs flow from us toward the animals. At the end of any long frozen period of mutual locked gaze with a wild animal, I am always intrigued to see which slight sign from me will trigger flight. A lifting of a foot prompts action before a hand movement, and both are normally beaten by a head tilt, but each animal has its idiosyncrasies.

Dogs have learned to beat us at our own game. Everyone will have seen a dog tilt its head as it looks up at us. A tilted head can aid a dog's vision and hearing, but some researchers believe that this is a sign dogs use to elicit the response they want from us. A dog with a tilted head is cute, and we tend to give more love and attention to animals when they look cute. So, when we cuddle the adorable dog with the tilted head, we don't realize we are reacting to a sign in the way that the dog wants. We are being played with—a sign we've met a real character.

Umwelt

WE HAVE ALL BEEN ANNOYED BY a housefly and tried to swat one away. Have you ever felt that your hand will get close to it, but that you'll never make contact with it? Perhaps you've also had the strange sensation that the fly knows this is what will happen and is being casual about your assault. There it sits on your plate of food even as your hand accelerates toward it. It squats there for much longer than is prudent, goading you, waiting until the very last moment before taking off; yet it always evades your angry sweep!

If we unpack this chain of events, it will reveal extraordinary new worlds. We discover them by understanding the *Umwelt*, the environment as perceived by another organism.

Whenever a family walks into a large shop, each member is drawn to different things within it, but they also see the inside of the shop differently. At the most basic level the smallest child will notice more of the lower part of the shop than the tallest adult. Companies spend millions researching how to take advantage of these small differences: We buy what we choose to buy, but often because it was put in front of us.

Eyesight, hearing, smell, touch, and taste will vary from one person to the next. But the perception of the shop will be different for each person because they have different life experiences and psychology. Some will have positive associations with being in a large shop; others will find it stressful or boring. Think of your own family and imagine taking each of them to a large shop. You know who will be keenest to stay or leave. In short, no two people will sense or experience the shop in the same way, and this is a difference within the same species. In nature, the world is our shop, and we have to consider how the environment is perceived across the species. If there are differences in how a simple environment is perceived within the same family of one species, imagine the differences in how a complex environment is viewed between a spider, a fish, and an orangutan.

Jakob von Uexküll, who pioneered the idea of the *Umwelt*, wrote:

> *Standing before a meadow covered with flowers, full of buzzing bees, fluttering butterflies, darting dragonflies, grasshoppers jumping over blades of grass, mice scurrying and snails crawling about, we would instinctively tend to ask ourselves the question: Does the meadow present the same prospect to the eyes of all those different creatures as it does to ours?*

This concept is important if we are to develop our understanding of biological signs, because we need to improve our feel for how others sense the world, what they are attuned to, and the key differences. We already do this sometimes within a domestic setting—the cat's low back means it has spotted a mouse, and I trust my dogs' barking means a delivery has arrived half a minute before the doorbell rings. I also know that an angry sound from my wife early in the morning means I've forgotten to put the toilet seat down.

The ancient Greek philosopher Anaximander asked what a falcon sees. Wittgenstein opined that if a lion could speak we wouldn't understand him, his point probably being that the lion's view of the world would be so alien to us that a common language wouldn't be enough to bridge it. It's a conundrum that evolves but doesn't go away. In 1974 the American philosopher Thomas Nagel wrote an essay titled, "What Is It Like to Be a Bat?"

In 1978 a chimpanzee called Sarah demonstrated to researchers that she was considering what the humans intended to do next. This sounds academic, and it is, but it's also fascinating in the context of the *Umwelt* because it is evidence of an animal with a "theory of mind." A creature can be said to have such if it considers how another animal is thinking. If one animal forms ideas about another's goals and takes these into consideration, it has a theory of mind. It is, of course, fascinating to consider to what extent animals can think, but the relevance here is only in terms of how complex and predictive signs may be. If an animal has a theory of mind, it is a potential extra stepping-stone in the world of signs. For example, a primate may respond to signs not just in the present—that is, to what an animal is doing—but by understanding what another animal plans to do. For practical purposes the psychology is a step too far at this stage, and we will focus on the physical biology, which is more accessible.

All animals sense the world differently from us, and some of the striking biological differences feed into our language when we say someone is "hawkeyed" or "as blind as a bat." But even as we acknowledge these differences we highlight another hurdle. Two of the biggest challenges for nature studies and a particular obstacle to understanding animals' *Umwelt* are anthropomorphism and anthropocentrism: seeing the animals as humanlike, and viewing their world from our perspective.

If you have ever felt that a singing bird sounds happy, you have succumbed to anthropomorphism: The bird sings to establish its territory; we sing for other reasons. Just the word "bird" leads us to assume certain things, but we know that within this category there are vast differences in biology, both visible and hidden: pigeon forebrains have half the neural density of corvids'.

We credit the ant with little intelligence, yet the colonies achieve extraordinary things and thrive in places that beat us. Perhaps our anthropocentrism leads us to focus on the small individual organism, when in fact it is a cog within a bigger collective—an insect example of us not seeing the wood for the trees?

If we combine the biological differences with the perspective problems, it takes us back to the fly that had the temerity to land on our cookies, then not take off until the last moment. This is anthropocentrism based on ignorance about the fly's *Umwelt*. The fly is neither showing temerity nor waiting until the last moment. It takes off as soon as it perceives the threat, which is only as our hand comes within twenty inches of it. We raise our hand to swipe, but it sees no danger in that. We bring our hand down quickly, still nothing, and when we feel it's showing a total disregard for our hand as it rapidly descends, the fly doesn't perceive a danger at all—its world of risk is only twenty inches in each direction. The fly, like every other animal, including us, lives within a perception bubble. We routinely make the mistake of thinking our bubbles are alike when they are not. There are always differences, and we're not always worse off: A fly finds it easy to evade our hand, but will head straight into a spider's web that's invisible to it but easy for us to see.

Many insects' bubbles are much smaller than ours, but ours is much smaller than many other animals': A polar bear can smell a whale twenty miles away and detect a seal through six feet of ice. We saw earlier how a vulture can tell the difference between a dead and sleeping animal from thirteen thousand feet.

Some birds and possibly badgers can hear the sound an earthworm makes as it breaks the surface. The perception bubble applies to all the senses we normally think of and many that we don't. Sand crickets can sense predators from air movement; they pick it up through tiny hairs. Stefano Lorenzini, a seventeenth-century Italian ichthyologist (fish scientist), noticed that many sharks and rays have dark regions near the fronts of their heads. These are called the "ampullae of Lorenzini," and we now know a lot more about how these organs help the creatures to sense the world using electromagnetic signals, which can pass around objects; the shark can "see" the fish hiding behind the coral. Each year we learn more about how birds and other animals use the Earth's magnetic field to navigate.

The *Umwelt* is partly about the sense that is used and partly about sensitivity, and this is not always intuitive to us. The bigger the creature, the greater the temptation to think of it sensing a cruder world, but a bowhead whale asleep at the surface can startle when a bird lands on it. The smaller the creature, the more likely we are to see its world as small, but a male silkworm moth can detect a mature female miles away.

Some animals have been credited with psychic or mathematical talents, like "Clever Hans," the horse that did arithmetic. But in his case, as in so many others, it transpired that the trainer was unaware he was giving the answers to the horse through tiny body-language cues. It appeared almost magical to those observing, but the horse was aware of the trainer's subtlest movements, invisible to observers even when they were studying the trainer for these exact signs, because horses are more sensitive to them than we are. A horse will notice part of our face move 0.2 millimeter. It's intriguing to think that it may be able to tell when we are happy, sad, annoyed, or lying before the people closest to us can.

Each morning I watch the birds peck at our lawn. Today our local pair of green woodpeckers were out again, peck, peck, peck, head up, then cocked as I move behind the glass. Peck, peck, peck. It amazes me that there is so much to peck at—what are they seeing? Whenever I venture out to the same spot and peer down, I struggle to notice anything that may be worth the effort. But, of course, their vision is greater, not just in acuity, but in color.

By detecting ultraviolet light, some birds and insects can see colors that are invisible to us. I feel a tinge of envy knowing that birds have four types of cones, the color-sensitive cells, in their eyes to our three. And if that wasn't enough, the science writer Jennifer Ackerman adds salt to the wound: "In each of a bird's cone cells is a drop of oil that enhances its ability to detect differences between similar colors."

For some reason, I feel less envy for the equally impressive ability of some vipers to detect infrared light and heat, or the way dolphins can build a map using clicks and echoes. This is probably because I find it easier to imagine being a bird than a snake or a dolphin. I also imagine birds leading a more "interesting" life than snakes or dolphins. But if I stop to think about it, dolphins have more complex brains than birds, so they may well have more interesting lives. Although, as Wittgenstein would doubtless say, we might be too baffled by either species' experience of the world to understand what was going on, let alone whether it was interesting.

The *Umwelt* is also about time. We can sense the world about eighteen times per second, which is why a series of twenty-four images per second of TV or cinema appears as fluid motion to us. It's also why anything that vibrates more than eighteen times a second becomes a single sound to our ears—you can try this by flicking the pages of a book: We can see and hear individual pages flick past at up to eighteen per second, but beyond that it becomes a blur and we hear only the collective sound of pages flicking.

Some fish see the world fifty times per second, so they'd find our TV screens unbearably flickering. (I'm not going to anthropomorphize them to the point where I think they'd be upset about this.) By clamping a snail and then testing how it responds to a stick, researchers discovered that it sees the world between three and four times per second, so we must expect snails to be oblivious to most subtle quick motions. Snails aren't credited with psychic or mathematical abilities.

Speed forms an important part of many animals' view of the world. It can be an efficient way of tuning to predators, particularly if you're not given to complex thinking. A scallop needs to be wary—there I go, anthropomorphizing again—alert to its predator, the starfish. We may think a starfish is fairly easy to identify, with a shape and colors that give some helpful clues, but it isn't to the scallop. The scallop's most efficient way of telling a harmless creature from a deadly starfish is actually the speed of that animal's movement. Something that looks exactly like a starfish to us will not trigger a defensive response in a scallop unless it moves with the same speed as a starfish.

We are unlikely to feel that we see the world in the same way as a scallop does, but a little closer to home we may observe something that we think looks straightforward yet makes no sense. Imagine a bird sees an insect it would like as a meal, perhaps a sparrow and a grasshopper. The bird stands over the insect, staring at it for many seconds as we watch them both. Why doesn't the bird eat the insect? Isn't it hungry? Has it gone off grasshoppers? No. It's much simpler: The grasshopper doesn't become identified as a meal until it moves. It doesn't really show up on the bird's food radar when it's still. That may appear crazy to us, but we're not so very different: We, too, have images we identify as food and others that we don't. Someone who is happy to eat hamburgers every day will drool at the sight of the Golden Arches, but will pass a field of cows without reacting.

These search images form an important part of each organism's perception, and this applies equally to humans. We have a limited ability to notice things, so the image we are searching for is the one we are more likely to find. The flip side of this is that we are likely to miss things that are similar, but don't fit the image we're searching for. I once spent half an hour looking for a book, during which time I picked it up at least three times. I'd forgotten I'd taken off its dust jacket the night before—my search image didn't match the book, even when it was in my hand.

The search image is why we always notice other people in the wild, because we're programmed to spot them by evolution and culture, but we might miss a significant animal or plant. Animals behave in a similar way: If the image fits, it fits, and if it doesn't, it doesn't. A bird searching for a grub is more likely to overlook us than one in a general state of vigilance, which is usually easy to tell from its location and its head and body positions.

Animal search images are associated with threats, food, mates, and territory, and can have many attributes, including shape, color, speed, odor, and so on. But no animals use a full picture—we all have quite large blind spots. We can't tell when an upwind badger is behind us, a lack of awareness that a badger might find extraordinary.

For a demonstration of extreme *Umwelt* differences, let's compare our view of the world and its challenges with those of the earthworm. It likes to take some things into its tunnels for food or protection, including pine needles. Many pine trees have paired needles that are always narrow at the closed end. Have a look at the problem below and consider how you might solve it.

How can you get the pine-needle pair down the tunnel without it getting stuck?

This puzzle isn't too difficult for us: We would pull the narrow end down first. But now let's level the playing field: Work out how to solve the problem without using your eyes or sense of touch. In other words, how could you work out which end to pull down the hole if you could sense nothing about the shape of the object?

Worms are able to pull pine needles and other leaves the right way down their narrow tunnels by tasting them—the closed end tastes different from the open end—and only the closed end tastes right for pulling.

By delving into the *Umwelt* of other animals, we start to learn that many things that initially appeared complex to us are much simpler to the animals we're observing. This is the upside to ridding ourselves of anthropocentrism: We stop projecting our complex cognitive world onto animals that are reading and reacting to simple signs. Experiments conducted with a hen and her chick demonstrated this effectively, albeit, almost inevitably, with a little cruelty.

A chick is tethered to the ground by one foot, understandably causing it some distress. It gives its alarm call, an urgent repetitive peep sound. The hen rushes to the scene and starts pecking furiously around the chick. Witnessing this, we would be tempted to weave a melodramatic narrative: "Oh, no! The chick is in danger! She's been captured and, look, she's tied up! Quick, Mom! Rescue her!"

But something much simpler is going on: The chicken hears a call that prompts her to peck randomly around the chick that issues it. That's it. There is no narrative, no rescue, no bigger picture. Researchers proved this by tying the chick to the ground again and this time placing a transparent glass bell jar over it. The chick reacts to this effrontery in the same way as before, emitting her loud peeps. This time the hen walks past the bell jar, sees the chick tethered to the ground, peeping away in distress, and continues on her way. She can't hear the signal and therefore doesn't sense the danger or react.

This is not a one-off. It is typical. Thought is not necessary for most animals, where a simple sign and reaction will do the job. Jackdaws are known to react to visual signs that are much simpler than those we would perceive. It can lead to behavior that makes little sense to us until we appreciate that a simple chain reaction is going on: The animal has seen an image and identified it as a sign, which triggers the action. When seen in this context, bizarre animal behavior can start to make sense.

For example, a mistake in identification of the image will set off the wrong action.

A jackdaw will quickly identify a cat as a dangerous predator and not approach it. However, a jackdaw that spots a cat that has snatched one of its colleagues sees a different image: This is a cat that must be attacked. The cat is less dangerous to the observing jackdaw at that moment as its mouth is full of bird, but it remains unwelcome and must be harried away from the area. Jackdaws have evolved a pair of very different responses to the two different images, cat with empty mouth and cat with bird in mouth, to improve the chance of the group surviving. But we can see how the image acts as a trigger, not careful study or thought, when we discover that a jackdaw that lets a cat with an empty mouth pass will later attack the cat if it walks back with a pair of black shorts in its mouth. The black shorts look enough like a captured bird to act as the sign to attack.

Before I laugh at the jackdaw, I recall that time on a night walk in low moonlight when I saw a large hunched man blocking my path. My pulse quickened as I flicked on my headlamp—which I am loath to do as it sets back night vision so dramatically. My pulse went up another twenty beats and I may have uttered some profanities as I was confronted by a monstrous badger, the size of a man. Within a second the drama faded and I was standing opposite a tree stump, with an outline not unlike that of a hunched man. It was covered with dark and light patches of lichens and fungi that could, at a stretch, resemble a badger's face. It turns out that meeting a hunched, six-foot badger in the woods on a dark night is the sign for me to swear and for my heart to palpitate.

Once we know how an animal perceives the world and combine this with its preferences, we can start to sense what is about to happen. Honeybees are attracted to flowers by scent, but when they get closer they are sensitive to shape and prefer stars and crosses to circles or squares. This knowledge allows us to sense where a bee is about to land.

Thinking back to the scallop and starfish or the bird and the grasshopper offers us a better insight into the importance of motion and stillness when we're in the wild. Within this context of images and signs, an animal freezing now makes much better sense: It's possible for animals to disappear from some other animals' searches by changing their patterns of motion or stillness.

Our chance of getting close to any animal will improve when we understand its *Umwelt*. Will our masking of color, scent, sound, or motion give us our best chance of creating an invisibility cloak? If we see a mammal ahead and we want to approach, we need to take care of our appearance, movement, scent, and wind direction, and make sure that no twigs snap under our feet. But trying to approach a moth silently is a waste of stealth; it won't hear you, even as you smash through bracken while playing the trombone. Moths detect the 20 kHz frequency of a bat's echolocation and use this to take evasive action, but that narrow frequency is the extent of their hearing.

We know that animals are less likely to spot us when they are searching for something, like food. When this knowledge is combined with the visual impairment of head-down body positions, we have a huge advantage in understanding how to approach them without scaring them off. Studies have shown that predator detection drops by 25 percent when a bird is searching for food, and by a further 45 percent when it's pecking that food. It is entertaining and instructive to test this by playing Red Light, Green Light with them.

In the human version of the game, someone stands with their back to a group and tries to catch people in the act of creeping toward them by turning suddenly. Play it with birds, and you'll notice that if you step as they peck, you get a lot closer before they fly off than otherwise. This game is educational fun for us, but the technique within it would have been the difference between life or death for our ancestors.

The game is instructive in a couple of other ways, too. First, it is harder to play it with horses, sheep, or deer than humans because with these animals we need to be sensitive about our scent and the wind direction. And also we are more likely to be spotted even when the animal is not looking at or for us because it has much better peripheral vision. The simple act of considering whether an animal is predator or prey will give us a good idea of the breadth of its visual world.

The lateral eyes of many prey animals mean that they can see almost all around them—horses can see, with at least one eye, everything that surrounds them, except the ten degrees directly behind them. Creeping up on a horse from behind would in theory rely on it not turning its head by five degrees. To get a feel for how little this is, hold your left fist out at arm's length. Now look at its left side and, without moving your eyes, move your head until your eyes rest on its middle knuckle (it's surprisingly hard to do this, because our eyes want to lock onto something, like a knuckle, but you get the idea—don't challenge a horse to this particular game).

Second, as we saw with the housefly, each species has its own relationship with danger and distance. An animal has a maximum distance at which it can detect a predator and an average distance at which it does so, and these are influenced by the locality and the experiences of those animals. I know that I can approach to within a couple hundred yards of most deer in my area before I need to be extremely stealthy, but in more open areas, where cover may be harder for a deer to reach and human contact rarer, the distance may be far greater. The point is that every animal has its own patterns of detection, and we can learn these through experience. The chance of a house sparrow detecting us grow steadily as we move closer, but doesn't change much for a starling, which is almost as likely to spot us from forty yards away as it is from ten.

One of the main benefits of considering the *Umwelt* of other animals is that it gives us new perspectives on the world of signs. A rattlesnake may be of interest or concern to us, but it's a serious threat to a California ground squirrel. For survival, the squirrel needs to find out as much as it can about the predator as quickly as possible. From this *Umwelt*, the rattle ceases to be solely a means of identifying the snake and instead becomes a form of Morse code: from the volume, pitch, and rate of the rattle, the squirrels can glean the size and temperature of the snake, which is valuable information because, as we saw earlier, temperature has a direct relationship with the likelihood of action in reptiles. The rattle is audible to us, so there is no reason why we shouldn't at least attempt to interpret the sign.

Understanding the *Umwelt* gives us a better sense of what animals will do next and how we can shape this by tailoring our motion or appearance. Embracing the idea of the *Umwelt* is also an act of generosity. We give the animals back their worlds by acknowledging them. But we also provide ourselves with a thousand new landscapes in the one before us. The hill is not only ours, but a richer-colored bump to the falcon, a mountain to the beetle, a refuge to the deer, and a wind shadow to the cold, wet sheep. Let us begin to sense and imagine what else.

Treachery

WE ARE BUILDING A PRACTICAL VIEW of nature as a world of signs that give instant meaning and trigger predictable actions. But evolution dictates that nature never stands still and will always incorporate changes that offer a competitive advantage. A few organisms have learned that by emulating certain signs they can prompt a desired reaction in another creature. Now that this is out of the evolutionary bag, a certain amount of trickery is to be expected.

Roosters allure hens by giving the call that indicates food, even when there is none, the sort of cheap trick that finds the impecunious and shallow singleton arriving at a date driving a car they can't afford. Some female finches grow weary of their mates staying too long away from the nest—*plus ça change?*—and imitate the sound of the male, which predictably brings them scurrying back.

Presumably after trying more direct pleas for company, Achilla, a lonely gorilla at the Basel Zoo in Switzerland, learned that deception worked where other efforts failed. By pretending to get her arm stuck in the wire mesh at the top of her cage, she could repeatedly force a keeper to come in to free her, giving her companionship for a short time at least.

Golden plovers will feign injury to draw trouble away from their young, and snakes go one step further, playing dead until they sense the danger receding. The saber-toothed blenny fish does a fake dance. Some fish allow "cleaner fish" to eat the parasites off their skin, but there is a protocol to this arrangement. The cleaner fish must offer its services, which it does with a choreographed dance. If the host is happy to be cleaned, it signals its willingness and the deal is done. The blenny has learned the cleaner's dance, but has no intention of eating the parasites: When the dance allows it to get close to an unwitting victim, it uses the opportunity to bite lumps out of it. Charming.

Animals don't have a monopoly on deception. Carrion flowers stink of rotting flesh to attract beetles and flies, which leave smothered in pollen. Carnivorous plants give off sweet smells to attract insect visitors that never leave. And passion vines grow a yellow spot on their leaves that looks like a butterfly egg to trick others into not laying.

The latest research is uncovering some impressive sophistication in the world of plant treachery. Some carnivorous flies like to feast on bees, particularly bees that are near death. Parachute plants draw in *Desmometopa* flies by brewing four chemicals that exactly mimic those given off by honeybees in trouble. The flies are tricked into thinking that a struggling bee lies in the bell-shaped flower, but all it finds are lots of hairs that make escape impossible, and so the diner becomes dinner for the flower.

Before we launch into sermons about the immorality of nature's deceitful behavior, we need to remember that we've long been in on the game. The Penobscot Indians of Maine drew moose within arrow range by using a cone made of birch bark to imitate the sounds of their mate. Ainu hunters in Japan and elsewhere have played a similar trick on deer.

Does this trickery undermine the foundations of what we are trying to do? No: The opposite is true. The deceptions only work because the signs are powerful, but honest ones will always dominate. Otherwise, the system fails.

A Storied Creature

THERE ARE MANY TRUTHS AND FALSEHOODS in folklore, but to see its purpose purely through that lens is too narrow. Folklore has roles beyond stocking the larder of our minds, and it performs them better than the raw facts can in isolation. The very best folklore contains truths, often wrapped in fiction, and delivers them in an entertaining and memorable way. Stories access parts of our brain that facts or instructions on their own fail to reach. That is why health advice often contains short stories instead of instructions. Cigarette packs say "Smoking Kills," not "Stop Smoking." Our fast-thinking limbic system is in charge of emotion and learning, so it is no surprise that we recall wisdom that makes us feel something, which is the job of stories.

What's more, folklore is something with which we should feel a special relationship because it is unique to our species. Green monkeys have been known to trick and lie—one was seen giving a lion alarm call, leading another to drop its banana, which the first then stole. Other animals are capable of language, invention, and deceit, but they do not tell stories. To enjoy stories is to be human. They allow us to share a greater truth amid small fictions.

The best messages outlive the inventor of the story, the storyteller, and even the story. Our morals have been shaped by true and fictional stories in ways that we cannot trace. The story does its job in a modest way, then may leave our memory.

Children would get bored of being told to "keep chipping away," but a story about a tortoise beating a hare in a race goes down better. Life can be tiring, tough, and tedious for all of us, so education is sometimes best served up disguised as entertainment.

Folklore has been part of every human society of which we have any knowledge, which makes a case for it having been necessary, not voluntary. It is one face of the wisdom of those societies. If we consider the different roles of folklore—entertainment, education, inspiration, and guidance—we can see why some work better than others and what role they can play in our aim of fast thinking outdoors.

Some of the most famous stories passed down to us are credited to the ancient Greek slave storyteller Aesop, who "made use of humble incidents to teach great truths . . . by announcing a story which everyone knows not to be true, told the truth by the very fact that he did not claim to be relating real events," wrote Philostratus. Many of the fables are etiological; they purport to explain the cause of some natural phenomenon—how the tortoise got its shell or why ants steal.

Etiological tales demonstrate the educational values and difficulties perfectly: We are given a colorful false reason for a true aspect of nature. We may remember this attribute and give no weight to the fiction, in which case we are better off. But some, of a literal mind-set, might recall the false reason and not the attribute, in which case they have been led down a bogus path. Some enjoy the story and think no more of it.

With no written record until recently, the only thing that would ensure folklore's survival was its own merit. If it was especially entertaining, informative, topical, surprising, or inspirational, it was more likely to be promulgated and survive—meaning all folklore was either viral or on its way out.

The cormorant was once a wool-merchant. He entered into partnership with the bramble and the bat, and they freighted a large vessel with wool. She struck on some rocks, and went to the bottom. This loss caused the firm to become bankrupt. Since that disaster, the bat skulks in his hiding-hole till twilight, in order that he may avoid his creditors; the bramble seizes hold of every passing sheep, to make up for his loss by retaining part of its wool; while the cormorant is for ever diving in the waters of the deep, in hopes of discovering whereabouts his foundered vessel lies.

This story is typical of much folklore: It is not the best story you will ever hear, but it is gently entertaining, even amusing, and envelops a little light education. Three animals' characteristics are woven into a tale about a plot gone wrong.

The entertainment was not always in story form. Sometimes it was more physical. For thousands of years, awareness of seasonal changes was enhanced by ritualistic celebrations. Nobody was going to forget the passing of the winter solstice when it was accompanied by a fire festival and the biggest party of the season, in the way that its successor, Christmas, does not go unnoticed now. And there is the pleasure of art: Understanding about animals was passed on via cave paintings tens of thousands of years before John James Audubon inspired so many with his magnificent paintings of birds.

But words transcend pictures and parties for the passing on of outdoor wisdom, as they are the most portable and easily spread form of lore. Think of the winter sun in high latitudes. In the Arctic, the sun may barely peep above the southern horizon before disappearing for another twenty-three hours.

The American author Barry Lopez adds a layer to this by showing us how it feels to witness it: It's like watching "a whale rolling over," an image that does more than facts alone. If this image works for you, if it creates a satisfying mini-story, then you will be more likely to share it, as I have done here. It becomes a piece of micro-lore. Sometimes we are lucky enough to feel our own lore forming.

When sailing off Iceland a few years ago, we were enjoying the sun near the middle of the night when we were hit by strong winds that surprised us. The boat heeled over and we scrambled to put reefs in the sails. As skipper, I was alarmed; the wind strength had shot up and the cause was not immediately apparent, but a few seconds later I saw the culprit on the horizon.

Katabatic winds were flowing down off the ice of the mountains to our east. When air comes into contact with cold surfaces, like snow-capped mountains, it cools, becoming denser than the surrounding air, and gravity pulls it on a downhill journey. It picks up pace until a blast of icy air reaches the bottom of the mountain. I had known the geography and meteorology of this phenomenon for many years, but it is not geography, meteorology, or any other "ology" that leaps into our minds at such times. We reach for something deeper: characters. I saw an invisible yet frightening wind monster rolling down the mountain. It is not a creature with distinct physical features, not one I know from other stories (I don't think), but whenever I see the cold slopes of mountains nearby I imagine it rolling down them. That image reminds me of the dangers better than any formal text could. If I were to pass this on as lore, I would need to name the monster and work on the story, but here it is on display not as lore, but as its precursor.

Before Aristotle and company began to observe and codify nature, folklore was how wisdom was passed on. And we exist as a species because we are both more intelligent and wiser than other species. Intelligence on its own is not enough outdoors: Those with the highest IQs are unlikely to last long without wisdom. The modern human in an industrialized society is probably every bit as intelligent as our ancestors (although this is not certain) and we have access to infinitely greater amounts of knowledge about the outdoors than they had. Yet we are less wise about nature than they were, and there can be only two reasons for this: a lack of outdoor experience and a lack of instantly accessible wisdom. If we look at a contemporary application of this idea, without resorting to technology, it will come to life.

Imagine you are planning a walk and a picnic on a summer day. You wake up excited by the day ahead, but on looking outside you see the landscape hugged by a thick mist. Mist is water vapor. It is direct evidence of wet air, and it appears to be a very poor weather omen. You are about to cancel your picnic, but then you remember an old shepherd's saying, "Morning mists carry away the rain." And you venture out to enjoy watching the mist clear and sun ruling the day. The meteorology may be of interest: Morning mists are more likely under clear night skies, which make clear daytime skies later more likely as the sun warms the land, but the facts are long-winded and easily forgotten. By giving the mist a character and making it responsible for an action, the shepherds encapsulated all that was useful in a piece of lore that was succinct, memorable, and helpful.

Another example might be the ancient idea that snakes guard treasure. Snakes couldn't care less for precious metals, yet there is value in lore: Humans need to be wary of some snakes, and they love riches. By putting something highly valued, a goal, on the other side of a genuinely dangerous foe, we have the makings of a very short story that is memorable and useful.

We may not recall it daily, but it will probably fly back into our conscious mind if we go digging for something on a warm day. In terms of awareness and survival, such lore is more valuable than a whole book's worth of knowledge on snake behavior that we don't recall in that instant.

Landscape features become mythical characters and are tied together in our memory by narratives of their relationships. This is oral cartography, and it has many forms, from the sea shanties that remind sailors of the next coastal feature to expect around a headland to Aboriginal song lines. The thread of each story will be dictated by the most vital feature or resource. An academic researching in Australia in the middle of the last century put it like this: "The whole Western Desert is criss-crossed with the meandering tracks of ancestral beings, mostly though not invariably following the known permanent and impermanent water-hole routes."

One of the great advantages of blending myth with physical features is that they support each other. The landscape feature jogs the memory while the story triggers another memory, then a prediction. A rocky outcrop may earn the character of a bat in a story, which reminds the traveler of the caves they will reach next. For Aboriginal peoples, the stories were practical resources, much as a map can be to us. A group in unfamiliar territory was able to find water because "some old fellers had been . . . and knew the stories."

On a much smaller scale, we are encouraged to notice details. An impression in a rock is a famous footprint; boulders are the baggage of giants. If the story is good enough, we will remember the smallest landmarks. And certain places in any landscape are associated with par-ticular animal behaviors. From a practical perspective, anything that helps us predict a behavior is worthwhile, regardless of its scientific accu-racy. This explains the many stories of places being haunted because, for those who are persuaded, the evidence is clear: At that exact spot animals sense a ghost or other macabre force and react badly. If a horse is regularly spooked at the same spot on a track, every rider will want to know about it. Stories of menacing phantoms would once have spread quickly among the locals and made riders wary of that spot, possibly saving them from harm. That there is a patch of darker ground next to the track—inconspicuous to humans but alarming to horses—is not the sort of story to travel as far or as fast.

Rhymes, scanning, and all of the tools of the poet help lodge lore in our minds, which is why the few that contain some truth have value. We are most likely to recall rhymes. Our weather typically arrives from the west, so a red sky at night means we can see far in the direction of the setting sun. It is a sign of clear skies to the west and therefore a good weather omen. A red sky at night is a shepherd's delight—and a folklorist's master class.

At its most effective, folklore enhances our outdoor wisdom by weaving an extra layer into the fabric of the landscape, helping us to remember, notice, understand, and predict things we may otherwise have ignored. In a scientific age, where the written word is given more authority than the spoken, we can still learn from the stories we hear about what lies ahead. When they rise up from our unconscious and give us helpful insight into a situation beyond our slow analysis, their value is beyond debate.

The Ikus

IEMERGED FROM A PINE FOREST UNDER a dull grey sky and followed a path of sand, dark mud, and dead pine needles out of the forest, then went on through the heather. There were scattered saplings, but the sky was now open. A solitary gorse bush added a sprinkling of yellow to the scene, and I leaned in to smell its coconut fragrance. I smiled, remembering that the strength of the scent is influenced by the levels of sunlight the plant receives—the more sun, the stronger the smell. I circled the bush and there were more flowers on the sun-soaked southern side, which is typical, but it would be fanciful to pretend that I could pick up changes in the scent. I will one day, though.

The sounds of the birds faded as I walked out onto the heath and a new quiet arrived. It was broken by the voices of children carried to me from another copse by the northerly breeze. I walked until I reached the edge of the heath and there was met by a wall of rhododendrons. Pushing through a gap, I picked my way between silver birches and holly, then the canopy darkened again and I listened to the mumbling and grumbling of spent pine cones underfoot.

On the other side of the pines, the land opened up once more and I saw an oak tree, the first for a long time. In the space of a few steps the soil had darkened and lost its sand. The sounds of birds returned, as I'd expected. Coal tits and song thrushes were singing close by. The tree, the color of the earth, and the sounds of the birds had joined together.

Habitat: *The natural home or environment of an animal, plant, or other organism.*

Ecology: *The branch of biology that deals with the relations of organisms to one another and to their physical surroundings.*

Biotope: *The region of a habitat associated with a particular ecological community.*

Habitat, ecology, biotope . . . Each of these words does a job, an overlapping and clinical job. And they each have weaknesses. Critically, they do not point us toward a way to experience the signs they envelop. That is why I prefer a different word: "ikus." Don't bother looking it up in a dictionary—you won't find it.

Ikus: *A habitat niche experienced as a collection of interwoven signs.*

I neither properly invented the word nor stole it. I borrowed it, broke it, then fashioned something from the pieces. I have been using it in my notebooks for so long that it took me a while to work out where it had come from. By flicking back through old scribblings I was able to trace its strange etymology. It turns out that I had used a foreign word, then allowed a corruption. It evolved to take on the meaning set out above.

About five years ago I learned that the Hai||om people of southern Africa refer to their home area as !hus—that word was an attempt to transliterate the local dialect into our alphabet. It wasn't very memorable to me. I started writing it as "ihus," which became "ikus." But the concept I liked was that the Hai||om saw their surroundings as a blend of sky, plant, animal, and human influences, and the land; for example, Tsabo!hus, meaning "land of the hard ground." Experiments with versions of it blended with my growing fascination for outdoor signs to create the concept "ikus."

We know that recognizing a plant or animal is also to see a sign, but there is much more to this than a single hop from observation to sign. Each organism indicates the likelihood of certain other organisms, and all of those are signs, too. These pointers are not restricted to other plants and animals. Each organism also indicates the likelihood of certain environment and landscape features. And it flows both ways: Each terrain feature indicates the probability of our encountering other terrain features and particular organisms. Every small patch of landscape is a network of interrelated and interconnected signs, and each time we notice a change in one, it is giving us a clue as to how the tapestry around us is changing.

On one level, this is how naturalists have always viewed the world. As Richard Jefferies wrote in 1879: "Crows frequently build in oaks, and unless they are driven away by shot will return to the same neighborhood the following year. They appear to prefer places near water, and long after the nesting-time is past will visit the spot."

Here we see a relationship between crow and landscape: It favors a certain tree species and likes to nest near water. Unsurprisingly, it does not like being shot at. Seen from one perspective, we have a habitat preferred by a bird. Finding an oak near water should increase our probability, especially at certain times of year, of finding the bird. Viewed from another perspective, the sight of a nesting crow is a sign that an oak and water may be close.

To appreciate the potential of the ikus view, all we now have to do is to realize that the crow, the oak, and the water are signs to dozens of other things, all interconnected. The full complexity may be daunting to our conscious minds, but need not be for our unconsciouses, which thrive on joining dots, monitoring patterns, and alerting us to surprises and inconsistencies. You are already so good at this that you may not even be aware of it.

If a person in your neighborhood begins dressing strangely or acting oddly, you will pick up on this as surely as if you saw a kangaroo reclining on the grass at your local park. The former is a sign to which we've retained some sensitivity; the latter is a glaring and ridiculous example of the sort of thing we have lost touch with—a sign in nature that something is not as we had expected. In both cases, our unconscious has told us that a familiar pattern has been broken. With practice, an unusual leaf shape will stand out like the kangaroo would. But to see the anomalies, first we must learn to see the normal patterns.

In 1936 Harley Harris Bartlett, a botanist, studied how the Maya people, an indigenous group of Mesoamerica, read their landscapes. He recorded how they recognized plant communities and their respective dominant species. Since then a lot more research work has been done, and wherever in the world it takes place, we discover that indigenous people can recognize individual species, but also view their surroundings as a collection of distinct landscape types. Shortly after the Second World War, the anthropologist Donald Thomson wrote about the naming culture among the Wik Monkan, an Australian Aboriginal tribe. He found that they had names for individual people, plants, and animals, as well as manufactured objects, like tools and weapons. But they also had a system of landscape classification and divided their country into "types," each determined by its geography and botany.

It turns out that the Wik Monkan customs are the rule, not the exception. When a pair of anthropologists looked at studies of indigenous awareness in investigations that ranged from Alaska to Australia, they found a common theme. Social scientists Eugene Hunn and Brien Meilleur discovered that the indigenous communities identified dozens of—and, in some cases, more than a hundred—different landscape categories, or "ecotopes." Some were focused toward the plant communities, but most included landscape types that were distinct from the plants.

In industrialized societies, it is clear that we have allowed many distinct landscapes to blend into one. We may still choose to go for a walk in the "dark woods." We tend not to walk from *heridzololima* to the *iitsaapolima*—from "high, closed canopy forest on moist soils near streams" to "high, closed canopy forest in secondary vegetation of old garden sites," in the way that the Baniwa Indians of the Amazon do.

A practical approach is to notice simple associations, starting with pairs, then slowly working outward. I often see the mounds created by yellow meadow ants on my walks. Something about the way they build them suits wild thyme, and I started to notice that the flower is often growing on them. This is an association, a nice simple pair. Importantly, I haven't solved any great ecological mysteries here, just noticed one small, pretty flower growing in one distinct place.

I practice noticing that the mounds mean I will probably see the flower, and soon the sight of the mounds prompts me to look for the flower without thinking about it. It becomes apparent that the wild thyme is a fussy flower: It loves lots of sunlight and is much more common on the sunny, south-facing side of these ant mounds. Another simple pairing—plant and aspect. But now we have a three-way association: insect home–plant–direction, ant–thyme–south.

When wild thyme is in blossom in summer, its small pink-purple flowers stand out, adding a sprinkling of color to the southern side of the mounds. I enjoy noticing this and look for it on my walks, making this association—mound, color, aspect. Then there comes a moment when I see south in a pink shade on a bump on the hill. This is not a dramatic moment; it slides in gently. The conscious thought fades and the sense of seeing direction in color emerges. It doesn't scream and it is not a robust sensing, just a shy prompt, but it's definitely there. And there is joy to it, as though the synapses between my ears like this game.

This is not about the ants, the flower, or even the direction. It is about the noticing of pairs. The species are different all over the world, but the approach is the same. It is about the associations we experience and developing familiarity with them.

Equally, it is not about always needing to explain the association. It is very satisfying to be able to say we will see a holly blue butterfly after Pegasus overtakes the sun in the east at dawn because we understand the relationship between Earth's orbit of the sun and the star calendar, but . . . the butterfly and the stars will still do their thing without our explanation. I'd encourage us all to understand the connection where we can, but not to place this above the observation and experience.

The observation remains valid and valuable *even if we get the explanation wrong.* Wherever we see bluebells, we are likely to see badger sets. This is another basic association and pairing, and such a dependable one that it was once believed the two were symbiotic. We now know there is little direct causal relationship between the very different organisms and see them cohabiting only because they happen to share a love of the same calcareous soil. But the thing to bear in mind is that our forebears *noticed* the association, even if they saw causality where there was none. They knew to expect badgers where they saw bluebells and vice versa.

Nature is always making connections where we would struggle to predict one. A wasps' or ants' nest might generate a healthy revulsion in us, forcing us to back away from the worrying frenzy. But at least a hundred species of bird like to build nests within five feet of these stinging, biting creatures—one animal's wariness is always another's opportunity. Wrens are more likely to fledge young if their nest is near a wasps'. Rooks are impressive defenders of territory, and birds of prey such as hawks are repelled by a rookery. This creates an umbrella of safety below rookeries for any creature, like the pheasant, that fears hawks but not rooks.

Aboriginals have proven extraordinary abilities for finding water in remote, arid parts of their country. They do this by noticing any changes in plant life, the behavior of birds and other animals, and also by being forensically attuned to the shape of the land. "I could find waterholes in rocky country by the shape of the rocks," Wintinna Mick told researcher David Lewis in the 1970s. And another Aboriginal tribesperson indicated that he would look on the lee side of escarpments.

It is only our lost awareness, a love of landscape detail that has absconded, that makes these skills seem superhuman. The Maya notice every minute shift in color and character of the soil: *sahkab lu'um* is a deep-black soil while *ch'ich lu'um* is a deep-black fertile soil, with small stones in it. In the Sahaptin language of the Indians of the Columbia Plateau, the word *xaat'ay* indicates the place where a stream shallows and passes over flat rocks. It came into existence only because this landscape feature is valuable. The Indians had observed a useful pairing between landscape and animal behavior: Shallow water and rocks expose the migrating salmon, making them vulnerable to the hunters' spears. It is analogous to an observation made by the Palauan fishermen of Micronesia, who use the word *hapitsetse* to describe the area where currents converge downstream of an island, creating rough waters that act as a sign of where tuna might be found.

We have touched on how the land, water, climate, plants, and animals are part of the fine matrix that makes up each parcel of habitat that we pass through, but one other important consideration is human influence. Humans have a habit of forcing an impact on their ecosystems. It is generally seen as negative—we have not been the most conscientious of guardians over the past few centuries—but the true picture is always more complex. It is not a case of human = bad, wilderness = good.

In the French Alps, the Alluetais, a rural peasant community, change their landscape as all settled people do. They see their world as being composed of niche microhabitats in the way that indigenous people do. The land in Les Allues is rocky, and most of the large stones must be removed before any field can be cultivated. This leads to piles of rocks at the edges of the fields, known to the locals as *les mordjes*. The Alluetais have noticed that the rock piles take on their own life and that some plant species prefer the disturbed earth and piles of rocks to either the worked field or the untouched land. The rock piles draw raspberries, bramble, and elder that in turn draw birds that enjoy the berries.

When farmers chooses a crop, they dictate not only the plants, but also the wildlife that will share the space. And that choice will stamp the land long after the farmers have themselves returned to the soil. As Richard Jefferies noted, the crops outlast the farmer:

> *These orchards are a survival from the days when the monks laboured in vineyard and garden, and mayhap even of earlier times. When once a locality has got into the habit of growing a certain crop it continues to produce it for century after century; and thus there are villages famous for apple or pear or cherry, while the district at large is not at all given to such culture.*

Our motives may be different: We do not rely on noticing the shapes of the rocks for a lifesaving drink, or ripples in the water's surface to catch our supper, but our ability to notice these things is not lost because of that—if we choose to look. This is the only major obstacle to our rekindling these skills: It's optional. There is no strong argument that can be made to say that they are necessary in a physical sense anymore. The Fulani people of the Sahel desert region of Africa have no choice but to monitor their environment for the subtlest changes in habitat; their lives depend on finding pasture in the land they move through. It's unsurprising, therefore, that they are sensitive to the ways that landscape, water, soil, plants, animals, and humans influence each small patch of that land. Only this level of interest could spawn a word like *hanhade*, meaning a very small area of compressed soil that tastes both salty and bitter. The Fulani have about a hundred environment classifications of this kind.

It is tempting to think of these signs as being more prevalent in exotic locations like the Sahel because the people there remind us, via pioneering anthropologists, of these lost skills. But a bridge in a suburb where we live can trigger a search for spraints, a sign of otters. The reaction of pigeons in a city can help us understand the behavior of gazelles in the Serengeti and vice versa.

Drawing all of the potentially complex pieces together, we can still see a simple approach. Every patch of Earth's surface is a tapestry of land, water, climate, plant, animal, and human signs. Trying to see the full interwoven matrix in one go is impossible, so we start by noticing simple associations: Certain soils mean that certain plants are likely; stagnant water means we'll see particular insects. Slowly and with practice, the pairs become triplets, which begin to touch each other's influence. At this point we have begun to tune in to the local ikus. We have a sense of place.

As we move through the landscape, our sensitivity to our ikus means that we have inbuilt expectations of the land, water, weather, plants, animals, and human behavior we will experience. We are seeing the patterns. If our senses feed us things that match these expectations, we feel attuned to our ikus—we have a fine sense of where we are. It also means that we have a baseline; any novelties or anomalies will stand out as dramatic signs.

The simplest, easiest to detect, and most dramatic change of ikus comes when we move between places of very different geological influences. Cross from an area with base rocks like chalk or limestone to an acidic area and the soil, water, plants, animals, and even human signs change rapidly. We can't fail to notice it. About the only thing that won't change immediately is the weather.

But the ikus viewpoint is really about encouraging an approach that allows the smaller signs to resonate. The nibbled plant that indicates the rabbit, which makes sense of the rustle in the leaves, which is a sign of the dry weather, which means the rabbit is heading to the rare large puddle behind us.

Part VI

Epilogue

The Room

T
HE IDEA OF A KEY WORKS well for unlocking some-
thing, in our case a sign that allows our fast thinking to reign
again. But what happens next? If each key opens its own
locked door, where do they all lead?

Our interest in the clues and signs in nature need not stop at the practical application. We can derive a lot of satisfaction from working out
where north is by using a shape in nature or predicting from its body language what a squirrel will do next. But there is another, headier feeling
when we start to sense that these observations are pieces that fit together.
The puddles we see are a reflection of time, both daily and seasonal, and
this is the metronome that the squirrels, birds, and wildflowers follow.
The vole ventures into the field because there is little moonlight, which
indicates a spring tide, which is why the fish can be seen jumping out
of the surging waters at the same time as the voles hop over the stubble
in the field.

In the middle of the last century, the colonial administrator Arthur
Grimble noticed that hundreds of tiger sharks gathered at one Pacific
lagoon for a day or two each month. He was intrigued as to why this
might be and began an investigation, pairing his observations with any

gems of wisdom he could glean from the secretive locals. He found his answer by following a long chain.

A minute marine organism, too small for him to identify, was brought closer inshore than normal by the high spring tide. This was the food of a minuscule crab, which was then tempted in great numbers to head a few inches deeper into the water than normal. The sardines, perhaps cued by the spring tide, launched in their thousands at this ephemeral crab feast. The grey mullet did not wait for a second invitation to gorge on the sardines. The mullet drew in the larger fish, like the trevally and also the tiger sharks.

Look at a jug. Notice how it appears different from each angle: It presents a different form to your eyes when viewed with the handle on the left or right, and a very different one when viewed from above or below. If you are sitting at the table and someone passes the jug in front of you, then pours the water, your eyes will see a hundred different shapes in a few seconds. But our brain has learned to solve the puzzle—it makes sense of the different perspectives and forms a single vision of a jug for us. Our brain cuts through the changing shapes and patterns to forge one meaning.

If the metaphor of keys is stretched a little, perhaps we can think of a vast circular room, with a million doors that touch each other around this strange space. Each key unlocks a door that allows us one perspective of the same room.

The extraordinary beauty of what we see in the room is complex and appears different from each door, but we know we must be viewing the same thing from slightly different angles. Sometimes we are fortunate enough to glimpse how what we see in that room is the same entity, even as it appears different from each door. And at this moment, nature makes sense. We experience something profound, an insight that is often accompanied by euphoria. It is an experience that transcends easy description, which is what many writers are conceding by reaching for the words "sublime" or "numinous." The contents of the room have been glimpsed from different angles over the years. For the English poet Thomas Traherne, this was the "real whispering" of nature.

The line between subjective experience and objective recording blurs when either nears this deeper appreciation. Alexander von Humboldt sketched his *Naturgemälde*, a three-foot-by-two drawing of the mountain Chimborazo. It outlined how the plants to be found in each zone would be decided by factors that ranged from temperature and humidity to the blueness of the sky. A poet might have said the same thing by recording how our sweating and squinting invite certain plants to appear.

The desire to care for our environment leads to another perspective, albeit a familiar view of interconnection. We may learn of the extinction of a bird and discover that it was inevitable once deforestation altered the flow of a river in another country. The fungicides used in southern Europe affect the ultraviolet light in Lapland.

Another perspective would be nature as theophany—a manifestation of God. The word "God" may repel those uncomfortable with orthodox religion, or other people's orthodox religion, but in this context, it is only shorthand for the belief that there is some deeper meaning behind the things we sense and beneath the universe as a whole. The shape, flavor, or name it takes may tie us in knots, but we either feel it or we don't.

Samuel Taylor Coleridge felt it. He differentiated between "abstract" knowledge and "substantial" knowledge. Coleridge's abstract knowledge is more technical; it sees us as standing outside nature, looking at it as a giant box, the contents of which can be understood by peering in and analyzing. His substantial knowledge is "that intuition of things which arises when we possess ourselves, as one with the whole . . ." Abstract knowledge is found in the guidebook that tells you which route to take for a good view of a mountain. Substantial knowledge comes from time spent immersed in that landscape. Coleridge saw an intuitive view of nature as necessary to more profound insights and a better path to that deeper meaning.

For all who are deeply immersed in nature, whether out of necessity or drawn there for other reasons, the line between the practical and philosophical disappears. In the case of traditional indigenous people, there is rarely a division. There is no purpose in a philosophy that is separate from the need to thrive within a landscape, so thought exists within that framework. Those of us from a different, less practical, tradition soon find that the act of navigating, foraging, hunting, or making shelter becomes philosophical. We start by finding north, using the wind, and end up appreciating that the path we are following is shaped by the way deer move between brambles, which is governed by the sun's own path through the trees. The practical act becomes a window into the whole.

Our brain collects these connections and sorts them, making good sense of them even as our conscious minds weave mad courses between more modern obsessions. In Mesoamerica, directions were paired with symbols, colors, and broader qualities: east is red, a reed, and masculine; west is white, a house, and feminine; north is black, flint, and death; south is a rabbit, blue, and life.

It is ironic that a practical approach to nature allows a change in thinking, one that a cerebral approach doesn't. Philosophy is fixed firmly in the slower part of our brains. It can discuss the fast part, but is forbidden entry. Discovering that everything in nature is a sign with meaning is a practical way of sensing connections, and these functional insights are whisked through to the fast brain. The act of noticing the relationship between a bird's behavior and a cloud, one that allows weather prediction, forges new patterns of thought. A broader, deeper, faster, more instinctive view of nature is formed: a new and ancient philosophy.

The dark line through silver dew connects us to the rabbit that has passed by. And the pairings spread until they touch each other. The dew is a sign of the clear skies of the vanishing night, and the grass that it lies on is paired with the rabbit. Near Venus, the cloud above the rabbit indicates the growing breeze, a sign that explains the rabbit's body language, itself a sign that we can tiptoe until we can nearly touch it.

We find that dew, grass, Venus, east, cloud, breeze, and rabbit become connected.

One cold January morning, I walked up Black Down, one of the higher hills in the low range of the South Downs in southeast England. I was drawn there before dawn by the heavy snow and the opportunities it offers. As the sun rose above the last clouds of the snowstorm, I met a gorse bush that brought me close to tears. I was offered such a strong sense of meaning that I felt unsteady with happiness. The experience of sensing direction, animals, and weather patterns without thinking, of feeling it so powerfully, so unambiguously, triggered a surge of emotion. I could see the room.

My slow thinking caught up and analyzed the signs. The storm's northwest wind formed familiar drift shapes in the snow on the windward and downwind side; the bush itself had been sculpted by years of exposure to the southwest wind; the gorse flowers dominated the southern side. The first warmth of the early sun had thawed snow on the southeastern side of the bush. A sound was two species, a squirrel and ivy. Tracks revealed where animals had sheltered overnight. I felt the breeze from the southwest now. The storm had passed.

My fast thinking gave my slow thinking a slow clap.

Notes and Further Reading

INTRODUCTION

In the past second your senses have picked up eleven million pieces of
  information: L. Cron, p. 7.

hearing honey: C. Turnbull, pp. 14–15 and 241.

the strange inscriptions of Assyria: R. Jefferies, from
  richardjefferiessociety.co.uk/downloads/THE%20OPEN%20AIR.pdf
  (Accessed 12/14/17).

WILD SIGNS AND STAR PATHS I

William Cowper: en.wikiquote.org/wiki/William_Cowper (Accessed
  8/22/17).

If an insect lands on the back of your neck: N. Tinbergen, p. 209.

The San people in the Kalahari dessert report experiencing a powerful
  burning sensation when they are getting close to an animal they are
  hunting: L. Liebenberg.

"I have a feeling . . . Feel in my head. Been in the bush since small . . .": D.
  Lewis, p. 265.

Joel Hardin: J. Hardin, p. 278.

Gary Player, a very successful golfer, was practicing difficult shots out
of a bunker: G. Yocom, "My Shot: Gary Player," August 12, 2010,
golfdigest.com/story/myshot_gd0210 (Accessed 8/24/17).

THE SUN ANVIL

Based on notes taken during a walk in Crete with Ed Marley in
September 2016.

WILD SIGNS AND STAR PATHS II

"The first great mistake that people make in the matter, is the supposition
. . .": J. Ruskin and J. Rosenberg, p. 24.

An RSPB warden once explained to me that the most common word used
to describe their reserve on feedback forms was "quiet": Steve Hughes,
personal correspondence.

"It is very likely some ploughboy who thinks nothing of it, except to
immediately imitate it, hears the cuckoo . . .": R. Jefferies, *Wild Life in a
Southern County*, pp. 314–15.

Carl Jung believed it was this process that explained . . . "distracted
psychological state": C. G. Jung, pp. 108–9.

"He who's bitten by a viper jumps from a spotted rope": C. Bailey, p. 34.

"I did not even know myself. There was something about him . . .": in
"The Police and the Thieves," *Quarterly Review*, 1856, quoted in K.
Summerscale, p. 83.

"sensitiveness—that peculiar, apprehensive detective faculty": Charlotte
Brontë, quoted in K. Summerscale, p. 83.

scientists in Iowa proved that gamblers can sense a pattern in the cards:
M. Gladwell, p. 9.

Firefighter story: M. Gladwell, pp. 122–4; G. Klein; and D. Kahneman.

We recognize snakes more quickly than we do other animals: N. Kawai
and H. S. He, "Breaking Snake Camouflage," PLOS One, October 26,
2016, journals.plos.org/plosone/article?id=10.1371/journal
.pone.0164342 (Accessed 8/25/17). My thanks to Arran Jacques for
making me aware of this.

macaques: T. Caro, p. 14.

Bird of prey neck shape: N. Tinbergen, p. 31.

RSPB . . . merlin: P. Holden and T. Cleeves, p. 103.

Butterflies that are searching for particular flowers might use the scent as the sign that they are near to them: N. Tinbergen, p. 82.

Hawk moths use colors to guide them: N. Tinbergen, p. 43.

I have read authors' definitions of "wild" as any place you can walk for a week: B. Krause, p. 5.

THE WIND ANCHOR

The mood of hunters may change with a shift in the wind and a hunt may be canceled: H. Brody, p. 119.

The Inuit check the wind first thing in the morning, when they step outside for their first pee of the day: L. M. Johnson and E. Hunn, p. 188.

"Guard your herd, O Amr, from the rings around the moon!": C. Bailey, p. 56.

WILD SIGNS AND STAR PATHS III

Pyrrhocoris apterus: Alban Cambe, personal correspondence.

"universe is perfused with signs": C. S. Peirce, quoted in A. Siewers, p. 1.

"perhaps the most international and important intellectual movement since the taking root of science . . ." John Deely, quoted by Dorion Sagan, in J. von Uexküll, p. 4.

"meaning-seeking creatures": K. Armstrong, p. 2.

"pansemiotic web of cosmic meaning": A. K. Siewers, p. 33.

"musical harmony of varied shapes and colors with a certain order and rhythm": St. Gregory of Nyssa, quoted in A. K. Siewers, p. 45.

"a red rag to a bull" is a myth: "Does the Color Red Really Make Bulls Angry?" discovery.com/tv-shows/mythbusters/mythbusters-database/color-red-makes-bulls-go-ballistic (Accessed 8/28/17).

Robins: D. Lack, pp. 162–5.

"associative activation" . . . David Hume: this section is indebted to D. Kahneman, pp. 51–2.

THE SHEAR

The seventh-century English monk Aldhelm claimed that the wind was invisible: A. Harris, p. 39.

THE SKY MAP

Coniferous trees release chemicals called terpenes: D. Adam, "Chemical Released by Trees Can Help Cool Planet, Scientists Find," October 31, 2008, theguardian.com/environment/2008/oct/31/forests-climatechange (Accessed 5/25/17).

Alaskan hunters have reported being able to locate caribou herds from miles away: D. Pryde, p. 192.

"water sky": B. Lopez, p. 291.

THE INVISIBLE HANDRAIL

the belief that jaguars in the Ecuadorian rainforest do not attack a person who sleeps face up: E. Kohn, p. 1.

Imshi sana wala tihutt rijlak fi gana: C. Bailey, p. 230.

THE LIGHT AND DARK WOODS

In the Congo, decades ago, a Pygmy stepped out of the forest onto open plains: C. Turnbull, p. 231.

One bright-orange maritime lichen found in the US: ocean.si.edu/ocean-life/invertebrates/seaside-lichens, and eol.org/pages/196085/details (Accessed 6/11/18.)

"wood blindness": J. Humphreys, p. 141.

THE EDGE AND MUSIT

studies have revealed that predators are more active at the edge than in the interior: M. Breed, p. 189.

"'Tis as hard to find a hare without a muse, as a woman without a scuse": E. of Norwich, p. 243.

THE FIRE

Funaria hygrometrica: my thanks to those who have written to me about this moss, including Paul Lane.

THE BROWSE, BITE, AND HAVEN

This chapter was aided by research done by the Forestry Commission, and my thanks goes to Robert Thurlow for his time discussing my findings.

"Furthermore ye should know a great hart by the fraying . . .": E. of Norwich, p. 135.

THE CELEBRATION AND SHADOW

receive twenty times more light than the northern: T. Kozlowski, et al., p. 125.

dog's mercury . . . had thrived in a narrow strip: I was inspired to look for this by the observations of that great naturalist, Oliver Rackham, in his book about Hayley Wood.

THE FRIEND, GUEST, AND REBEL

Scots pines were once planted in clumps in the UK to send a signal to drovers that they could stay for the night: R. Mabey, p. 23.

"By old farmhouses, mostly in exposed places (for which there is a reason), one or more huge walnut trees may be found . . .": R. Jefferies, *The Amateur Poacher*, pp. 8–9.

THE REAPER

Honeysuckle grows clockwise, while others, like bindweed, grow counterclockwise: D. Derbyshire, "New Twist on Plants That Grow in Spirals," May 9, 2002, telegraph.co.uk/education/3296579/New-twist-on-plants-that-grow-in-spirals.html (Accessed 6/16/17).

Suckers, lots of young shoots, emanating from the base of an oak mean it is struggling: P. Wohlleben, pp. 68–9.

the temperature difference between the south and north side of trees in winter can reach 45 degrees Fahrenheit: K. Wagner, *Sunscald Injury or Southwest Winter Injury on Deciduous Trees*, digitalcommons.usu.edu/extension_curall/1239 (Accessed 12/14/17).

Female woolly spider monkeys in Brazil: J. Shurkin, "Animals That Self-Medicate," pnas.org/content/111/49/17339.full (Accessed 6/16/17).

THE PERCH AND SENTINEL

Species of crow, blackbird, pigeon, and wren are known to use sentinels: T. Caro, p. 159.

When it is time for the sentinel meerkat to stand down, the sounds alter: T. Caro, pp. 161–2.

When the male red-winged blackbird is guarding a nest: T. Caro, p. 159.

The higher any sentinel is, the more those in the group know they can rely on it and the more time they spend focused on foraging: A. N. Radford, L. I. Hollén, and M. B. V. Bell, "The Higher the Better: Sentinel Height Influences Foraging Success in a Social Bird," *Proceedings of the Royal Society B*, Vol. 276, pp. 2437–42, April 1, 2009.

THE FACE AND TAIL

FACS: imotions.com/blog/facial-action-coding-system and en.wikipedia.org/wiki/Facial_Action_Coding_System (Accessed 7/18/17).

birds or reptiles . . . fish gills . . . amphibians' . . . Snakes: T. Maran, et al., pp. 133–4.

Australian magpie . . . Lesley Rogers: K. Shanor and J. Kanwal, p. 101.

Horses, cats, deer, and elephants reveal a lot through their ears . . . "temper yawn" . . . crocodile's smile: T. Maran, et al., pp. 129–34.

many primates and dogs can follow our stare . . . but wolves apparently don't: "The Zoosemiotics of Sheep Herding with Dogs," Louise Westling, p. 38

Dog tail signs: S. Coren, "What a Wagging Dog Tail Really Means," psychologytoday.com/blog/canine-corner/201112/what-wagging-dog-tail-really-means-new-scientific-data (Accessed 8/21/17).

Deer and antelope, as well as some lizards and many water birds, flick their tails to indicate: T. Caro, pp. 250–60.

Some monkeys will hold their tail out horizontally behind them when afraid, but baboons: T. Maran, et al., p. 88.

THE PEEK

Predators are finely tuned to vigilance and will target animals that are foraging over those that are vigilant: T. Caro, pp. 141–2.

Many birds, including favorites such as sparrows starlings, robins, and blackbirds: T. Caro, p. 163.

Grey squirrels will pause more frequently when moving out of woodland: T. Caro, p. 117.

Adults are more alert than youngsters: T. Caro, p. 166.

ringed seals . . . Weddell seals: T. Caro, p. 119.

Willow tits scan their surroundings less when they are in a flock with coal tits: T. Caro, p. 144 (table).

house sparrows make a specific call, a chirrup: T. Caro, p. 125.

ducks on the edge of the group open the eye that faces outward: T. Caro, p. 119.

THE FREEZE, CROUCH, AND FEIGN

Studies in the US have found that fox squirrels that inhabit: T. Caro, p. 47.

the bittern . . . Before it turns into a statue: T. Caro, p. 37.

Raptors and owls that hunt rodents: T. Caro, p. 414.

the francolin: L. Liebenberg.

"There might perhaps have been fifty birds": R. Jefferies, *The Amateur Poacher*, p. 110.

Crouching . . . is clever in another way, too, as it covers any shadow: T. Caro, p. 59.

Crouching can be triggered in birds by calls: T. Caro, p. 414.

Crows tend to hunker down: N. Tinbergen, p. 162.

In one study of fifty ducks that feigned death: T. Caro, p. 439.

THE FLIGHT

A rodent falling off a twig in blind panic at detecting a weasel nearby: C. Elford, p. 33.

A small bird will use about thirty times as much energy: J. Ackerman, p. 50.

FEAR—Flee Early and Avoid the Rush: W. Cooper and D. Blumstein, p. 338.

Animals are also sensitive to season, hunger, location, experience, and social rank: S. Laskow, "Animals Don't Just Flee—They Make Surprisingly Careful Escape Plans," atlasobscura.com/articles/animals-dont-just-flee-they-make-surprisingly-careful-escape-plans (Accessed on 5/16/17).

Studies have shown that animals are 60 percent more likely: T. Stankowich and D. Blumstein, "Fear in Animals: A Meta-analysis and Review of Risk Assessment."

it would lead to too many false alarms and a lot of wasted energy . . . the flock is sensitive to the difference between one and two birds taking off: T. Caro, p. 139.

"When the wolf seeth them [the greyhounds], and he be full, he voideth both before . . .": E. of Norwich, pp. 62–3.

Animals are sensitive to the body language of flight preparedness, and we
can see this spreading through groups of geese or ducks: D. Lack, p. 44.

If we spook a fallow deer on a hillside: Rob Thurlow, personal
conversation.

springtails and mosquito pupae . . . Mallards: W. Cooper and D.
Blumstein, p. 212.

"Therefore he fleeth oft forth with the wind so that he may always hear
the hounds . . .": E. of Norwich, p. 32.

Birds are more likely to fly directly away from a slow attack and
perpendicularly away from a fast one: W. Cooper and D. Blumstein, p.
211.

blue tits fly more steeply upward away from attacks that come in from the
side than from above: T. Caro, p. 421.

In the wide-open landscapes of the tundra, animals as diverse as hare and
ptarmigan: N. Tinbergen, p. 164.

California ground squirrels jump sideways as they go about their escape
while African squirrels leap vertically: W. Cooper and D. Blumstein, p.
422.

Blue tits that are attacked by a bird of prey will more often than not
execute a "roll and loop": T. Caro, pp. 420–1.

THE REFUGE

Prey animals retain an awareness of the distance to their nearest refuge
and this influences the timing of any flight decision: T. Stankowich and
D. Blumstein.

Songbirds approach trees head-on and woodpeckers, creepers, and
nuthatches flee to the backs of tree trunks: T. Caro, p. 419.

THE CACOPHONY

Elephants can detect a female in heat six miles away through the
vibrations on the ground: K. Shanor and J. Kanwal, p. 34.

parrots can say everything we can and make many noises we can't: Y. N. Harari, p. 24.

Ravens are territorial, and a dominant pair may occupy an area where an abundant source of food: M. Cocker, *Crow Country*, pp. 177–8.

When the Prussian naturalist and explorer Alexander von Humboldt was exploring: A. Wulf, p. 71.

Deer are joined by other cloven-hoofed animals, such as sheep, goats and antelopes: T. Caro, p. 250.

The fear or distress call: W. Cooper and D. Blumstein, p. 219.

will also make defense calls—carnivores that are cornered by a predator usually growl or hiss: T. Caro, p. 416.

Rabbits and hares sometimes do this too—it may be mimicry: T. Caro, p. 416.

Green monkeys react to a lion by scampering up a tree, but to the eagle's call by looking up: Y. Harari, p. 24.

Niko Tinbergen . . . Gull chicks: N. Tinbergen, p. 82.

Vervet monkeys react to starlings, mongooses to hornbills, squirrels to blackbirds: T. Caro, p 202.

"This elegant little bird is used, not to attract the hawk": T. Birkhead, pp. 3–4.

chickadee: K. Shanor and J. Kanwal, p. 100.

Vervet monkeys have different calls for the threat of a snake, a leopard and an eagle: T. Maran, et al., p. 158.

Great tits that find a quarrel of sparrows all bunched around a food source have been known to issue a false alarm call: T. Caro, pp. 219–20.

THE TRACK

indigenous tribespeople might go for a week without seeing a right angle: L. Pedersen, p. 9.

Thomas Magarey . . . encountered Aboriginal mothers putting lizards in front of their infants: R. Moor, p. 138.

A polar bear's prints may run parallel to a pressure ridge on the sea ice: B. Lopez, p. 97.

THE CIRCLING

Bruce Chatwin: B. Chatwin, p. 14.

A circling crow with a raucous blackbird beneath it might suggest a fox: C. Elford, p. 82.

THE STOTTING

some squirrels and deer flag their tails and lizards wag them: W. Cooper and D. Blumstein, p. 275.

Occasionally the animals make these signs when they strongly suspect a predator is lurking nearby: W. Cooper and D. Blumstein, p. 275.

When skylarks are being pursued by merlins: T. Caro, p. 258.

The gazelle that does the inspecting is less likely to be attacked by a cheetah: W. Cooper and D. Blumstein, p. 279.

THE GUIDE

The Bedouin prize secrecy: C. Bailey, p. 396.

Gamekeepers keen to control the numbers of stoats or weasels on a property might see one of these animals: L. Rider Haggard, p. 118.

Richard Nelson: D. Abram, p. 197.

honeyguide bird: D. Lack, p. 216.

A robin will follow a badger, pheasant, wild boar: D. Lack, p. 215.

THE SQUALL SQUAWK

Sharks will flee the area a hurricane is about to pass through . . . elephants pick up thunder a hundred miles away through their feet: K. Shanor and J. Kanwal, pp. 105–6.

Gilbert White learned to forecast the weather by observing the behavior of his tortoise: A. Harris, p. 211.

"We did learn later to accept cockroaches as domestic pets": A. Grimble, p. 16.

FLOCK, BUBBLE, AND BURST

Frogs will hop into gaps to get away: T. Caro, p. 267 and p. 289

Derek Scrimgeour: L. Westling, p. 43.

If the dog lowers its head, ears, and tail: "The Zoosemiotics of Sheep Herding with Dogs," Louise Westling, p. 44.

a dominant corvid entering a group with lower status: T. Angell, "Body Language in Crows," psychologytoday.com/blog/avian-einsteins/201208/body-language-in-crows.

In 1981 a pair of researchers, J. E. Treherne and W. A. Foster, published: T. Caro, p. 274.

birds . . . are capable of monitoring the actions of up to seven: J. Ackerman, p. 34.

starlings, which come together if a falcon is looming, and it has been noted in other common species: N. Tinbergen, pp. 169–70.

THE RETREAT AND REBOUND

Raptors tend not to hunt in the immediate area of their nest: J. von Uexküll, p. 105.

THE JINK

Butterflies have evolved a technique to change direction more sharply by using the turbulence their own wings create, and monarchs are able: L. Villazon, "Why Don't Butterflies Fly in Straight Lines?" sciencefocus.com/qa/why-dont-butterflies-fly-straight-lines (Accessed 6/13/17).

When a hen robin is making a new home with a cock and learning her new territory: D. Lack, p. 49.

a "blencher": E. of Norwich, p. 206.

THE EDDY

"One may guess the power of the north wind blowing over the edge": E. Brontë, *Wuthering Heights* (1847), Vol. 1, Ch.1, p. 2, read in A. Harris, p. 12.

TWO FROSTS

"A great frost is always quiet": R. Jefferies, *Amateur Poacher*, p. 217.
"The Frost performs its secret ministry . . .": Samuel Taylor Coleridge,
"Frost at Midnight."

THE CLEPSYDRA

The Anishinaabe of Canada see six seasons . . . *tagwaagin* marks the
autumnal color change and becomes *oshkibiboon* when the leaves have
fallen: L. M. Johnson and E. Hunn, p. 232.

the Fulani people of the Sahel: L. M. Johnson and E. Hunn, pp. 57–8.

Pele . . . Her face was spotted, apparently, in a photo of an ash cloud above
the Kilauea volcano as recently as 2017: F. Parker, "'Goddess of Fire'
Seen in Dramatic Volcano Eruption Photographs," April 18, 2017,
metro.co.uk/2017/04/18/goddess-of-fire-seen-in-dramatic-volcano-
eruption-photographs-6582812/ (Accessed 6/23/17).

"For three hundred years, the oak grows and grows . . .": personal, based
on conversations during a walk in Windsor Great Park with those who
work for The Woodland Trust.

there is one spruce in Sweden that is reputedly 9,500 years old: P.
Wohlleben, p. vii.

Hunters in the north know that you can age a seal or polar bear: B. Lopez,
p. 118.

"Better a wolf in the field than a fine February": C. Rhodes, p. 22.

"March sustains the crop or March destroys the crop": C. Bailey, p. 73.

in the past ten years the area devoted to vineyards in England and Wales
has more than doubled. There was a vicious late frost in 2017, which
killed off three-quarters of the crop in some areas: Z. Wood, "English
Vineyards Report 'Catastrophic' Damage After Severe April Frost,"
May 2, 2017, theguardian.com/business/2017/may/02/english-
vineyards-frost-champagne-bordeaux-burgundy (Accessed 6/27/17).

Close to the ground, the temperature is higher on average in spring than
higher up, and this . . . gives the smaller trees a head start, bringing them
into leaf about two weeks before the taller ones: P. Wohlleben, p. 143.

we might sense the sap rising in the dark holes that grow around the trees: R. W. Kimmerer, p. 64.

The Bedouin know to sow crops when the Pleiades appear . . . "O happy valley flowing with Aldebaran's showers . . . while it is rich in flowers": C. Bailey, pp. 22, 31–2, 54, 71.

zeitgeber: M. Breed, pp. 71–2.

One of Alexander the Great's admirals, Androsthenes, noted that tamarind leaves open during the day and close at night: en.wikipedia. org/wiki/Nyctinasty (Accessed 6/28/17).

jellyfish go to sleep at about four PM, sinking to the ocean floor: K. Shanor and J. Kanwal, p. 130.

Horses can get by with as little as two hours per day but bats need twenty: K. Shanor and J. Kanwal, p. 131.

we *do* know that bees learn to time their visits to certain flowers to arrive when the nectar is most available: N. Tinbergen, p. 168.

LABELS THAT COME TO LIFE

"She did not even know . . . which vines to follow to find the delicacies hidden": C. Turnbull, p. 132.

In the Amazon the wisest are called "vegetalistas": J. Griffiths, p. 17.

"more worthless than tamarisk": C. Bailey, p. 21.

"moths have feathered antennae, butterflies don't . . . millipedes": R. Fortey, p. 52.

They know that a female roe deer can be easily identified: C. Elford, p. 15.

Habitat, Ecology, and Biotope: definitions from en.oxforddictionaries.com.

"Crows frequently build in oaks, and unless they are driven away by shot": R. Jefferies, *Wild Life in a Southern County*, p. 308.

THREE LUMINARIES

The Gwi: L. Liebenberg.

a horse with its head down, a hanging bottom lip, and a slumped hip: K. Shanor and J. Kanwal, p. 133.

Adam Shereston: personal conversations and correspondence.

The ears and head are flags to the horseperson: equusmagazine.com/
behavior/how-to-read-your-horses-body-language-8577 and localriding
.com/equine-body-language.html (Accessed 5/9/17).

Lions are much easier to read than tigers or leopards: T. Maran, et al.,
p. 135.

A NOBLE PURSUIT

!xo: L. Liebenberg.

"solitary, poor, nasty, brutish, and short": T. Hobbes, en.wikipedia.org/
wiki/Thomas_Hobbes (Accessed 6/5/17).

the Bedouin looked down their noses at the Solubba hunters of northern
Arabia: R. Lee and R. Daly, p. 389.

Yuval Noah Harari: Y. N. Harari, pp. 56–7.

farmers worked harder and longer than foragers and were rewarded . . .
less varied diet: Y. N. Harari, p. 90.

Other academics have gone further, claiming that hunter-gatherers are
"the most leisured people in the world": E. Service, pp. 12–13.

"The Golden Age ended when men stopped hunting": B. Chatwin, p. 136.

"The Romans, unlike the Greeks, and still more unlike those mighty
hunters of old . . .": Theodore Roosevelt, p. xxi of E. of Norwich.

managed so well with so little for fifty thousand years: R. Lee and R. Daly,
p. 1.

Feeding antelopes move from bush to bush, following a zigzag pattern into
the wind: L. Liebenberg.

Kutchin hunting example: L. Liebenberg.

Aboriginal peoples learned to map water by taking an interest in whether
any slain animal had drunk recently: H. W. Wilson, pp. 105–6.

There is a difference between hunting and killing: R. Moor, pp. 152–9.

chimpanzees have been observed following prey stealthily for more than
an hour: L. Liebenberg.

Hunting literature of the Middle Ages refers to: E. of Norwich, pp. 7–8.

etymology of the word "nobility" . . . *nobilité*, meaning "high rank; dignity, grace, great deed": etymonline.com/index.php?term=nobility (Accessed 6/6/17).

Some sources list as many as seventy-two such signs, including the slot: E. of Norwich, p. 225.

"well advised of his speech and of his terms, and ever glad . . .": E. of Norwich, p. 124.

The San people of the northern Kalahari are expected to shun arrogant behavior: L. Liebenberg.

Common among indigenous communities is a sense that the environment is generous and benevolent: R. Lee and R. Daly, p. 4.

"The experiences I share with the deer in weather and places": C. Elford, pp. 16–17.

TOMORROW'S HUNTER

Based on a visit to the Joint Intelligence Training Group and conversations with Squadron Leader R. Jones, in Chicksands, Bedfordshire, in June 2017.

MORE THAN MACHINES

Ivory Coast chimpanzees use a stick to dip for water in narrow tree holes: V. Gill, "Primate Tool-Use: Chimpanzees Make Drinking Sticks," January 10, 2017, bbc.co.uk/news/science-environment-38524671 (Accessed 25/07/17).

Mice have learned sequences of movements through a maze to find food, then remembered them up to eight weeks later: D. Thomson, p. 247.

have taught honeybees how to tell the difference between a Picasso and a Monet: D. Kennedy, "Scientists Discover Bees Can Tell a Picasso from a Monet," October 28, 2012, bbc.co.uk/news/av/science-environment-20114359/scientists-discover-bees-can-tell-a-picasso-from-a-monet (Accessed 7/25/17).

"machines without a soul": T. Maran, et al., p. 23.

"squeaking parts in an unfeeling machine": J. von Uexküll, p. 21.

Pigeons are brilliant at navigating and poor, relative to crows, at working out rules for solving problems: J. Ackerman, p. 22.

"over-scenting": J. von Uexküll, p. 106.

"producer-scrounger": M. Breed, p. 177.

"open field": M. Breed, p. 193.

jackdaws . . . Konrad Lorenz: N. Tinbergen, p. 148.

In 1978 some laboratory rats were confronted with a swimming task: M. Breed, p. 166.

In the Kalahari, if an animal has been shot with poison, its character and personality: L. Liebenberg.

Australian Aboriginal peoples can tell whether an animal is tame by the tracks it leaves: D. Lewis, p. 280.

"The harts bellow in divers manners, according as they be old or young": E. of Norwich, pp. 161–2.

UMWELT

"Standing before a meadow covered with flowers": J. von Uexküll, from J. Hoffmeyer, p. 54.

In 1978 a chimpanzee called Sarah demonstrated: M. Breed, p. 168.

anthropomorphism and anthropocentrism: C. Foster, p. xiv.

We credit the ant with little intelligence, yet the colonies achieve extraordinary things: R. Moor, pp. 74–6.

which is only as our hand comes within twenty inches of it . . . spider's web: J. von Uexküll, p. 82.

a polar bear can smell a whale twenty miles away and detect a seal through six feet of ice: K. Shanor and J. Kanwal, p. 81.

Some birds and possibly badgers can hear the sound an earthworm makes as it breaks the surface: C. Foster, p. 51.

Sand crickets can sense predators from air movement: W. Cooper and D. Blumstein, p. 322.

a bowhead whale asleep at the surface can startle when a bird lands on it:
B. Lopez, p. 4.

but a male silkworm moth can detect a mature female: J. von Uexküll, p.
22.

A horse will notice part of our face moves 0.2 millimeter: T. Maran, et al.,
p. 92.

Human, fish, and snail perceptions per second: J. von Uexküll, pp. 70–2.

Worms are able to pull pine needles and other leaves the right way down
their narrow tunnels by tasting them: J. von Uexküll, p. 82.

pigeon forebrains have half the neural density of corvids': J. Ackerman, p.
232.

Researchers proved this by tying the chick to the ground again and this
time placing a transparent glass bell jar over it: J. von Uexküll, pp.
88–9.

Something that looks exactly like a starfish to us will not trigger a
defensive response in a scallop unless it moves with the same speed as a
starfish: J. von Uexküll, p. 82.

when we discover that a jackdaw that lets a cat with an empty mouth pass
will later attack the cat if it walks back with a pair of black shorts in its
mouth: J. von Uexküll, p. 109.

Moths detect the 20 kHz frequency of a bat's echolocation: J. Hoffmeyer,
pp. 53–4.

Studies have shown that predator detection drops by 25 percent when a
bird is searching for food, and by a further 45 percent when it's pecking
that food: W. Cooper and D. Blumstein, p. 323.

ultraviolet light . . . birds have four types of cone . . . "In each of a bird's
cone cells is a drop of oil that enhances its ability to detect differences
between similar colors": J. Ackerman, p. 224.

The chance of a house sparrow detecting us grow steadily as we move
closer: W. Cooper and D. Blumstein, p. 328.

rattlesnake . . . California ground squirrel: W. Cooper and D. Blumstein.

TREACHERY

Roosters allure hens by giving the call that indicates food: K. Shanor and
J. Kanwal, p. 211.

Achilla, a lonely gorilla at the Basel Zoo: T. Maran, et al., p. 135.

Some female finches grow weary of their mates staying too long away from
the nest: K. Shanor and J. Kanwal, p. 240.

"cleaner fish": T. Maran, et al., p. 88.

The Penobscot Indians of Maine drew moose within arrow range: L.
Liebenberg.

Ainu hunters in Japan: R. Moor, p. 150.

Carrion flowers stink of rotting flesh to attract beetles and flies . . . passion
vines: "Summoned by Screams," *Economist*, October 6, 2016, p. 79.

A STORIED CREATURE

Green monkeys have been known to trick and lie—one was seen giving a
lion alarm call . . . Other animals are capable of language, invention,
and deceit, but they do not tell stories: Y. N. Harari, p. 35.

"made use of humble incidents to teach great truths": Apollonius of
Tyana, wikipedia.org/wiki/Aesop%27s_Fables (Accessed 6/21/17).

"The cormorant was once a wool-merchant": "Cormorants,"
Spectator, December 28, 1895, archive.spectator.co.uk/article/28th-
december-1895/13/cormorants (Accessed 6/19/17).

"The whole Western Desert is crisscrossed with the meandering tracks":
R. Berndt, cited by D. Lewis, p. 254.

"some old fellers had been . . . and knew the stories": D. Lewis, p. 254.

THE IKUS

In 1936 Harley Harris Bartlett, a botanist: L. M. Johnson and E. Hunn,
p. 23.

a system of landscape classification and divided their country into "types":
D. F. Thomson.

heridzololima to the *iitsaapolima*: "Beniwa Habitat Classification in the White-Sand Campinarana Forests of the Northwest Amazon, Brazil," M. Abraão, et al., from L. M. Johnson and E. Hunn, p. 90.

it was once believed the two were symbiotic: P. Barkham, p. 96.

But at least a hundred species of bird like to build nests within five feet of these stinging, biting creatures: T. Caro, p. 83.

"I could find waterholes in rocky country by the shape of the rocks": D. Lewis, p. 278.

sahkab lu'um is a deep-black soil while *ch'ich lu'um* is a deep-black fertile soil: L. M. Johnson and E. Hunn, p. 261.

the word *xaat'ay* indicates the place where a stream shallows and passes over flat rocks . . . It is analogous to an observation made by the Palauan fishermen of Micronesia, who use the word *hapitsetse* to describe the area where currents converge downstream: L. M. Johnson and E. Hunn, p. 21.

the Alluetais . . . Les Allues: L. M. Johnson and E. Hunn, pp. 164–7.

EPILOGUE: THE ROOM

For the English poet, Thomas Traherne, this was the "real whispering" of nature: J. Wright, p. 220.

Alexander von Humboldt: A. Wulf, pp. 88–90.

"that intuition of things which arises when we possess ourselves as one with the whole": A. Siewers, p. 24.

Arthur Grimble: A. Grimble, pp. 112–14.

The fungicides used in southern Europe affect the ultraviolet light in Lapland: J. Hoffmeyer p. vii.

In Mesoamerica, directions were paired with symbols, colors, and broader qualities: A. Siewers, pp. 217–19.

Bibliography

Abram, David, *Becoming Animal*, Vintage, 2011.

Ackerman, Jennifer, *The Genius of Birds*, Corsair, 2016.

Armstrong, Karen, *A Short History of Myth*, Canongate, 2006.

Bailey, Clinton, *A Culture of Desert Survival*, Yale University Press, 2004.

Barkham, Patrick, *Badgerlands*, Granta, 2014.

Barnes, Simon, *Bird Watching with Your Eyes Closed*, Short Books, 2011.

Bell, Matthew, Hollén, Linda, and Radford, Andrew, "Success in a Social Bird," *Proceedings of the Royal Society B*, Vol. 276, 2009.

Birkhead, T., *Bird Sense*, Bloomsbury, 2013.

Breed, Michael, *Conceptual Breakthroughs in Ethology and Animal Behavior*, Academic Press, 2017.

Brody, Hugh, *Living Arctic*, Faber & Faber, 1987.

Caro, Tim, *Antipredator Defenses in Birds and Mammals*, University of Chicago Press, 2005.

Chatwin, Bruce, *In Patagonia*, Pan Books, 1979.

Christie, Agatha, *Appointment with Death*, HarperCollins, 1996.

Cocker, Mark, *Crow Country*, Vintage, 2007.

Cocker, Mark, *Claxton*, Penguin, 2014.

Collins, Sophie, *Why Does My Dog Do That?*, Ivy Press, 2008.

Cooper, William E., and Blumstein, Daniel T., *Escaping from Predators*, Cambridge University Press, 2015.

Cron, Lisa, *Wired for Story*, Ten Speed Press, 2012.

Elford, Colin, *A Year in the Woods*, Penguin, 2011.

Fortey, Richard, *The Wood for the Trees*, William Collins, 2016.

Foster, Charles, *Being a Beast*, Profile Books, 2016.

Gibson, James, *The Ecological Approach to Visual Perception*, Psychology Press, 1986.

Gladwell, Malcolm, *Blink*, Penguin, 2005.

Gooley, Tristan, *The Natural Navigator*, The Experiment, 2011.

Gooley, Tristan, *The Natural Explorer*, Sceptre, 2012.

Gooley, Tristan, *How to Read Nature*, The Experiment, 2017.

Grimble, Arthur, *A Pattern of Islands*, Eland, 2010.

Griffiths, Jay, *Wild*, Penguin, 2006.

Harari, Yuval Noah, *Sapiens*, Vintage, 2011.

Hardin, Joel, *Tracker*, Joel Hardin Tracking Inc., 2009.

Harris, Alexandra, *Weatherland*, Thames & Hudson, 2016.

Hatfield, Fred, *North of the Sun*, Virgin Books, 1991.

Hemingway, Ernest, *Green Hills of Africa*, Vintage, 2004.

Hoffmeyer, Jesper, *Signs of Meaning in the Universe*, Indiana University Press, 1997.

Holden, Peter and Cleeves, Tim, *RSPB Handbook of British Birds*, Bloomsbury, 2014.

Humphreys, John, *Poachers' Tales*, David & Charles, 1992.

James, P. D., *Death in Holy Orders*, Faber & Faber, 2001.

Jefferies, Richard, *The Amateur Poacher*, Tideline Books, 1985.

Jefferies, Richard, *Wild Life in a Southern County*, Thomas Nelson & Sons, n.d.

Johnson, Leslie Main and Hunn, Eugene S., *Landscape Ethnoecology*, Berghahn Books, 2012.

Jung, C. G., *The Earth Has a Soul*, North Atlantic Books, 2008.

Kahneman, Daniel, *Thinking, Fast and Slow*, Penguin, 2012.

Kimmerer, Robin Wall, *Braiding Sweetgrass*, Milkweed Editions, 2013.

Klein, Gary, *Seeing What Others Don't, Nicolas Brealey*, 2014.

Kohn, Eduardo, *How Forests Think*, University of California Press, 2013.

Kozlowski, Theodore T., Kramer, Paul J., and Pallardy, Stephen G., *The Physiological Ecology of Woody Plants*, Academic Press, 1991.

Krakauer, Jon, *Into the Wild*, Pan Macmillan, 1996.

Krappe, Alexander Haggerty, *The Science of Folk-Lore*, Methuen & Co., 1930.

Krause, Bernie, *Wild Soundscapes*, Yale University Press, 2016.

Lack, David, *The Life of the Robin*, Pallas Athene, 2016.

Lawrence, Gale, *A Field Guide to the Familiar*, University Press of New England, 1998.

Lee, Richard B. and Daly, Richard, *The Cambridge Encyclopedia of Hunters and Gatherers*, Cambridge University Press, 2008.

Lewis, David, "Observations on Route Finding and Spatial Orientation Among the Aboriginal Peoples of the Western Desert Region of Central Australia," *Oceania Journal*, Volume 46, No. 4, 1976.

Liebenberg, Louis, *The Art of Tracking*, David Philip Publishers, 1990.

Lopez, Barry, *Arctic Dreams*, Vintage, 2014.

Mabey, Richard, *Flora Britannica*, Sinclair Stevenson, 1996.

Maran, Timo, Martinelli, Dario, and Turovski, Aleksei, editors, *Readings in Zoosemiotics*, Walter de Gruyter, 2011.

Moor, Robert, *On Trails*, Aurum Press, 2016.

Naparstek, Belleruth, *Your Sixth Sense*, HarperCollins, 1997.

Norwich, Edward of, *Master of Game*, University of Pennsylvania Press, 2005.

Pedersen, Loren E., *Sixteen Men*, Shambhala, 1993.

Pryde, Duncan, *Nunaga*, Eland, 2003.

Rackham, Oliver, *Hayley Wood*, Cambridgeshire Wildlife Trust, 1990.

Rackham, Oliver, *The Ash Tree*, Little Toller Books, 2015.

Rhodes, Chloe, *One for Sorrow*, Michael O'Mara Books, 2011.

Rider Haggard, Lilias, *I Walked by Night*, Coch-Y-Bonddu Books, 2009.

Ruskin, John and Rosenberg, John D., *The Genius of John Ruskin*, University of Virginia Press, 1998.

Service, Elman R., *The Hunters*, Prentice-Hall, 1966.

Shanor, Karen and Kanwal, Jagmeet, *Bats Sing, Mice Giggle*, Totem Books, 2011.

Sheldrake, Rupert, *Dogs That Know When Their Owners Are Coming Home*, Arrow Books, 2011.

Siewers, Alfred Kentigern, *Re-Imagining Nature*, Bucknell University Press, 2014.

Song, Tamarack, *Becoming Nature*, Bear & Co., 2016.

Springthorpe, G. D. and Myhill, N. G., editors, *Wildlife Rangers Handbook*, Forestry Commission, 1994.

Stankowich, Theodore and Blumstein, Daniel T., "Fear in Animals: A Meta-analysis and Review of Risk Assessment," *Proceedings of the Royal Society B: Biological Sciences*, Vol. 272, No. 1581, 2005.

Stokes, Donald and Lillian, *A Guide to Animal Tracking and Behavior*, Little, Brown, 1986.

Summerscale, Kate, *The Suspicions of Mr. Whicher*, Bloomsbury, 2009.

Thomson, D., "Names and Naming Among the Wik Monkan Tribe," *Journal of the Royal Anthropological Institute*, Vol. 76, No. 2, 1946.

Thomson, J. Arthur, *The Wonder of Life*, Andrew Melrose, 1927.

Thompson, Harry, *This Thing of Darkness*, Headline Review, 2006.

Tinbergen, N., *The Study of Instinct*, Oxford University Press, 1958.

Turnbull, Colin, *The Forest People*, Bodley Head, 2015.

Uexküll, Jakob von, *A Foray into the Worlds of Animals and Humans*, University of Minnesota Press, 2010.

Westling, Louise, "The Zoosemiotics of Sheep Herding with Dogs," in *The Semiotics of Animal Representations*, Kadri Tüür and Morten Tønnesen, Rodopi, eds., 2014, pp. 33–52.

Widlok, Thomas, "Orientation in the Wild: The Shared Cognition of the Hai||om Bushpeople," *The Journal of the Royal Anthropological Institute of Great Britain and Ireland*, Vol. 3, No. 2, 1997.

Wilson, Helen Wood, *Bushman Born*, Artlook Books Trust, 1981.

Wohlleben, Peter, *The Hidden Life of Trees*, Greystone Books, 2016.

Wright, John, *A Natural History of the Hedgerow*, Profile Books, 2016.

Wroe, Ann, *Six Facets of Light*, Jonathan Cape, 2016.

Wulf, Andrea, *The Invention of Nature*, John Murray, 2016.

Young, Jon, *What the Robin Knows*, Houghton Mifflin Harcourt, 2012.

Acknowledgments

"My subconscious being was not prepared to take this risk and jungle sensitiveness came to my assistance and guided me away from the potential danger."

These are the words of the legendary hunter-turned-conservationist and author Jim Corbett. He was describing how he had felt the need to take an unusual route through the jungle, one that kept him at a safe distance from a tiger that he was not yet aware of.

At times writing this book has felt like the opposite experience. An unconscious urge drove me toward a subject that lurked in the bushes and then stared back at me like a cornered tiger. It was a subject that did not like me drawing too near and put up quite a wrestle. It is likely that the tiger would have got the better of me, were it not for the support of many kind people. The book is dedicated to them.

I would like to thank all the indigenous people, anthropologists, hunters, semioticians, ecologists, and others across the world who have kept the flame of our old wisdom alight and accessible. I don't know the names of many of those I am most indebted to, but of the few I do, I am particularly grateful for the work of Tim Caro, William Cooper,

Daniel Blumstein, Leslie Main Johnson, Eugene Hunn, Timo Maran, and Jakob von Uexküll.

I would also like to thank those who have offered their time, advice, gems, or encouragement, either in the field of the mind or the field of the field: Kate Jeffery, Zita Patai, Hugo Spiers, Rich Jones, Steve Hughes, Tracey Younghusband, Rob Thurlow, Mark Wardle, John Rhyder, Adam Shereston, John Pahl, and Richard Nissen. Thanks also to the many others who have come on courses or got in touch to share observations or experiences.

Thank you, Neil Gower, for your brilliant illustrations and cover, as always.

My sister, Siobhan Machin, offered sage advice at a critical stage and I will be in trouble if she has not been thanked over a decent lunch by the time of publication, and with a sincere thank you here.

A big thank you to Hazel Orme, Cameron Myers, Rebecca Mundy, Caitriona Horne, and Ben Summers and all at Sceptre for all your hard work. Any errors are mine alone.

I would like to thank my agent Sophie Hicks and editor Rupert Lancaster, whose enthusiasm and encouragement made embarking on this book possible and whose patience and assistance made completion much more enjoyable.

Finally, I'd like to thank my family and friends for their support, not least when I'm tired from tiger-wrestling.

Index

Page numbers in *italic* denote illustrations

drumlins, 209
ducks, 11, 50, 126, 132–33, 140, 187
dunes, 63, *64*
dung, 230–31
dusk. *See* dawn and dusk

E

eagles, 155, 157
early humans, 244–45, 252–53,
    289–90
ears
    body language, 116, 118, 120,
        247
    hearing, xv, 15–16, 55, 124, 274,
        276, 281
    See also sound
Eartham Pit, 219
earthworms, 274, 278–79
echolocation, 195, 281
ecology, defined, 294
ecosemiotics, 47
ecotones, 83–84
ecotopes, 296
Ecuador, 233
eddies, 71, 204–5
"the edge," 83–86
Edward of Norwich, 90, 138, 141,
    269–70
eggs, birds, xvii
egg timers, 216
elder trees, 97, 103
electromagnetic signals, 274–75
elephants, 105, 116, 138, 175, 268
Elford, Colin, 259
emotions
    in animals, 116, 154, 249, 268

limbic system and, 29–30, 31,
    286
reading signs and, 55, 56, 57
energy conservation, 135–36, 137,
    151
Enlightenment, 7
ESP (extrasensory perception), 32
evolution, 33, 53, 120, 149, 192,
    284
experience
    combined with knowledge, 54
    as pattern recognition, 263
    reading signs and, 31–34, 47,
        54–55
expressions
    in animals, 115–16
    facial, 55, 114–15
    in language, 16, 31, 33, 192
eyes
    gaze, 116, 118, 249
    sight, 79–80, 117–18, 195, 248

F

"the face," 114–18
Facial Action Coding System
    (FACS), 114–15
falcons, 131–32, 187, 264
fallow deer, 92, 140, 146, 195
farming, 223, 244, 253, 300
fast thinking, 9–16, 33–34, 51, 55,
    220, 240–42, 286–87, 305
fear, 30, 115, 118, 131, 154, 267
FEAR (Flee Early and Avoid the
    Rush), 136
fear bradycardia, 131
fearfulness, genetics and, 267

fungi
  colors of, 52, 239
  life cycle, 231
  as southeast compass, 231
  types of, 103
  as warning system for trees, 46
fungicides, 307

G

gamblers, pattern recognition in, 32
gamekeepers, 120, 172, 193, 195
games, 140–41, 281–82
gaze, 116, 118, 249
gazelles, 131, 142, 156, 169–70
geese, 50, 139, 186, 225
genetics, fearfulness and, 267
geocaching, 39
ghosts, sensing of, 291
Gilbert Islands, 175
goat's beard, 215, 227
go-away birds, 156
God, nature as manifestation of, 307
golden plovers, 284–85
golfers, 16
gorillas, deception in, 284
grass
  animal self-medication and, 105–6
  as light reflector, 80
  noise of walking on, 109
  "the ramp" and, 63, 64, 65
grasshoppers, 277, 280–81
grasslands, 89
great tits, 158, 239
green monkeys, 155–56, 286

Gregory of Nyssa, St., 49
Griffiths, Martin, 6
Grimble, Arthur, 175, 305–6
grosbeaks, 166
group behavior, 126, 166, 179–87, 266–68
"the guide," 171–73
gulls, 146, 155, 164–65, 166, 173, 186–87
Gwi people, 244

H

habitat, defined, 294
Hai||om people, 294
hand motions, and squirrels, 53
"the handrail," 73–77
Harari, Yuval Noah, 10, 252–53
Hardin, Joel, 13
hares, 90, 91–92, 120, 130, 146, 154. *See also* rabbits
Harting, James, 156–57
Hatfield, Fred, 149
hat-thrower fungus, 231
havens, 92–93
Hawaiian islands, 219
hawk moths, 53
hawks, 110, 156–57, 299
Hawksworth & Rose scale, 81
heads, in body language, 116–18, 123–24, 137–39
hearing, sense of, xv, 15–16, 55, 124, 274, 276, 281. *See also* sound
heather, 210–11
Heathrow Airport, 70–71
heat stroke, 17–18
hedges
  age of, 220

as barriers, 85
bird behavior and, 249–50
as friends to other species,
    99, 315
herbivores, 106
herd defense, 183–84
herds. *See* flocks
herring gulls, 155
hiking. *See* walking
hills
    anticipating drops on, 11–12
    drumlins, 209
    eddies and, 71
    "the handrail" and, 74, 76–77
hippopotami, 116
Hobbes, Thomas, 252
holly trees, 241
honey, xv
honeybees, 265, 280, 285
honeyguide birds, 173
honeysuckle, 103, 225, 230
Hooper's rule, 220
horses, 120, 160, 230, 246–48,
    275, 282, 291
Hughes, Steve, 240
humans, early, 244–45, 252–53,
    289–90
Humboldt, Alexander von, 151,
    237–38, 307
Hume, David, 56
humidity, 45, 207, 218
humility, in hunters, 258–59
humpback whales, 233
Hunn, Eugene, 296
hunter-gatherers, 219, 244,
    251–56, 259
hunting
    "the freeze" and, 130

humility and, 258–59
by indigenous peoples, 7, 244,
    252–56, 285
intelligence and, 254
vs. killing, 257, 259–60
leisure and, 253–54
pattern recognition in, 251, 256, 263
trickery and, 285
venery and, 258
wind and, 40–41
zenith of, 260
See also predators and prey
hurricanes, 175

I

ice
    color of clouds and, 71
    Inuit knowledge of, 44
    moon phases and, 232
    sastrugi, 63, *64*
identification, belief in wisdom as, 238
"the ignore," 201–3
ikus, 293–302
illness, signs of, 101–5
images
    identification of, 279–80
    search images, 277–78
indigenous peoples
    awareness in, xiv–xv, 7–9, 237–38,
        239, 296
    hunting by, 7, 244, 252–56, 285
    landscape reading by, 296
    tracking by, 159–60
    view of wilderness as a friend, 259
    wisdom of, 238–39, 254–56
Industrial Revolution, 244, 253

refuges of, 145, 146–47
"the shimmy" and, 198, 200
tails, 53, 114, 118, 168
vigilance in, 124, 125
standing waves, 71
stared at, sense of being, xi–xii, xv
starfish, 276–77
starlings, 125, 156, 186, 187, 258, 282
stars
associations with, 56
as compasses, 19, 23, 25–28
See also constellations; *individual stars*
stinging nettles, 56, 87–88, 93, 97
stonechats, 153
stone walls, 222–23
storms, 14–15, 174–75, 207, 309
storytelling and folklore, 245, 286–92
stotting, 168–70
streams, 218, 299
stripping, 89–90
substantial knowledge, 307
suckers, 104
sulfur dioxide, 81
summer triangle, 23, 27–*28*
the sun
cloud formation and, 69
as a compass, 20–22, 66–67, 229–30
damage to trees from, 104
haloes around, 44
rainbows and, 21–22, 215
rising, 66–67
setting, 262
See also light

sun scald, 104
superstition, 30–31
surgeons, caring in, 57–58
sweating palms, 32
Sweden, 220
swifts, 50, 199
sycamore trees, 65, 90, 315
symbols, in semiotics, 47–49
System 1 *vs.* System 2 thinking, 9

T

tag (game), 140–41
tails, 53, 114, 118, 168
tamarind, 227
tamarisk, 239
taste, sense of, 226, 238, 278–79
Taurus (constellation), 215, 225
teachers, caring in, 58
technological progress, wisdom as, 252–53
teeth
biting and, 91
horses' baring of, 246–47
telephone conversations, xii
temperature
cloud formation and, 69
damage to trees from, 104
light and, 95
plants reaction to, 223–24
temper yawning, 116
terpenes, 70
territory
defense of, 51–52, 188–90, 194, 267, 273, 299
marking of, 89–90, 266
of robins, 51–52, 188–89, 267

watched, sense of being, xi–xii, xv

water

eddies, 71

finding, 244, 291, 299

ponds, 43, 199, 217–18

puddles, 14, 217–18

ripples, 43, 144, 199

rivers, 71, 74–77, 84, 237

springs, 218

streams, 218, 299

tides, 232, 261–62, 305–6

time and, 216, 217–18

waves, 62, 63, 71

water clocks, 216, 217–18

"water sky," 71

water vapor, 68–69, 290

waves, 62, 63, 71

weasels, 146, 172

weather

folklore about, 289–92

forecasting, xv, 10, 175, 223

fronts, 44

frost, 212–14

lightning, 14–15, 104

rain, xv, 10, 69, 122–23, 290

"the squall squawk" and, 174–75

storms, 14–15, 174–75, 207, 309

See also rain; wind

Weddell seals, 125

wedge effect, 63, 64

wet wood, 103–4

whales, 233, 274, 275

White, Gilbert, 175

white-tailed deer, 141

Wik Monkan people, 296

"wild," definitions of, 36

wildcats, 23–24

wilderness

as a friend, 259

sense of, 36

wildflowers, 52, 56, 84, 97, 174, 297

wildlife. See animals

wildlife photographers, 260

willow tits, 125

wind

anchoring, 42–43

direction, 40–45, 60, 65, 141, 204–5, 248, 255

eddies, 71, 204–5

fronts and, 44

frost and, 213–14

horses and, 248

katabatic, 289

moose and, 255

predicting patterns of, 42–43

prevailing, 65, 69

"the ramp," 62–65

shaping trees, 63, 103, 180–81

"the shear," 60–61

sound of, 79

turbulence, 71–72, 192

waves and, 62, 63, 71

wind maps, 41–43

winterbournes, 218

Wintinna Mick, 7, 299

wisdom

belief in identification as, 238

belief in technological progress as, 252–53

in early humans, 244–45, 252–53, 289–90

folklore and, 286–92

of indigenous peoples, 238–39, 254–56